A WORLD RECAST

A WORLD RECAST

An American Moment in a Post-Western Order

Simon Serfaty

ROWMAN & LITTLEFIELD PUBLISHERS, INC.

Lanham • Boulder • New York • Toronto • Plymouth, UK

Published by Rowman & Littlefield Publishers, Inc.
A wholly owned subsidiary of The Rowman & Littlefield Publishing Group, Inc.
4501 Forbes Boulevard, Suite 200, Lanham, Maryland 20706
www.rowman.com

10 Thornbury Road, Plymouth PL6 7PP, United Kingdom

British Library Cataloguing in Publication Information Available

Library of Congress Cataloging-in-Publication Data
Serfaty, Simon.
　A world recast : an American moment in a post-Western order / Simon Serfaty.
　　p.　cm.
　Includes bibliographical references and index.
　ISBN 978-1-4422-1587-0 (cloth : alk. paper) — ISBN 978-1-4422-1589-4 (electronic)
　1. United States—Foreign relations—21st century. 2. Geopolitics—United States. 3.
　World politics—21st century. 4. Civilization, Western—21st century. I. Title.
　E895.S48 2012
　327.73009'05—dc23

2012024451

3/3

Printed in the United States of America

CONTENTS

ACKNOWLEDGMENTS

A *World Recast* began as a graduate seminar taught at Old Dominion University in Norfolk, Virginia. As part of the seminar, I agreed to write a paper of my own that would follow from our weekly discussions and related reading assignments. This book, in a sense, is my seminar paper, turned in a bit late. Those who attended the class will grade it as they see fit. Meantime, I want to acknowledge them all—Tasawar Baig, Steve Jones, Wiebke Lammer, Cindy Miller, Maxim Miroshnikov, C. J. Pelgram, and Tim Williams: where can better motivation be found than in a classroom? Thanks, too, to Aaron Sander, a promising doctoral student who raised useful questions as the manuscript was being completed; to my colleague at ODU, David Earnest, who made valuable suggestions and helped me tighten the entire manuscript; and to Regina Karp, the director of the Graduate Program in International Studies at Old Dominion, for her encouragement over the years.

Thanks also to John Broderick, the supportive president of the university that has been my academic home in Norfolk, Virginia, for the past twenty years; and to John Hamre and Craig Kennedy, who extended the hospitality and support of the institutions over which they preside and with which I have the privilege to be associated: respectively, the Center for Strategic & International Studies (CSIS) and the German Marshall Fund of the United States, in Washington, DC.

The issues covered in these pages are such as to make it difficult to acknowledge all. Ideas in this field have many sources, and the most thorough footnoting still overlooks the information and insights gained from known and unknown speakers at conferences and roundtables around the world—from early professors and former as well as current colleagues. My thanks, therefore, also go to the many I do not cite specifically even though my distinct memories of them and the arguments they made will appear throughout these pages.

Finally, a closing thought about dedications. After my first book, which was meant for my parents, of course, others went to my loving and tolerant lifetime wife, Gail—who gave me balance and unwavering encouragement; to my gifted and attentive son, Alexis—who is the lasting pillar of our afterlife; and to the many others—family members and friends, and also students, who gave life meaning. Now, and one more time, this book goes to all of them simultaneously, including the few who are no longer with us but whom I remember fondly.

❶

A POST-WESTERN MOMENT

To be on the side of history is desirable so long as we know where history is going. That is not always the case, however. Even now when there is much agreement and possibly some relief over the passing of the U.S. preponderance that defined the latter phase of the Western era—a short-lived "unipolar moment" of presumed omnipotence—there is little consensus about the post-Western world that is said to lie ahead.

Entering the second decade of the twentieth century one hundred years ago, there was a more widely shared sense of the world. There were at most fifty countries; few of them were dubbed great powers, and even fewer qualified as world powers—mostly European countries with decisive military capabilities. This was a Western world, as it had become apparent during the previous century after India and China far in the East, and Turkey at the margin of the West, had fallen increasingly behind.

The durability of that world, domineering and sure of itself, was not questioned seriously: this was a belle époque—a time when Rudyard Kipling's "fantasy was potent magic" that helped conquer empires in the morning and gather "home for tea" in the afternoon.[1] This looked like a good time to be alive—until, that is, a horrific and unnecessary war, which started in the summer of 1914, quickly gained worldwide dimensions, and lasted over three decades, made it a good time to die. "We were born at the beginning of the First World War," wrote Albert Camus of his generation. "As adolescents we had the crisis of 1929; at 20, Hitler. Then came the Ethiopian war, the civil war in Spain and Munich. These were the foundations of our education. . . . Born and bred in such a world, what did we believe in? Nothing."[2]

That the West stayed on top nonetheless, with the entire European state system in ruins, was owed to a massive investment of American power and leadership that tightly recast the West. While the European powers that had just been humiliated and defeated in war now assumed a supportive role, a triumphant America took over with the tacit consent of its new charges. Thus told, without any imperial intent from the United States, the history of the "short" century behind provides for a Western narrative that follows not only the rise of American power but also, and even especially, the collapse of everybody else.

Entering the second decade of the twenty-first century the past looks very distant, like a millennium away. In the previous epoch, the nation-state ruled and force prevailed, leaving the weak at the mercy of the strong. This was an epoch of state coercion and national submission, of conquests and empires, though few could anticipate that it would take only a lifetime to see them all gone. In the new epoch, institutions matter—occasionally more than their member states—and military force is rarely decisive. On the whole, wars are no longer in fashion and other forms of power are favored to shape the world rather than rule it.[3] This is an epoch when ter-ritorial overlaps facilitate a global public awakening to the "better" things available elsewhere and, therefore, more pressing demands for broader ac-cess to them—when half of the world must adapt to scarcity while the other half is rebelling against being too thin and too poor, as well as not free.

In the new epoch there is little time for a time out from a world that brings ever more quickly the over there of yesteryear over here. There are more than two hundred countries now, and many of them matter, with several more in a position to claim a moment of fame during which their in-fluence extends to the world at large. Having too many states thus featured by history above the others creates an unusual moment of zero-polarity: a world with "many communities, spheres of influence, hegemonic imperi-ums, interdependencies, and transnational loyalties that exhibits no clearly dominant axis of alignment and antagonism and has no central steering group or agency."[4] Across time, this sort of a world is haunted by the ghosts of the previous century's interwar years, another zero-polar moment whose ugly and brutal memories have not receded yet.

The specialists and country watchers of the Cold War decades seem a bit lost in this world; they were acrobats who juggled the arithmetic of weap-ons and other specific attributes of power. Generalists can now enjoy their overdue intellectual revenge; they are historical architects who mend the fragmentation of time and space. Staying out of consensual bandwagons fueled by the fashionable truth of the day, they shy away from mass-induced certainties and acknowledge instead the unpredictability of the moment. They are, wrote historian John Lukacs, "the creations of [their] time but, in a way, the creators of [the] time too"—judges and penitents, as Albert Camus put it, or the judged and judger, in George Kennan's words.[5] But be ready: much that is not known or only presumed will be cleared soon during the coming decade, which looms decisive. Remember, that was also the decade that conditioned the twentieth century whose history really started in full in the 1910s, with a war that the European Great Powers could neither avoid nor settle after it had ended, a revolutionary reset of neighboring Russia that its ideological masters could neither complete nor sustain, and an American surge to primacy for which the United States was not prepared and to which the rest of the world was not immediately responsive.

What is already known and widely acknowledged about the twenty-first century, though, is that the Western era is ending. As a post-Western era is said to begin, its final character is unknown, which means that there is no final evidence yet of irreversible decline for the West and irresistible ascendancy for everyone else. Indeed, this book suggests that the West can stay ahead of the rest because the rest cannot afford moving away from the West. That is not without some irony. Even with an ill-defined post-Western world lurching ahead, the West won! North Americans and Europeans, together with wartime survivors like Japan but also South Korea, as well as former holdings of the British Empire including Australia and New Zealand, no longer dominate the rest of the world but the rest is struggling to become like the West.

Standing up to, and challenging or disrupting the geopolitical reach of the West, a confusing and expanding bag of powers is emerging, new influentials, and nuisance or failed states. Their number is astounding—a dozen and more, almost a distorted echo of the pre-Westphalian era that set the stage for a consolidation of territorial space in the middle of the seventeenth century, even before the American Republic was born.

Among these emerging powers China leads the peloton as the most obvious bidder for preponderant status. Back as a world power after a long leave of absence, China is acting as a power in the world that aims to be second to none. Flushed with money, it enjoys a buying spree around the world—acquiring commodities to sustain its voracious need for economic growth, companies to gain access to needed technologies, and real estate for military outposts. Its largesse in areas that were once the imperial backyards of the

West also buys China new friends. This is a floating power that goes where its interests take it, welcomed for what it brings but also feared for what it takes. But is this condition sustainable—meaning, more of the latter and less of the former? With a GDP per capita generously estimated at $7,600 in 2010 (one hundredth in the world) China ranks behind Albania and barely ahead of Algeria: as China pulls its immense rural population out of poverty, organizes its giant urban centers into a coherent whole, preserves its vital access to commodities and export markets, and keeps its huge boundaries safe from fourteen neighbors, will it become a reassuring champion of the status quo or a restless challenger to world order? What is known now and thus can be said with some assurance is only that China has the potential to be as much of a power as it wishes to become, but it has not become yet the superpower it is already said to be. And although Chinese power is ample it is still balanced by weaknesses and vulnerabilities that are no less compelling. "They" are not the way we used to be, and much of what "we" still are remains what they can only hope to become.[6]

That the Chinese would be more aware of their unsettled condition than their Western interlocutors is not the least surprising feature of the moment. Unlike China, however, there are other emerging powers that show less patience with the pace of history and can hardly wait to exploit the opportunities it affords. These countries want to move history and make it go faster—so fast that in some cases their future is being lived in full before its time. The risks these states face from within, and the dangers they raise for others, are not caused by their power but by expectations that exceed their power: countries that attempt to do too much too early, or from which too much is asked too soon, fall victims of their own vulnerabilities. For the acquisition of power takes time and this is the odd thing about the long term: it cannot afford to take less than the time it needs.

Consider Russia, which is ranked behind Uganda for its easiness of doing business, and behind nearly everyone in the world on the issue of corruption. Although its GDP in 2010 dollars is ranked seventh in the world, Goldman Sachs forecasts that it will approach the EU levels by 2050 only—and even that is viewed as an achievement since no other emerging market is expected to achieve such a feat earlier.[7] Or consider India, whose performance has been praised by President Obama as "one of the most stunning achievement in human history."[8] India is ranked behind Bangladesh for the average years of schooling per capita, and ahead of most on the sensitive matter of poverty—with the eight poorest states in India home to more poor people (an estimated 421 million) than all fifty-three countries in Africa; or reflect on Brazil, whose slums in the nation's capital serve as a reminder of a country whose infant mortality rate is ranked ninety-third in the world, and where the education standards fall below those of Zimbabwe; or think about Turkey whose secular style of governance looks like a model for many of its Muslim neighbors even though it still lacks a credible constitution and even a shared understanding of what it means to be a Turk—beyond the populist assumption that "Lucky is the one who is a Turk."[9] In short, the jury is still out as states everywhere must demonstrate their ability to keep things together from within before they can better engage their neighbors and the world. At best, would have claimed former secretary of state Dean Acheson, this is what used to be known as the Scotch verdict—"Not proven yet."[10]

For much of the recent past, changes in the global structure of power have been announced periodically—often, if not always, at the expense of American and Western power. Such announcements proved premature, and the changes that were announced did not go in the directions that had been anticipated, as Japan can testify. Still the conditions of ascendancy elsewhere are real this time, although they are not as irresistible as they are made out to be and need not imply irreversible decline elsewhere. As recently as 2008, Kishore Mahbubani declared the Western era over—a death sentence he and many of his readers applauded but which is yet to be carried out. Ironically, it is Libya that was used as prime evidence—the "intellectual smugness" of American foreign policy that, Mahbubani wrote, spent several decades working to bring Colonel Qaddafi down before coming to terms with him.[11] Well, with Qaddafi gone with a UN-mandated, Western-managed, and NATO-enforced send-off, who looks smug now?

How will the Western powers live the post-Western moment and adapt to a post-Western world? We ought to know but not forget that there is an easy answer to this question: more comfortably and better than anywhere and anyone else. The relative decline of American power, as well as the institutional travails of Europe and the marginalization of Japan, is real. The rise of many new powers in Asia and elsewhere is also beyond question and generally for the good. But so are—real and for the good—the resilience of Western states from within, and their capacity to respond to challenges from without. Where are the people who dream of a summer house in the Chinese countryside where standards of living remain below those in Uganda, or want to have surgery in India where the health budget of $20 billion (1.4 percent of GDP) represents a bit more than $1.50 a day for each citizen, or do their schooling in Brazil or Turkey, which both ranked 104th in the world a few years ago? There is little need to insist: on these societal issues at least, aggregate statistics for all conceivable indicators do not lie. French Marquis de Custine's *Journey to Russia*, published shortly after Tocqueville's magisterial work *Democracy in America*, urged readers to "go to Russia." Quoting from Karl Marx, Custine praised such a journey as "very useful . . . for any foreigner. It is always well to know that a society exists where no happiness is possible."[12] The invitation went then to those who despaired of conditions in postrevolutionary France, but it would also suit today's skeptics who despair of the Western place in the post-Western world.

For the United States this is not decline but adjustment. The American economy accounted for nearly two-fifths of the global output in 1960, and such domination could not last. Nor could the United States sustain indefinitely the rates of growth it had during the thirty years from 1950 to 1980 when they topped 5 percent a year four times in each of these three decades—and only once more since. That, too, had to come down—just like the extraordinary growth of the Chinese economy over the past three decades will also slow down, which is already the case with a growth rate projected at "only" 7.5 percent in 2012. As to Europe, the institutional disarray of the past few years is legitimate cause for concern. But now like on so many earlier occasions when forecasts of Europe's impending death proved premature, a crisis which is possibly existential may yet prove to be once again the catalyst for the sort of *relance* that has defined the process of European integration over the past sixty years.

Remembering the destitute Europe that had to surrender to history sixty years ago is as difficult as remembering the dominant Europe that still prevailed one hundred years ago. "The nations of Europe," wrote Jean-Jacques Rousseau even earlier, "touch each other at so many points that no one of them can move without giving a jar to all the rest." This condition, which Rousseau attributed "to nothing better than chance," ceased to be cause for wars and became the glue needed to cement a union when, halfway into the twentieth century, Europe starkly understood that it had run out of suicidal options. Without the union that has been built since, Europe's death from war wounds would have been certain, and without it now its future in the twenty-first century would be dim. But the intimacy described by Rousseau no longer applies to Europe only; it also involves Europe's renewed ties with the United States, which had barely been born when the eighteenth-century French humanist, who was called a *philosophe*, wrote those lines.[13] And these ties, in the end, are what will help keep the West ahead of the rest—no longer decisive, admittedly, but still indispensable; and no longer exclusive, to be sure, but willingly inclusive.

An insistence on the continued primacy of transatlantic relations also distinguishes this book from the prevailing emphasis on a redirecting of U.S. primary relations toward Asia. As Hillary Rodham Clinton noted in November 2011, the U.S. "post–World War II commitment to building a comprehensive and lasting trans-Atlantic network of institutions and relationships has paid off many times over—and continues to do so."[14] Although it is equally true, as Clinton further argued, that "the time has come for the United States to make similar investments as a Pacific power," it is important to remember that entering the 2010s the terms of engagement with ascending powers across the Pacific involve states that do not share the same values and traditions, and whose adjustments to each other will be, therefore, more difficult and polemical than was the case when Americans and Europeans resumed their relations with fallen powers across the Atlantic after 150 years of separation and neglect.

Two decades after the end of the Cold War, the U.S. rise to preponderance need not be remembered with an excess of humility—the wars that might have been avoided, the crises that could have been better managed, and the better world that had been hoped for quicker. Without falling into triumphalism, there is also ample space for satisfaction and even pride in the many achievements behind. For half the world at least history was forced to change its ways: regions were pacified, states were recast, and people were pampered. That goes for much of Europe, but it also fits most of Central and South America; Africa, whose states gained sovereign independence if not, or not yet, affluence and dignity; and Asia, where hundreds of millions of people are waking up from their Western-induced long sleep into a changed world that the Western powers helped free and which they will now hopefully help make whole. Were Woodrow Wilson to come back to life and cast an eye on what has become of the world since he brought America back into it, in 1917, he would be on the whole rather satisfied. The "tedious climb that leads to the final uplands" proceeded at a heavy cost for more than "a generation or two"—an estimated 150 million deaths, increasingly noncombatant civilians slaughtered for power and greed. But early on in the twenty-first century we stand closer to "those great heights where there shines unobstructed the light of the justice of God" than we did one century, one millennium, one epoch ago.[15] This is still an American moment.

That the uphill climb ahead will remain Sisyphean is likely. For a bit of the world at least there is tragic evidence of a temptation to return to the old ways of history and reassert forcefully a long-gone primacy, by the state over its people and by the stronger powers over those that are weaker.

That is what makes the current moment pivotal, as well as urgent. Going from euphoria to hysteria, between 1911 and 1914, did not take long. Unbeknownst to the then heads of state and government, the "long peace" they had enjoyed for the previous ninety-nine years had little time left. In a sense, twenty years after another long peace, lived in fear during the Cold War, there is also little time left for another time out as a post-Western world is remodeled and refurbished with Western help.

The text that follows may occasionally seem to meander in time and in space: after all, no moment, least of all one that is expected to lead to a post-Western order, can be expected to unfold predictably. Still there is an organization that goes as follows.

Chapter 2 sketches the gradual transformation of the twentieth century and the drastic reduction in the number of Great Powers from many to two until the one-power structure that followed the collapse of the Soviet Union before turning, post–September 11, 2001, into the zero-polar moment of the past several years. The chapter insists that the two halves of the twentieth century cannot be remembered separately, not only for what became of Europe and the rest of the West but also for what has become of the West in the rest of the world. As part of a global tour that continues in chapter 3, this chapter assesses briefly the main attributes that define power—including critical mass, military capabilities, and economic resources with organization and steering as subjective modifiers. A ranking of world powers based on these attributes confirms the continued primacy of Western powers, but also the unquestionable but yet unfinished ascendancy of other powers in Asia and elsewhere.

A tentative blueprint for the post-Western world highlights a core group of five and a half major powers—the United States and Europe with China, plus Russia and India with, possibly, a crippled Japan maintained near the top by the resilience of its people; that landscape is surveyed briefly in chapter 3. But in the current geopolitical transition many other states also matter, either because of their capabilities and influence or because of their potential for nuisance and even failure. These states form a peloton of undetermined size. The sight of the many powers that expect to ride ahead of others is blurred by signs of their weaknesses that might pull them behind others. Ironically, the attribute that the major powers used to find most decisive, which is military power, is turning into the attribute that is losing its relevance most quickly. Yet, that the use or the threat of military force may well be getting obsolete does not mean that force has ceased to be a fundamental dimension of power. Many more decades will pass before that point is reached, if ever. But coercive power has already become largely out of date for major powers: in all cases involving them, and in most cases involving others, because it has proven to be increasingly inconclusive relative to the costs of using or even merely threatening to use it.[16] "The fast fish, not the big fish, eats the small fish," Vice President Joseph Biden was told when visiting Turkey in early 2011. That may well be true, but beware of what happens if the whale chooses to harass the small and weak shark.[17]

"After a difficult decade that began with war and ended in recession," President Barack Obama told the British Parliament on May 28, 2011, this is "a pivotal moment." And so it is: chapter 4 insists on the central role of the United States, which will remain the world's lone superpower during the decisive decade ahead. In the twentieth century, too, it was the decade of the 1910s that proved decisive, with the start of a suicidal war that brought Europe down, America up, and Russia astray—thus setting the stage for a failed peace that framed a fatally flawed League of Nations. From that point on, the U.S. rise to power unfolded by default rather than by design, and by invitation rather than by coercion. Bound to lead at birth, because of its attributes but also because of the character of its people, an imperial America was meant to be defensive in nature, to remain persuasive in action, and to be limited in duration. There was more to national security than the defense of the nation's territory, however. Protecting and enhancing the core values that defined America's way of life and ensured its people's well-being was also important and demanded an external milieu compatible with the country's domestic vision.

"On issues close to home, [Americans] feel at home," writes Johns Hopkins professor Michael Mandelbaum.[18] But, he adds, on issues of the world they feel far away—out of place, ill-informed and uninterested. Lacking historical depth and geographic anxieties, their preferences lack consistency and rely on a specific view of themselves more than on a broad appreciation of others. The laissez-faire temptation to leave the world is only part of a never-ending dialogue about the nation's role. For while awaiting the time when the world can be abandoned to its bad ways, others prefer a *laissez-nous faire* approach (let us do it) aimed at making them more like us. Meantime, the general public responds to immediate results. Don't tell me but do show me: a good policy is one that works, preferably on the quick and on the cheap. Trying is not good enough, especially as the costs of regulating some kind of order among more and more powers aiming to be above others mount to the point of exceeding America's capacity to face them.

Chapter 5 acknowledges the multipolar future that lies ahead and reviews the various alliance handicaps faced by some of the most readily identifiable powers that are likely to populate it. The self-imposed handicap defined by the forthcoming moment—maybe an era—of fiscal austerity in the United States and elsewhere in the West is recognized for the limits thus placed on external priorities. That, however, reinforces even further the centrality of the transatlantic alliance and its role as an axis of stability for the emerging new order: not only because of its continued primacy as the world's most complete partnership—that which is best endowed with all the attributes of power—but also because of a lack of competitive partnerships involving either the United States and Europe with a third party, or the rest without or against the West, however these other states might be grouped, at two or more and many. Unlike what proved to be the case during the various structural configurations of the previous century, there is little prospect of diplomatic triangulation between the main powers in the West and the rest (including India), or between the rest (including Russia or China) and parts of the West.

In lieu of a conclusion, chapter 6 returns to the urgency of the moment, which leaves no time for a time out from the world. That urgency will be most dramatically tested in the Greater Middle East, including the Persian Gulf and extended all the way to Pakistan. In this region, the new Global Balkans that defined the earlier part of the twentieth century, a new Sarajevo instant—even shorter than a moment—is faced: an instant, that is, during which a small regional clash can erupt at any time, and escalate in no time into a major conflict with global ramifications that would define the next several decades.

NOTES

1. Simon Schama, *Landscape and Memory* (New York: Vintage Books, 1985), p. 3. Some of these ideas appear in my essay, "The Folly of Forgetting the West," *Policy Review*, no. 174 (August & September 2012): 35–48.

2. Albert Camus, "Humanity at Zero Hour," quoted in Jeffrey C. Isaac, *Arendt, Camus and Modern Rebellion* (New Haven, CT: Yale University Press, 1994), p. 21.

3. Robert A. Pastor, ed., *A Century's Journey: How the Great Powers Shape the World* (New York: Basic Books, 1999), pp. 333–34.

4. Seyom Brown, *New Forces, Old Forces, and the Future of World Politics* (Glencoe, IL: Scott Foresman, 1988), p. 242. Joseph S. Nye, Jr., *Bound to Lead: The Changing Nature of American Power* (New York: Basic Books, 1990), p. 237.

5. John Lukacs and George Kennan are quoted in William Pfaff, "Wise Men against the Grain," *New York Review of Books*, June 9, 2011, p. 60.

6. Thomas L. Friedman and Michael Mandelbaum, *That Used to Be Us: How America Fell Behind in the World It Invented and How We Can Come Back* (New York: Farrar, Straus and Giroux, 2011).

7. Anders Aslund and Gary Clyde Hufbauer, *The United States Should Establish Permanent Normal Trade Relations with Russia* (Washington, DC: Peter G. Peterson Institute for International Economics, 2012), pp. 1–2.

8. Quoted by Chico Harlan, "Obama Ends Asia Tour with Ailing Nation," *Washington Post*, November 12, 2012.

9. Robert D. Kaplan, *The Coming Anarchy: Shattering the Dreams of the Post Cold War* (New York: Vintage Books, 2000), p. 36.

10. Dean Acheson, *Fragments of My Fleece* (New York: W.W. Norton & Company, 1971), p. 86.

11. Kishore Mahbubani, *The New Asian Hemisphere: The Irresistible Shift of Global Power to the East* (New York: PublicAffairs, 2008), p. 111.

12. Astolphe-Louis-Léonor, Marquis de Custine, *Empire of the Czar: A Journey through Eternal Russia* (New York: Anchor Books, 1989). Karl Marx is quoted in David Mayers, *The Ambassadors and American Soviet Policy* (New York: Oxford University Press, 1995), p. 25.

13. Quoted in Kenneth N. Waltz, *Man, the State, and War* (New York: Columbia University Press, 1969), pp. 183–84.

14. Hillary Rodham Clinton, "America's Pacific Century," *Foreign Policy* (November 2011).

15. Quoted in John Lamberton Harper, *The Cold War* (Oxford and New York: Oxford University Press, 2011), pp. 10–11.

16. Robert E. Osgood and Robert W. Tucker, *Force, Order, and Justice* (Baltimore: Johns Hopkins University Press, 1967), p. 3.

17. Mark Landler, "In Turkey to Strengthen Ties, Biden Refuses to Ignore a Host's Boast," *New York Times*, December 3, 2011.

18. Michael Mandelbaum, *The Frugal Superpower: America's Global Leadership in a Cash-Strapped Era* (New York: PublicAffairs, 2010), p. 29.

2

RECASTING THE
GLOBAL SYSTEM

The demise of the European state system during the first half of the twentieth century did not result from the rise of American power but from the combined fall of every Great Power in Europe and everywhere else. In effect, the decline of the latter conditioned the ascendancy of the former. In 1945, after two suicidal wars waged in slightly more than a single generation, the New World was invited to rescue the Old World from itself, and thus give the West a new lease on life.

That the transfer of Western power and leadership across the Atlantic was not done after World War I was due only partly to America's unwillingness to step up because of its eagerness to come home. No less important was Europe's reluctance to let go of its historically dominant position, and its resistance, therefore, to an American rise to the top and on its own terms. That was in 1919, though, and the mistake was not repeated in 1945. For the remainder of the century, a gradual fusion between Europe as Not-America and America as Not-Europe created a new sense of the West, which even during the Cold War remained distinctive from the idea of a Free World that included a growing number of liberal democracies inspired by Western values.[1]

Now, entering the twenty-first century, the West is said to be fading, and even going if not gone yet. Regretfully, there is no one to which the United States can hand the baton for the twenty-first century, as was done by Europe for the previous period. But should the history of the post-American, post-Western world ever have to be told in the future, emphasis will be placed this time on the combined rise of new or renewed Great Powers rather than on the decline and fall of the current Western powers.[2] And should trends currently discerned fail to be confirmed during the coming years, it will not be because of an American or Western reluctance to permit and even invite other states to share their preponderance but because of the inability of other states to do so.

HOW MANY POWERS ARE ENOUGH?

The unipolar moment that followed the Cold War was expected to start an era. It was inaugurated in January 1991 when the first Gulf War set the stage for an awesome demonstration of U.S. power, as well as an impressive display of U.S. leadership and diplomatic competence in a region of global significance. The facts of American primacy were beyond question in virtually every area: superior capabilities (military, but also economic and institutional) that no other country could match or even approximate in their totality; worldwide interests that no other regional power could embrace, let alone challenge; and a universal saliency that confirmed America's legitimacy to intervene decisively wherever it chose to be involved on behalf of its interests or values, as well as those of its allies and friends.

With history having thus come to the end of its ideological evolution, as political scientist Francis Fukuyama wrote in a polemical essay on the end of history, historians who believed in the uniqueness of the United States' primacy were taking their revenge over theorists who had insisted on the iron laws of countervailing power.[3] For relative to the costs of balancing such overwhelming American power, other states viewed the threat it raised as distant physically and modest strategically—sufficiently benign and not threatening to live in a condition of inferiority, at least for a while. And why would it be otherwise? The American formula that linked democracy with peace, and peace with prosperity, appeared to work well enough. After 1919, few efforts to adapt democracy to the changed conditions of the postwar world proved successful: twenty years later, before the start of World War II, democracies only survived in the dozen countries that enjoyed the highest per capita income.[4] But now, after the Cold War and with the twentieth century near completion, history was sketching a fairy tale ending—an irresistible urge by "the rest" to be free and affluent, like the West. All that was needed now was to accommodate that urge: powerful and principled, "we" had all become hardened Wilsonians while "they" were all recast into soft Westerners. With any challenge to American power thus made either futile or needless the most that other states might consider was a bit of soft balancing that would be designed to "signal a commitment to resist the superpower's future ambitions" without suggesting a resolve "to coerce or even to impede" with "territorial denial, entangling diplomacy, economic strengthening . . . or resolve to participate in a balancing coalition." But that would be hard work.[5]

Now, however, the talk of America's decline is combined with the sight of power everywhere else to confirm the end of the unipolar moment before any sort of era had the time to get started. That transition, too, was forecast earlier—and often. Immediately after the Cold War, skeptics and critics of unipolarity favored Japan and Germany (with or in Europe) as the leading peer competitors, which kept a decisively Western flavor for the presumed post-American order, as had been the case for the post-European world after World War II. But widely mentioned, too, were China, inevitably; a recast Russia, surprisingly soon; a surging India; and others like Brazil and, more recently, a resurgent Turkey. These "emerging powers" still form the core roster of applicants for preponderant status but the requirements have been diluted to make room for a larger entering class of upstarts elsewhere—as many as "dozens of others" according to some analysts.[6] What is surprising about the demise of unipolarity is not, therefore, that it happened, although even as a "moment" it was admittedly short-lived. What is even more surprising is what is taking its place—where the successor states are assuming their new role, and how a new international order might be organized and regulated, with and against whom.

Power Transitions

In and of itself a change in the global structure of power is not surprising. Power moves, relentlessly—up, down, and sideways. Ends typically outrun usable means and available time. Along the way, choices must be made, therefore, among priorities that are not always well picked relative to what is most immediately necessary or most readily manageable. Such choices are not easy, and even when made on behalf of the most desirable goals they often carry unexpected consequences that can derail the best plans. Moreover, unipolar systems of the type that emerged late in the twentieth century have been historically rare and geographically confined. When found, as with China in the Far East several centuries ago, such systems were never global in scope and thus had little in common with early U.S. expectations to extend to the rest of the world what had been achieved for the Western world during the Cold War. That, wrote Tony Lake, the then national security advisor to President Clinton, would require a will to confront "backlash states" that were bucking the global trend toward democracy, free markets, and civilized conduct.[7]

The reason why one power alone cannot suffice or last can be stated succinctly. An international order will not endure for long if it caters exclusively or primarily to the interests of the one while remaining indifferent and even hostile to the aspirations and needs of the many other smaller and weaker states. If entering the twenty-first century an unprecedented U.S. zeal for military intervention was nonetheless accepted for a short while, it was because of the horrific events of September 11, 2001. Reprisals from the United States were thought to be justified on grounds of self-defense, and the war in Afghanistan, where those events had originated, was acknowledged as an American action that deserved universal support. But lacking a common understanding of the historical significance of these attacks—whether as an unrepeatable aberration or as a new kind of conflict standing between war and terrorism—support from the rest of the world to engage into collective defense in Afghanistan did not include a war for regime change in Iraq as well. Such a preemptive military action might have been legitimate abroad only if the real enemy had been credibly (let alone correctly) identified for the unequivocal and immediate threat it raised to all; and the war that followed might have remained popular at home only if it had remained short and relatively painless, as had been promised.[8] Neither of these propositions was met, and in the confusion that followed the unipolar moment thus unraveled.

Even analysts who welcomed the unipolar moment at the close of the past century forecast it, therefore, only as a geopolitical interlude pending a return of multipolarity, however constructed, or another bipolar face-off, however composed. No unipolar power can outlive for long the constant pressures of discontented states: every challenge must be met, and none permits failure. That, predictably, is too much to ask, however abundant the power of the preponderant state. On the whole, the most optimistic projections gave the unipolar moment twenty to forty years, during which the United States would be gradually tied down, like Gulliver, in "an iron cage of multilateral rules, safeguards, and dispute resolution procedures."[9] That such would be the case was not only a matter of U.S. power and policies; even in the specific circumstances of the post 9/11 conditions, it also showed a deeper resentment felt in much of the world for the moral and historical righteousness and certainty that the United States was now displaying: the reflection of a "universalist political philosophy and a strong evangelical streak" that made America dangerously intrusive not only because of who and what it was but also because of what it might do and how, now that the assault of September 11, 2001, had unveiled America's vulnerability to unprecedented acts of terror.[10]

Power and the various attributes that define it never stays in place, and history has been cursed by states that resisted their decline for too long or, conversely, made use of their nascent power too early and, on occasion, so abusively as to prompt unwanted responses from concerned rivals that fear a lack of balance, or neglected allies that fear different priorities. In the multipolar world that opened the twentieth century, an ascending and increasingly assertive Germany, which had threatened to impose its own unipolar moment in Europe after unification in 1871, was surprised by the Entente Cordiale between France and Great Britain in 1905; and after France enlarged its bilateral entente to Russia—to make it the Triple Entente—the German state did not find enough capable partners for an effective counterweight of its own, notwithstanding the addition of Italy to the alliance the German state had signed with Austria-Hungary in 1879. With all major powers now fearing that time worked against them, except possibly for Britain, war soon erupted, after ninety-nine years of relative tranquility. That proved to be a death sentence for Europe and the Westphalian state system that had defined it for over three hundred years. In the bipolar organization of power that next emerged midway through the twentieth century, expansion and containment defined an increasingly hostile dialogue between two extra-European powers, the United States and the Soviet Union, across a European continent that was prepared for neither. With both superpowers reasonably confident that in such a structure time worked on their side, war was avoided along a partition line that kept both halves of Europe separate.

In a traditional multipolar context, the prolonged agony of the Austrian-Hungarian Empire is an example of a power's vain attempt to reverse its fall from primacy. After the Congress of Vienna in 1815, and thus long before its war with Prussia in 1864, Austria-Hungary never had much of a future. In the spring of 1914, no negotiated settlement would have been enough to restore life to an empire whose state was too weak for the too many nations it housed and claimed to represent. Instead, the Austrian emperor hoped that a short and triumphant war waged with the support of Germany against Serb nationalism would be a catalyst for redemption and renewal. But as we know now, even a German victory, which seemed within reach before the U.S. entry in the war in 1917, would only have meant an earlier German takeover of a worn-out and spent empire—earlier, that is, than the

Anschluss engineered by Adolph Hitler two decades later, as Germany's first step for its own national redemption and a resumed imperial march into its *Lebensraum*.

Troubling the agony of dying empires can be dangerous. The nineteenth century was shaped in the mid-1810s by the Great Powers' commitment to a prewar order based on the ancient principle that had just been painfully endured during nearly thirty years of revolutionary wars: namely, that the ideological dangers posed for all powers by revolution outweighed the strategic opportunities brought by any one of them.[11] That is what a young Harvard doctoral student named Henry Kissinger called "a world restored"—which kept Europe going, America growing, the West ahead, and a Eurocentric world relatively at peace while the rest of the world (including China, India, and the Ottoman Empire) declined steadily. In August 1914, a general European war was probably overdue forty to fifty years after the unification of Germany had decisively changed the balance of power in Europe. The twentieth century was "short" if identified with World War I, but it is significantly longer if the war is linked to Germany's unification, which occurred in 1871. Nor, in 1939, can World War II be separated from the first world war and its flawed outcome at Versailles twenty years earlier. These wars' legacies also include the rise of the Soviet empire whose ultimate collapse was forecast in the bipolar world that followed the fall of the Third Reich. This is what George Kennan did, notwithstanding the "orgy of good feelings" about the United States, which he wishfully witnessed in Moscow for the "lend-lease" of its abundant power to an admittedly unnatural ally, while in the United States, too, there was appreciation for the indispensable Soviet contribution to the triumph of the Western democracies.[12]

Getting the Polarity Count to Zero

The two halves of the twentieth century must be remembered jointly, not only for what became of Europe and the rest of the West but also for what became of the West in the rest of the world. Early in the 1900s, a growing interaction between Europe, Asia, and North America already pointed to the rise of a post-Europe, post-European global order organized by states that did not know each other very well and needed to get acquainted without the imperial lenses they wore to see afar.[13] Midway through the century, a geopolitical transition, started earlier but somewhat ignored, was completed as the European state system was reduced to a cluster of fallen and powerless states, including an exhausted France that had never recovered from the Napoleonic wars, an overstretched Britain that was crumbling under the weight of its imperial burdens, and a destroyed Germany that had brought shame on its people and the very idea of Western civilization. Indeed, even without World War I the primacy of Europe would not have endured much longer. That it lasted so long is already remarkable—a tribute to moderation and prudence, which both died an ugly death during half a century of total wars.[14]

In the bipolar structure that emerged out of these wars, the U.S.-Soviet competition produced an abusively global contest that wasted the seemingly inexhaustible capabilities of the United States and overlooked the vulnerabilities of the Soviet Union. As noted by political scientist Kenneth Waltz, a bipolar world does not mean that either superpower is obligated to assert a positive control everywhere in the world—including in "the interstices of the balance of power" where live the weaker and smaller states but over which the intensity of the competition does not abate in the absence of agreed peripheries.[15] Whether the United States in Vietnam or the Soviet Union in Afghanistan this is nonetheless what was done too often. But Moscow, and Washington, to an extent, seemingly assumed that time was on their side—the former because of a presumed U.S. lack of will and intent, which would inevitably drive it away, and the latter because of a Soviet lack of renewable capabilities and internal soundness, which would inescapably bring it down.[16] For both superpowers, this is what containment was all about: a mixture of vigilance and resolve that would permit either side to wait the other out and win without the messiness of a war.

The Soviet views were grossly shortsighted. "The steady character of our countrymen," had noted Thomas Jefferson in early 1801, "is a rock to which we may safely moor." A lifetime later, America's resiliency, and its ability to overcome moments of relative decline and public fatigue, was confirmed again when President Ronald Reagan overwhelmed the Soviet ability to match, let alone exceed, an open-ended American capacity for the renewal of its power. As a result, the Soviet overreach, which had been noted first in the Caribbean in the early 1960s and felt next over Angola, in Central West Africa in the mid-1970s, was conclusively exposed in South Asia in the 1980s with a war in Afghanistan that proved catastrophic. The final ideological collapse of the Soviet regime, and territorial dismantlement of the USSR, followed. In retrospect, asserting a global role that had little to do with the history of Russia was the wrong thing to do. Soviet leaders would have been better inspired to accept the offer of a Cold War tie, which President Richard M. Nixon extended at the bipolar summit held in Moscow in May 1972. That offer took the form of a negotiated "statement of principles of international conduct" designed to "incalculate habits of moderation" on both sides.[17] If enforced, it would have assured the Soviets of regional parity with their main adversary in their immediate neighborhood—obviously a much better outcome for them than what unfolded less than two decades later after the balance had shifted to the benefit of the United States.

As power moves, which is always the case, the world changes, as it always does. How we are to adapt to these changes can be distorted by self-serving complacency (the "indispensible-power" argument), abusive dominance (a latent "America-uber-alles" temptation), and even self-defeating indifference (a latent "post-America" prediction).[18] Still, beyond such broad misrepresentations of Great Power status, there is some logic in assuming never-ending shifts from many or several powers to fewer—a logic that was lived in full during the past century. When the power count gets down to one there is also some logic to anticipate new shifts as the preponderant power feels the pressure, endures the torments, and questions the limits of a moment it had previously welcomed as a well-earned reward for past imperial "services." That was the case for the United States when President George H. W. Bush outlined a strategy of preponderance shortly after his impressive triumph in the first Gulf War—a strategy, that is, explicitly designed to maintain a favorable balance of power that would keep the main allies content, the defeated adversaries down, and the emerging powers behind. Admittedly, such a strategy would raise real risks of overextension. Rome is an especially good example of less-than-global unipolar preponderance: it managed these risks well, or at least longest—its rulers understood the need "to conserve force and use military power indirectly, as the instrument of political warfare" rather than as the psychic satisfaction of meaningless victories in purposeless but costly wars of choice.[19] Yet Rome too fell, though less quickly than any other empire since.

A paradox of preponderance is that even countries with much more power than all or most of their rivals can be denied influence on, or have less influence than, weaker countries on a whole range of significant issues and as if the difference in power was of no consequence. In other words, superiority measured in terms of available capabilities can still fail to produce the desired outcomes. Thus, in 1914, World War II grew out of a small incident in a weak nuisance state that larger empires were unable to manage. As the crisis quickly escalated, neither Serbia nor Austria-Hungary could be controlled by their stronger patrons, Russia and Germany respectively. For the prewar diplomats, as well as for wartime military strategists, events proved to be more decisive than the plans of men. In 1939, the war was started by a previously defeated German state whose leader had acquired an image of demonic invincibility that blinded his victims to his country's unpreparedness for a war that none of the still-stronger Western democracies wanted to wage. Memories of the previous war had produced a European culture of appeasement that still appears to prevail today.[20] During the Cold War, the power of the weak was surely a lesson both superpowers learned the hard way, in Vietnam and in Afghanistan. But that is also the harsh lesson the United States was taught in the unipolar structure that followed—President George H. W. Bush in Iraq, in a war he chose not to end after he had won it; President Clinton in Somalia, in a war he chose not to win after he had waged it; and George W. Bush in another war with Iraq he chose to fight seemingly without a strategy to win it.

The states' instinct is to balance, whether defensively for security or offensively for preponderance. That alone is enough to limit the duration of the unipolar power to a moment. What comes after unipolarity can be a final drop of the power count to zero, meaning a transition to a more traditional world with one, two, or more identifiable powers. A zero-polar world is not a world without Great Powers, and it can even have too many of them, but it is hardly a recipe for order. Instead, it can produce, as historian Niall Ferguson put it, though in a different context, "an anarchic new Dark Age" during which long and barbaric conflicts imposed by the very weak on the strong to test its endurance are waged by the very strong and increasingly angry gathered "into a few fortified enclaves."[21] That the most recent zero-polar moment emerged during the interwar years of the twentieth century is not a comforting thought. The peace treaty signed at Versailles in 1919 did not end the war. Rather, it left victorious and defeated states alike weak and with enough discontent to resume the war twenty years after it had been fought—especially as America's self-denial caused a power vacuum that favored a *revanchiste* Germany.[22] To an extent, therefore, going from one dehumanizing war to the next was preordained; but still, there were some serious blunders, as well as a bit of bad luck, that reinforced the drift from one war to the next.

Among such blunders one deserves special mention: less than three years after World War I, a small "coalition of the willing" was organized by France to invade the Ruhr, Germany's crucial coal region. Italy and Belgium gave the French-led coalition a semblance of legitimacy in the absence of support from the League of Nations. Regime change was not the goal of the French assault, but its impact on the fledgling Weimar Republic was expected to be secondary to ending the "formidable danger" allegedly raised by the German objections to the Versailles peace treaty, including its disarmament and financial clauses for reparations. As we know now, the French action was a monumental strategic error. While an angry Britain argued bitterly against France's "inherent perfidy and insincerity," a moribund President Wilson reportedly wished he could "tell the French ambassador to his face that he would like to see Germany 'clean up' his country [namely, France]." In Germany, meantime, the French invasion and the two-year occupation that followed ended any remaining hopes of reconciliation with moderate German leaders, and any plausible expectation of a peacekeeping role for a League of Nations already crippled by the U.S. abstention. The short postwar era ended then. What replaced it was to be Europe's long death watch. For by then, in the spring of 1923, another war in Europe was all but unavoidable. There was no stable German government ready or able to control a dangerously erratic and increasingly popular Hitler, no single power capable to contain an increasingly restless and bellicose German populace, and no coherent alliance able to deter the upcoming war with a remilitarized German state.[23] The stage was set, and the cast was eventually enlarged to Imperial Japan, another revisionist state that was prepared to commit whatever amount of force might be needed to achieve the changes it sought.

Power Unleashed

Entering the twenty-first century, the war in Iraq played an equally significant role as a decisive catalyst for system change. The decision to wage war on Saddam Hussein was made by George W. Bush with the broad support of a vengeful nation that the events of 9/11 had made aware of the existential risks raised by such aberrant regimes. Throughout 2002, and up to the invasion, opinion polls showed a large majority of Americans in favor of military action—as many as 69 percent in CBS/New York Times polls concluded in early 2003 before and after the war began. Admittedly, there was ambivalence regarding the timing of the operation, as many believed that the UN should be given more time to look. With an overwhelming number of Americans (85 percent) convinced that Iraq had such weapons, and a clear majority skeptical that they would be found, the two-thirds public support Bush received for acting without waiting for specific UN approval was more than a mere rally-round-the-flag phenomenon.[24] Only later did the evidence of failure transform it into a war of choice that was said to have been launched deceptively in the name of nonexistent weapons of mass destruction.

What made of the war the divisive issue it became was less the decision to start it than the inability to end it promptly and successfully.[25] In 2002, America stood sure of its right after a horrific day that was not attributable to Saddam Hussein but might be repeated by or because of him; and as Americans viewed Saddam's Iraq as an imminent danger they used circumstantial evidence for a preemptive action that was compared to John F. Kennedy's in the Caribbean in the fall of 1962. This was a far-fetched analogy, to say the least.[26] But like the French government in the Ruhr some eighty years earlier, the Bush administration was determined to seize the moment, and do away at last with an adversary that it expected to defeat on the quick and without tears.

Why the Iraqi government chose to fight rather than to agree to a settlement that might reassure the United States without a war is puzzling. The superiority of American power and the president's will to use it was beyond doubt: Iraq, on the other hand, lacked the power it claimed to have, and Saddam could hardly depend on the will of his oppressed people to fight against America and on his behalf, as they had fought against Iran but on behalf of their country. In the United States, the risks of doing nothing were perceived to be much above the costs of a military action: even if Saddam had not been directly involved in the planning of 9/11, the risk that he had access to weapons of mass destruction (WMDs) had now become too high. Note that the few former senior officials who argued against the use of force in the spring of 2003 for the most part sought the postponement rather than the cancellation of the war: many of them because more time was needed to prepare for "the days after" and some of them because of a need for additional intelligence about Iraq's capabilities and intent.

More likely, Saddam's miscalculation was based on the security dilemma he faced. Showing weakness and acknowledging that his country was not WMD-capable unlike what was widely assumed would have left Iraq vulnerable to Iran. Saddam had gone to war with each country once before: with Iran, his regime had been saved only after hundreds of thousands of casualties had been incurred on each side. With the United States, there had been only a few thousand casualties and his regime had survived his humiliating defeat. A decade later, in 2001, Saddam remained convinced that no U.S. president would dare do away with him: so long as he was seen as a rampart against Iran, a war with the United States was a rationally low-risk option that would leave Saddam, in his estimation, with the ability to simply lose and move on. In other words, Saddam Hussein thought that he had analytical information about the

United States and its intentions that others did not have. This in turn gave him the incentives to resist, which others could not understand.[27] Of course, he was wrong because like many others, including some of America's closest allies like France and Germany, he ignored the depth of national anger and security concerns in the United States at the time. The war about to take place was not designed to complete some unfinished business left by the president's father ten years earlier, or to *prevent* a repeat of the horrific events of 9/11. Rather, this new war in Iraq intended to *preempt* a risk, now deemed by many to be a threat, that had escaped the country's imagination since at least the collapse of the Soviet Union: namely, a direct attack on U.S soil.

In a sense, this war was also a fortuitous convergence of time and people as the veterans of the first Gulf War who populated the highest levels of the Bush administration had emotionally prepared, but not planned, for this moment during much of the previous decade. Now, 9/11 provided convincingly an irresistible rationale for making of Iraq a threat sufficiently urgent to bypass another protracted negotiation over sanctions at the United Nations. As was to be shown, the U.S. calculation proved correct at first: the invasion proper was relatively easy—arguably the most effective U.S. military operation since the landings at Inchon in September 1950, less than three months after the North Korean aggression. The difficult part came afterward, with an ill-planned occupation for which neither the United States nor the coalition of the willing, which had been hastily formed for the military mission, was either prepared or "adequately resourced."[28] (See table 2.1.)

During the initial phase of the war, this new demonstration of U.S. power was intimidating and appeared to extend the unipolar moment unveiled during the first Gulf War in 1991. American power, said to be "awesome"— which it was—was used in order to "shock"—which it did. With the U.S. military mission "accomplished" in less than six weeks, few states were able or willing to stand in the way. Even Iran, which was itself sufficiently preoc-

Table 2.1. The War in Iraq, 2003–2012

	2003	2003–2006	2007–2011	2011–2012
Mission	Invasion	Occupation	Reconstruction	Withdrawal
Mood	Supportive, vengeful	Restless, skeptical	Critical, angry	Relieved, bitter
Tool	Coalition of the willing	Antiterrorism	Counterinsurgency	State-building
Outcome	Successful	Fiasco	Improving	Unclear

cupied with al-Qaida to look the other way had U.S. planes or missiles entered its air space, was now sufficiently impressed to seek a comprehensive and unconditional dialogue on such major U.S. goals as "decisive action" against terrorists (meaning, presumably, Hezbollah in Lebanon), the end of its "material support" for Palestinian militias (meaning, possibly, Hamas in Gaza), and joining the Saudi initiative for a two-state solution in the Israeli-Palestinian conflict.[29] Bush's failure to respond to Teheran's opening was further evidence of the triumphant mood that prevailed at the time. Unipolar preponderance was now equated with unilateral omnipotence. In any case, with no WMDs found anywhere in Iraq and with regime change about to be completed in Baghdad, the invasion had been successful and the war was thought to be over—there at least, with others likely to come elsewhere.

But instead of the quick withdrawal that had been anticipated, the invasion was followed by a disastrously mismanaged occupation that failed to produce either the rehabilitation or the reconstruction of a stable Iraqi state. Faced with a divided and increasingly violent country that was culturally and politically alien to the United States, the public mood quickly turned from supportive and permissive to skeptical and restless. For any preponderant state, little is worse than the evidence of failure, and for the United States specifically, little is more politically damaging than the mere appearance of failure. Thus, the inefficacy of American power in ending the war after it had been easily won caused a broad rejection of the leadership of the U.S. president at home and of his country in the world. And even though the shift from antiterrorism to a counterinsurgency strategy during the waning years of the Bush administration proved effective, it was not enough to restore the U.S. reputation for efficacy.

From Bush to Bush, the war in Iraq ended a unipolar moment that President Obama neither could nor wished to restore. But if not the United States, who? Early in the 2010s, as the United States painfully steps out of the quagmire of preponderance into which it fell in Iraq, a zero-polar moment is lived in "a bifurcated world" in which areas where the state does not exist clash with others where the state exists for the benefit of its people.[30] That clash—in the name of civilization rather than between civilizations—will be for the West to sustain and ultimately help win, not because of a model it would impose but because of the failings it can help others overcome. How many powers will be enough to manage such conditions is not clear; what is clear, however, is that only one such power, let alone none, is not enough.

HOW MUCH POWER IS ENOUGH?

"A structure," notes Harvard political scientist Joseph Nye, "is simply an arrangement of all the parts of the whole."[31] What this arrangement is like depends on how power is assessed and where it is located—not power for its own sake but relative to the outcomes it aims to achieve and the states it is designed to influence. But can power be measured—and, for that matter, how is it assessed?

The facts of power are elusive, and from time immemorial these facts have been deceptive. No one in 1672 who "computed the relative forces of France and England," wrote Winston Churchill, "could have foreseen . . . the noble colossus of France [lying] prostrate in the dust, while the small island [of Britain] would emerge victorious." There were, added Churchill, "conflicting yet contributory forces."[32] In the multipolar structure of the Westphalian state system, the quest for balance and its related "exercises in cartography" were the work of accountants no less than of diplomats: for every partition of Poland, for example, each territorial inch—"the fertility of the soil and number and quality of the populations concerned"—was scrutinized to ensure that the acquisitions of the victorious Great Powers were completely equal and that no one was left at a disadvantage.[33] After 1945, Stalin expected no less: he equated victory with security and security with territory—the territory, that is, which would be taken from the defeated states with the immediate acquiescence of the allies. As plainly stated by historian John Lewis Gaddis, "what one had provided the other was expected to endorse."[34]

During the Cold War, notes former national security advisor Brent Scowcroft about a bipolar structure he helped master and end, "we had a competitor we could more or less measure."[35] This is true theoretically: the assessment of power is easier in a bipolar world that lacks the complexity of a more plural structure. In real time, however, the measurement by either side of its adversary's power remained the hostage of multiple complexities, which explain Scowcroft's qualifier—"more or less." Thus, after World War II the United States did not even attempt any comprehensive national assessment of the Soviet forces until 1960 when the Kremlin's own data had to be evaluated in their totality before responding to its unexpected proposal for cuts in armed forces. Prior to that time, bureaucratic battles tended to exaggerate Soviet air capabilities, including bombers and missiles, which the U.S. Air Force maximized while the other military services relied on the more moderate estimates provided by the intelligence community. Conflicting assessments produced periodic "gaps" that typically fa-

vored Soviet capabilities at the expense of U.S. capabilities.[36] Indeed, in the
fall 1962 Cuban missile crisis, arguably the most dangerous episode of the
Cold War, grew out of a Soviet reaction to an American strategic buildup
that was started because of its own misperception of Soviet forces. Robert
McNamara, who served as secretary of defense during much of the 1960s,
acknowledged the mistake he made when he based his threat assessment
on the Soviet potential rather than on Soviet intentions.[37]

Later in the 1970s, after arms control had assumed center stage in U.S.-
Soviet relations, analyst Ray Cline assessed power around three attributes
which he called mass, economic capacity, and military force—and which
he measured with more or less objective data. These, however, were next
modified by two subjective multipliers loosely identified as "strategic purpose" and the "will to pursue national strategy" and to which Professor
Cline ascribed arbitrary numbers. This power equation produced an elabo-
rate ranking of the "perceived" power of 158 different countries spread
over eleven regions. Reviewing these rankings with hindsight is puzzling:
the Soviet Union was ranked first, ahead of the United States; Brazil was
ranked sixth, behind Iran, but ahead of China and France; and India and Israel stood behind Pakistan and Egypt, notwithstanding their recent military
triumphs over their respective enemies.[38] While Americans worried and
a declinist school took off in the West with near Hegelian accents, Cline
became a bit of a celebrity in the Soviet Union whose number one ranking
had come as a surprise.

Power Attributes

According to Kenneth Waltz, the guru of realist theory, the main power
attributes are the "size of population and territory, resource endowment,
economic capability, military strength, political stability and competence."
Different analysts organize these attributes differently, but the fundamental dimensions of power do not truly differ among them. In the 1950s,
Hans J. Morgenthau, the grandfather of realism, highlighted "quality of
diplomacy" (a dimension of "competence") and "national morale" (an indicator of "political stability") as variables that modify the availability of
capabilities and strength. For Kenneth W. Thompson, another architect
of postwar realism, power attributes are "physical" (geographical position,
natural resources, productive potential, military capacity, and population)
and "non-physical" (national character, morale, leadership, and appeal).
In the same vein, the French sociologist Raymond Aron viewed power as
"milieu, resources, and collective action"—and one of his French disciples,

Thierry de Montbrial, makes a useful distinction between power (namely, force), potential (namely, resources), and "potency" (namely, the conversion of potential into capabilities for coercive action).[39] More practical, Chinese officials speak of "comprehensive national power"—what Nye calls "complete" power, to be steered for "co-optive" or "command" functions with a "smart" or "skillful combination" of "hard" and "soft" capabilities, and with the "contextual intelligence" of a competent leadership and apt organization.[40]

To each analyst his own matrix; more importantly, to each state its own approach to power and its own assessment of the stockpile it needs and can afford. However power is viewed, its measurement remains relative and rather subjective—easier, it is said, to experience and feel than to describe and define. Even its most tangible features are subject to under- or over-evaluations. As a result, the "quantity" of available power is always elusive. But so is its "quality," including the will to use whatever is needed for the task—and the organizational ability to steer it for the desired objectives.

Figure 2.1 assesses three main overlapping categories of power attributes: critical mass and milieu, force and military capabilities, and economic power and resources. These are multiplicative rather than cumulative: that is why each arrow starts slightly to the right of the one above it. All three are modified by a fourth attribute, which has to do with steering and points to the state's ability to translate the nation's capacity into actionable capabilities for the desired goals. The effect of steering on state power can be positive or negative, hence the two-way vertical arrow that completes the horizontal arrow—which is kept thinner to reflect the relatively limited

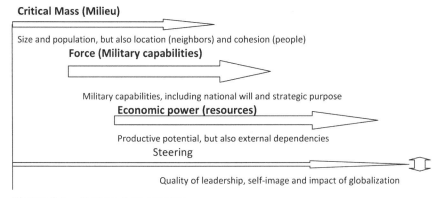

Figure 2.1.   Power Assessment

impact it can have on the other main attributes. Power assessment cannot escape any of these categories, even though each of them remains more or less speculative, depending on the variables and available data. Even the relative value of each category of power attributes varies, which explains the thickness of the arrow: thus, economic power stands between military capabilities (still potentially decisive) and the raw materials offered by the critical mass.

Critical mass stands primarily for size—of territory and population: in most instances bigger remains better and wars cannot be waged without people. That mass is not always well balanced, however. Canada, Australia, Argentina, and Saudi Arabia are all very big states with relatively small populations; Nigeria, Japan, and India are smaller states relative to their larger populations. Predictably, demographic trends stand out as significant modifiers of a country's critical mass: populations in India and Nigeria are getting bigger and younger, while Japan's is turning smaller and older, like the states of Europe and even China but unlike Russia whose population suffers not only from very low fertility but also from a declining longevity (respectively ranked 197th and 162nd in the world in 2011).

In an age when the Westphalian principle of national sovereignty was sacred, location, or milieu, was a main modifier of the state's physical characteristics. Shared borders, often disputed, were a cause for shared troubles—or at the very least shared concerns. As the legendary Otto von Bismarck reportedly liked to say, the test of a good diplomat for a country with five neighbors is to deliver three allies. But conditions have changed since. Territorial permeability and growing regional integration have muted past tensions from within and extended every neighborhood to the world without. In South America, for example, Argentina can now ignore Brazil's rise to military dominance in the area, while on the other side of the Atlantic even Greece can now escape its previous imperative to match Turkey's military capabilities: in 2011, Argentina's military power was ranked thirty-second in the world, as compared to Brazil's eleventh place, one spot ahead of Greece, which had fallen far behind sixth-ranked Turkey.[41] Yet, that Turkey's military power would have moved significantly ahead of Brazil made sense because of their respective milieu: lacking trust in the protection afforded by NATO, which Greece can block at will, Turkey faces a difficult neighborhood that also includes Iran, Iraq, and Syria.

The usefulness and effectiveness of hard military power has receded over time, but force remains a major category of power attributes. To an extent, military capabilities can be measured, combatant for combatant (available military manpower, but also manpower fit for service or reaching military age annually), and weapon for weapon (in all services, not only quantitatively but also qualitatively). These clearly matter: in 2012, numbers alone would help explain the different reactions to the quasi civil wars in weak (and fully disorganized) Libya and stronger (and much better equipped and battle-ready) Syria. The state's potential can also be assessed relative to the size of its population (and thus, available reserves) and demographic trends, but is also sensitive to historical precedents (which can help assess motivation and endurance) and geographic conditions (like location or topography). Aggregate defense spending is a useful indicator of the state's ability to execute its perceived intentions. Other significant variables include the availability of some strategic resources like oil (including oil reserves) and money, or even facilities like airports and harbors. In the end, though, no single variable is decisive. Very poor Pakistan and failed North Korea are nuclear powers, but even without accounting for their nuclear capabilities, they respectively rank as the world's 15th and 22nd military powers, but only 179th and 193rd in terms of GDP per capita. Meantime, tiny South Korea and (nuclear-capable) Israel are top ten world military powers. But insufficient size or wealth can also constrain the ability to acquire, renew, or use force for too long a time—and, on occasion, may even determine how and when to use it: for example, a weaker country convinced of the inevitability of a conflict with an adversary that enjoys better attributes can conclude that striking early and first is better. Consider, for example, the military balance between Israel and Iran. While the Israeli military is ranked slightly ahead of Iran (tenth and twelfth respectively), it lags sharply behind in most measurable areas, and its capacity to maintain its advantages in, say, total defense spending, is made questionable by a 1-to-10 ratio in population, and 1-to-80 in size. Yet few military analysts would bet against Israel in case of a war between both countries.

An increasingly significant dimension of power is not coercive, or hard. "You're waging war with Soviet arms," Henry Kissinger reportedly wrote Egypt president Anwar Sadat in the fall of 1973, "but you'll have to make peace with U.S. diplomacy." One of the most celebrated architects of *realpolitik* during the second half of the twentieth century, Kissinger was not wrong: the ability to convince, or even seduce, matters more and more because war now settles less and less. This is what Harvard professor Joseph Nye calls "soft power," which he defines as the state's ability to induce other countries to "develop preferences or define their interests in ways consistent with its own."[42] In the fall of 1990, George H. W. Bush's UN-driven multilateral diplomacy was the main feature of the U.S. response to Iraq's invasion of Kuwait: to build a universal coalition Bush's "tin cup diplomacy" cancelled $7 billion worth of Egyptian debt, convinced Saudi Arabia to extend a $4 billion line of credit to Russia, allowed Turkey to ship significantly more textiles and ensured confirmation of World Bank loans between $1 and 1.5 billion for each of the upcoming two years, ended an eighteen-month isolation of the Chinese government, brought Syria into the coalition even while shipping new defensive weapons to Israel, and secured financial commitments from Germany, Japan, and others for most of the war costs.[43] About twenty years later, the administration of George W. Bush was less skilled in achieving a universal consensus for an intervention of its own in Iraq, and the smaller coalition of the willing organized accordingly by the U.S. president proved capable to fulfill its military mission (with regime change as its central component) but grossly insufficient and untooled for attending to the occupation that followed.

There is nothing "fuzzy" about the idea of soft power.[44] This is not about Sister Teresa waging a triumphant moral campaign on General Patton. But as the use of military force grows less likely to be conclusive, even for foreign and security policy objectives to which it is best suited, other power attributes become more significant to coerce no less than to convince or seduce. For Russian analyst Andrei Tsygankov, this means more reliance on "political legitimacy, economic interdependence and cultural values." Significantly, little of this is characteristic of Russian power assets: a recent comprehensive assessment of soft power capabilities ranked Russia twenty-eighth in the world, immediately after India and barely ahead of Greece (ranked thirtieth). Although the same study also ranked China rather low, just ahead of Brazil, the facts of soft power may ultimately prove quite compatible with Chinese history and the works of their leading strategic thinkers.[45] Much richer and less dogmatic than the Soviet Union of old, but also less offensive (historically) and less normative (politically) than Western powers, China is organizing its own soft power game better than its former Soviet ally did during the Cold War. Especially in a moment of deepening austerity elsewhere in the world, huge amounts of Chinese sovereign funds can flow out to states that remember China as a successful challenger of the old bipolar structure, which now offers an alternative to cash-poor Western states without insisting on "politically correct" practices and values. China's appeal as a can't-miss-superpower, as well as its I-don't-care attitude, produce traction that is added attraction for people who have grown weary of Westerners pulling them to unwanted directions.

Economic power is a third category of attributes that has gained much importance over the past few decades, during which the definition of great powers ceased to be limited to the state's ability to prevail in war. Gross domestic output is a primary indicator that measures the nation's economy. That China's aggregate GDP passed that of Japan in 2010 is therefore important—but not decisive, or else China would have been the world's peerless power of the nineteenth century, when its share of the world's GDP reached 32.9 percent—far more than at the start of the previous century (22.3 percent) and also more than the United States or Western Europe at the close of the past century (21.9 and 20.6 percent respectively).[46] But no less significant, too, is the per capita distribution of the aggregate output. That GDP per capita in China will remain far behind that of Japan for many years and even several decades also matters—though, again, not decisively or else the ten miniscule states that had the highest per capita incomes (at purchasing power parity) in November 2010, ranging from $179,000 in number one Qatar to $48,900 for number tenth Kuwait, would top the United States, ranked eleventh ($47,200). That is not the case because despite their wealth these states clearly lack influence on the world economy—for stabilizing or disrupting financial markets, as market outlets, or for developing and contributing to coordinated responses to prop up the world economy as and when needed.[47]

The increasing influence effect of commerce (including trade but also foreign direct investments) also says a great deal about bilateral or regional relations. The United States annually sells about $1.5 trillion worth of goods and services to the rest of the world, which creates an estimated ten million high-paying jobs in America: it is estimated that every $1 billion of additional exports creates as many as seven thousand very good new jobs.[48] For an emerging economy especially, it is hard but indispensable to enter the competitive manufactured or agricultural and financial markets of matured economies. But it is even harder and consequential to be denied or lose those markets after they have been won. That is why economic sanctions can work. To escape or at least mitigate external dependencies—not only on exports, but also on commodities, capital, and technologies—alternative markets and suppliers are sought, which reinforces the new flexibility of the system's structure. Thus, according to the World Trade Organization (WTO), EU trade with China in 2010 ($544.7 billion) exceeded trade with the United States, still its most lucrative trade partner, by nearly $100 billion (with two-thirds of the excess caused by a much higher level of Chinese imports from the EU). Exports from Central and South America to the United States ($118 billion) or to the EU ($108 billion) still significantly exceed exports to China, but China's two-way trade with Brazil ($56 billion in 2010) now surpasses Brazil's trade with the United States ($45 billion that year), something beyond imagination ten years ago: in 2000, the United

States took 18 percent of Brazil's exports and provided 23 percent of its imports, and China was nowhere near Brazil's main trading partners.[49]

In 1947 trade negotiations involved only 27 countries, most of them rich and with an agenda mostly confined to manufactures. Now, over 150 countries negotiate over a truly global agenda that can be blocked by any of the poorest participants (like Chad, for example, on behalf of its cotton). Moreover, the influence of trade, which used to run from the industrialized North to the developing South, is now felt the other way, too—by Northern countries that need access to the expanding markets of the South. According to Goldman Sachs, the BRICs contributed 36.3 percent of the world's GDP growth during the first decade of the twenty-first century, as opposed to 27.8 percent for the United States.[50] As a result, a cohort of Western heads of state and government seeks privileged access to Southern economies for commercial contracts that the home economy demands. Meantime, countries in the South develop new trade patterns with third parties and among themselves, which are fraught with geopolitical significance. Thus, Turkey's trade with the then fifteen-member European Union accounted for over 56 percent of Turkish trade in 1999, but it was down to only 41 percent in 2011, after EU membership had expanded to twenty-seven countries. Meantime, Japan's trade has moved convincingly away from the West and toward China: between 2000 and 2010, the share of Japanese exports fell from 29.7 percent to 15.4 percent for the United States, and from 16.3 percent to 11.3 percent for the EU, while rising from 6.3 percent to 19.4 percent for China; as to Japanese imports, they fell from 19 percent to 9.7 percent for the United States, and from 12.3 percent to 9.6 percent for the EU, while rising from 14.5 percent to 22.1 percent for China. Elsewhere, the Euro-Atlantic share of Africa's exports declined from 67 percent in 2000 to 47 percent in 2010, but the Chinese share rose from 5 percent to 18 percent during the same period.[51]

Political scientist Karl Deutsch has assessed state performance "less as a problem of power and somewhat more as a problem of steering."[52] Steering depends on leadership, which inspires national will and strategic purpose. During World War II, Churchill was Britain's main asset—at least pending the U.S. entry in the war, when Franklin D. Roosevelt and the character of the American people became Churchill and Britain's main assets. When Roosevelt died, the Germans thought that this leadership change alone would end the "artificially-bolstered" Grand Alliance "with a gigantic clap of thunder" and Himmler promptly offered to surrender the German forces on the western front—a suggestion that was dismissed by Truman.[53] States can also steer and mold external perceptions of their power—willingly or inadvertently, for the better or worse. During the Korean War, Stalin, who did not think much of Truman, hoped to exhaust the president's will while diverting and even depleting America's capabilities away from Europe; after the war had ended, Secretary of State John Foster Dulles hoped to leave the Kremlin with "that nasty ultimate doubt at the backs of their minds, that some idiot in Washington might not after all loose off an atomic bomb, if Russia went too far."[54] Neither Stalin, who died in March 1953, nor Dulles, who died in May 1959, lived long enough to make the needed steering adjustment.

Steering demands knowing where to go and how to get there without being distracted by other and lesser events along the way; it also means adapting and responding to surprises, and knowing when one is lost or has lost— when it is preferable, that is, to try or stop trying to get there, wherever "there" might be, either because the desired outcome is no longer doable or because the rising costs of making it doable cease to make it desirable. Given what is now known, and could have been understood then, the U.S. intervention in Vietnam began too early and lasted too long: there was little need for the Eisenhower administration to stand in the way of the 1954 Geneva Accords calling for the prompt reunification of Vietnam, and there was little need, too, for the Johnson administration to dig in after manufacturing a North Vietnamese attack in the Gulf of Tonkin a few weeks before the 1964 presidential election. From the moment Johnson inherited the presidency in November 1963, he viewed his options too narrowly—"get in or get out, or get off," he argued hours after Kennedy's assassination; Johnson's conviction that he could not afford to "lose Vietnam" was reinforced by self-described "ex-historians" who reminded him of the damage endured by Truman after he was charged with the loss of China in 1949.[55] Yet too much of a bad war that got increasingly worse cost the United States dearly—an estimated $550 billion (in 2010 dollars).[56] That is less than the dollar cost of the shorter war in Iraq, which the Congressional Research Office estimated at $812 billion through fiscal year 2012—but with a loss in U.S. lives barely one-tenth of what occurred in Vietnam.[57]

In an era of generational austerity, the so-called guns-and-butter argument—Nation or Empire?—is strengthened. Domestic priorities cannot be ignored while attending to the pursuit of security needs and ideological pretensions abroad, or to the leader's ambitions and the nation's delusions at home: that has become true even for nondemocratic states. Only to the extent that both sets of priorities are reasonably satisfied can there be people sufficient in numbers, cohesive in action, motivated in intent, and responsive (or submissive) to the institutions that represent (or usurp) their collective identity. But such satisfaction cannot be complete without minimal respect for the nation's self-image. Win or lose, czarist Russia would not accept a demotion to a second-rate power status prior to 1914—no more so than Soviet Russia at Brest-Litovsk in 1917, or postcommunist Russia since the Cold War. In Moscow, Vladimir Putin understood this basic truth better than Boris Yeltsin, and in Washington, George W. Bush acted on it better than Bill Clinton. In 1961, Kennedy's ambition to keep U.S. military capabilities "second to none" was a challenge that Carter did not recognize during a national crisis of moral legitimacy he inherited from his predecessors. In 1950, the newly installed People's Republic of China was too weak but also too proud to remain indifferent to America's march to its frontiers, which it was unable to deter but which it was nonetheless able to contain. Fifty years later, a strong and united China is too strong (and still too proud) to even sniff the humiliating air of Western dominance and interference, whatever the nature of its regime: its "destiny" is not one of subjugation or even subservience in the Pacific, and its long fall from primacy is viewed as an unrepeatable aberration.[58]

Multilateral institutions can also have a reductive or multiplicative effect on power, making the small state feel big, but also the weak stronger and the poor richer. Consider the impact of the United Nations on the use of force. In the early days of the Cold War, getting the UN involved was a revealing sign of superpower indifference; now, it gives the stronger power universal legitimacy and the weaker powers relevance. In Libya in spring 2011, the Obama administration barely consulted with Congress for a constitutionally mandated approval of military action, but it sought UN authorization for a NATO intervention aimed at goals that the international community defined as humanitarian but which the Western powers enforced as regime change. On the other hand, one year later over Syria, the Russian and Chinese veto of U.S.-sponsored sanctions blocked the United States and other Western states from any sort of military intervention assuming they ever had any such intention.

Finally, a sharp increase in the pace of technological innovations and their potential for displacements and realignment has significance as well. Chinese claims that the label "made in China" will eventually be written as "conceived in China" after Western technologies are reinvented on the cheap outline the new geopolitical geometry to which China aspires. The boast is heard or repeated elsewhere with appropriate cultural adaptation. In this context, the spread of scientific research away from traditional Western centers highlights not only the like of China, which has upped its R&D spending by 20 percent every year during the ten years that followed 1999, but also new scientific powers like Turkey (which tripled R&D funding over a ten-year period ending in 2008) and Iran, where R&D spending is projected to reach 4 percent of GDP by 2030, as compared to 2.59 percent in 2006.[59]

In September 2001, war took a pagan turn for the worse—with acts of terror that seemed to redefine the meaning, ease, and cost of killing. Consider: the attacks of 9/11 cost their perpetrators an estimated half a million dollars, but ten years later the total costs of these attacks to the United States was estimated at $3,300 billion—or one-fifth of the total national debt.[60] Such costs discrepancy is unsustainable and leaves the United States, the West, and much of the rest at the mercy of other similar events that would be initiated by different groups and for different reasons but would have even worse consequences. One example of relative costs will suffice: defense against the primitive but deadly insurgent bombs used in Afghanistan, which consist of a plastic jug filled with ammonium nitrate fertilizer, require the expenditures of tens and hundreds of millions of dollars for such items as ground-penetrating radars, mini-surveillance robots, bomb-resistant underwear, and more. The risk, therefore, is that in this zero-polar moment the barbarians might force the West to abandon their own civilized ways and fight like barbarians as well. That would reduce the main attributes of power to the ability to kill and the willingness to be killed.

Power Assessment

This chapter began with a question: how many powers are enough? More than one is the answer, however peerless the preponderant power may be, and however flawlessly pure its intentions. For much of the twentieth century as other powers could do less and less, except to each other, the United States had to do more and more. It was, write journalist Thomas Friedman and political scientist Michael Mandelbaum, "a preacher, a healer, a philanthropist, a surgeon, and a doctor."[61] But even all that was not enough: it also became the architect that sketched the blueprint of a new world order, the contractor that managed its construction, the broker that financed its mortgage, the interior decorator that furbished it—and more. For this, the United States was rewarded handsomely, whether in cash with unparalleled prosperity or in kind with countries that now go the American way.

That will no longer be possible, however, or even desirable. As more and more states want to attend to some of these tasks, it is no longer indispensible for America to do it all—on its own or as a leader of what became of the West. That much is apparent. What is not apparent, however, is the answer to another broad question—how much power is enough and, indeed, how much power may also prove to be too much, not only how much but also where?

The Group of Twenty provides a good starting point. Its membership includes nineteen countries plus the EU. Organized after the financial crises of the 1980s in order to extend the Group of Seven (plus Russia), G-20 assumed preeminence ten years later, when another cycle of financial crises confirmed the central role of several emerging-market countries. G-20 makes room for the main Western states: the United States and the EU (on its own, plus Britain, France, Germany, and Italy), as well as much of the rest of the West (Japan, but also Canada and Australia plus Argentina); the four main emerging powers known as the BRIC states (Brazil, Russia, India, and China) plus South Africa (BRICS); and five pivot states that we label the KISMET states (South Korea, Indonesia, Saudi Arabia, Mexico, and Turkey), even though, contrary to the meaning of this Turkish word, their rise to renewed preeminence in the twenty-first century was hardly preordained. In 2010, G-20 covered most of the world's land area outside Africa, and housed two-thirds of the world's population; it produced nearly 90 percent of the world's GDP and represented 80 percent of global trade (including intra-EU trade); the world's fifteen top-ranked military powers are all G-20 members; and all G-20 members (and three other EU states that are not included in G-20) ranked among the world's twenty-six largest economies.

Still, the inclusion in G-20 of both the EU as a virtual political unit of twenty-seven states, and four of its largest members, is a source of multiple accounting. The states of Europe matter as a union. So considered, their core attributes have a dimension no single European state can match, including Germany whose economy is inextricably linked to the EU and whose lack of military power keeps it dependent on the goodwill of its partners, allies, and neighbors. A modified G-20 should not attempt to replace Britain, France, Germany, and Italy with countries of equal or superior power, but it can bring into a broad calculus of world powers a few more critical pivot states that are necessarily of interest for what they can do or might become.

On top of the list of such pivotal countries, there is Iran, which was a main beneficiary of the Arab Spring of 2011 and remains intent on joining Israel as a nuclear power in the Middle East. Its slow-moving confrontation with the United States and its allies is especially dangerous, with consequence on relations with and between all G-20 states. After a peaceful regime change in early 2011, Egypt is also facing a decisive period of political, economic, and societal reconstruction. The period is decisive because several decades of bad and corrupt governance by Hosni Mubarak make the risks of state failure real. As the first-ranked Arab country in the Middle East for military strength, and the third largest economy in the Middle East, Egypt is a state of consequence for the entire region: its radicalization, by way of the ascending Muslim Brotherhood, would have serious consequences for Israel, with which the Egyptians signed a decisive peace treaty in 1978 but which long-suppressed public sentiment for the Palestinians may now threaten. Israel's ties with the United States and other Western states also make it a test of future relations between the West and the rest of the world, including Russia but also China, which is torn between its needs for Iranian oil and American consumers. Finally, as the largest and most populated state in Africa and a major oil exporter, Nigeria is a significant state of concern—still haunted by the memories of its horrific postindependence civil war over Biafra in the late 1960s, and now torn between the emerging power it can be and the failed state it might yet become.

Any power assessment for this relatively small group of twenty states should account for the availability of all three core attributes discussed earlier—mass, military capabilities, and economic capacity. Making the core attributes multiplicative means that they must interact, which simply indicates that the effect of one core component depends on the value of another component. This makes obvious intuitive sense. For example, the effect on state power of both mass (territory and population) and a sizeable economy is greater than either a sizeable mass or a sizeable economy, and bigger, too, than the addition of both. Thus, a zero, or near-zero value for military capabilities would also reduce state power to zero or near-zero when introduced as a multiplier of mass and economic capacity—which also reinforces the idea of "completeness" when thinking about power in the twenty-first century.

As part of the critical mass, the size of the area is fixed, but that of the population evolves over time—although rather slowly. Few modifiers would likely change much the world power ranking for mass, and those that might produce a change find their way into other measures of military and economic power. For example, age and gender distribution impact military capabilities, not only with regard to the size of armed forces but also with regard to the willingness to use them. They also are significant variables in any assessment of economic power because of their consequences on the state's economic size and productive capacity. With data readily available, the ranking for critical mass is based on a combination of area and population sizes. As shown in table 2.2, Russia is the biggest country by size, and

Table 2.2.   Critical Mass

Country	Area (km²)	People (m)	Rank (1+2)
China	9.6 m (4)	1,130 (2)	1
U.S.	9.8 m (3)	310 (4)	2
India	3.29 m (7)	1,173 (1)	3
Russia	17.1 m (1)	140 (8)	4
EU	4.3 m (6)	492 (3)	5
Brazil	8.5 m (5)	201 (6)	6
Indonesia	1.9 m (11)	243 (5)	7
Canada	9.98 m (2)	33.8 (17)	8
Mexico	1.97 m (10)	113 (10)	9
Nigeria	923 t (15)	152 (7)	10
Argentina	2.78 m (8)	41.3 (16)	11
Australia	7.74 m (6)	21.5 (19)	11
Iran	1.65 m (12)	67 (13)	13
Egypt	1 m (14)	80 (11)	13
Japan	378 t (17)	126.8 (9)	15
S. Arabia	2.1 m (9)	29 (18)	16
S. Africa	1.2 m (13)	49 (14)	16
Turkey	774 t (16)	77.8 (12)	18
S. Korea	100 t (18)	48.6 (15)	19
Israel	22 t (20)	7.35 (20)	20

Source: The CIA World Factbook.
Note: m = million; t = thousand

India by population, but China comes first in the cumulative ranking that combines both. The United States, ranked second, is the most balanced state in terms of size and population, like Brazil, ranked fifth and sixth for area and people. Fertility-high Nigeria (now ranked tenth) and eighteenth-ranked Turkey are the states that are most likely to move up in coming years, although in both cases population growth may prove to be detrimental to their economy even if it proves favorable to their military potential.

The assessment of military capabilities and economic power is more subjective. Variables overlap. Some, like defense spending, rely on official data that are more or less reliable; others, like the will to fight, cannot readily be measured. For example, China tends to understate defense budgets, especially in the aggregate, but Saudi Arabia tends to overstate them, especially per capita. In any case, Clausewitz's "fog of war" continues to spread uncertainty on the assessment of military capabilities, and its leaders' capacity to make good use of them for any period of time. Also at play is what the Greeks called *fortuna* or fate: the inevitability of man-made blunders, the absurd significance of trivialities, the unpredictability of God-made events.

As Oliver Cromwell noted of statesmen: "He goeth furthest who knows not whither he is going"—which is why the British historian A. J. P. Taylor used to place considerable emphasis on the role of chance.[62]

A study by the group Global Firepower, a reliable source of comprehensive military data, has ranked the world's military powers on the basis of forty-five factors, including personnel (population and available manpower), weapon systems (but not nuclear weapons) and resources (including oil), logistics (roads, railways, airports, and motorways), and financial (budgets and reserves).[63] The exclusion of WMDs can be questioned: these have a meaningful deterring military value, and some failed or failing states with nuclear weapons have an unparalleled potential for harming the power structure irreversibly. Yet note that the top five military powers—the United States, Russia, China, the EU, and India—all have nuclear capabilities. They are ranked ahead of Turkey, South Korea, and Japan, while nuclear Israel, which comes next, is placed one notch before Brazil, which also comes immediately before Iran. Note, too, that impoverished Pakistan is ranked fifteenth (counting Great Britain and France rather than a single EU) without accounting for its substantial strategic arsenal. Thus, the ranking places the two former masters of the bipolar structure still far ahead of the rest. Midway into the ranking, Egypt and Saudi Arabia combine with Iran to keep Israel, ranked slightly higher than either state, sensitive to Iran's acquisition of nuclear weapons, Egypt's mood changes, and Saudi Arabia's interest in alternative allies among the non-Western emerging powers.

Economic power is especially difficult to assess and a large number of variables that affect it also apply directly to military power. Note that just as "critical mass" is different from milieu, economic power, which tends to be measured as an aggregate, is not the same as wealth, which is measured on a per capita basis. A recent attempt (2010) to measure economic power parsimoniously was made by a group of Indian economists. The study developed an index that is designed to "encapsulate the economic . . . power of a nation's government in the international arena." The index uses four broad variables: government revenues, foreign currency reserves, export of goods and services, and human capital. These variables "broadly reflect aspects that contribute to a government's economic clout, voice and negotiating leverage by capturing elements like its ability to raise resources, its creditworthiness and credibility in international financial markets, its influence on global economic activity and its potential in terms of human resources."[64] The 2009 results for a modified G-20 show that the top ten spots are occupied by the Western core, all five BRICS states, and two of the five KISMET countries: (1) the United States, (2) China, (3) EU (estimated on the basis of the rankings achieved by individual EU countries), (4) Japan, (5) India, (6) Russia, (7) Brazil, (8) South Africa, (9) South Korea, and (10) Mexico. The index captures well the recasting of the global power structure.

The results of ranking the modified G-20 on the basis of the core attributes—critical mass (based on the CIA *World Factbook*), force (based on the Global Firepower measurement of military strength), and economic power (based on the Indian study)—are shown in table 2.3.

No conclusive empirical claim can be made out of this final ranking. As noted, there are other subjective indicators that are much more unreliable and modify, for the better or for the worse, each core attribute. But at least the ranking can open a small yet credible window on the conditions it describes without distorting the complex reality the assessment aspires to convey. In any case, additional indicators for each category would not change this ranking significantly. With the United States and the EU joined by Japan and Canada among the top ten countries, the Western powers remain well positioned and even largely ahead. This

Table 2.3.   Core Power Ranking Formula: Pp = Mass × Force × Economy

Country	Mass	Economy	Military	Total
U.S.	2	1	1	2 (1)
China	1	2	3	6 (2)
Russia	4	6	2	48 (3)
EU	4	3	4	60 (4)
India	3	5	5	75 (5)
Brazil	6	7	10	420 (6)
Japan	15	4	8	480 (7)
Indonesia	7	11	13	1,092 (8)
S. Korea	19	9	7	1,197 (9)
Canada	8	11	15	1,320 (10)
Turkey	18	13	6	1,404 (11)
S. Arabia	16	14	16	1,496 (12)
Mexico	9	10	17	1,530 (13)
Australia	12	15	14	2,145 (14)
Egypt	12	18	12	2,808 (15)
Iran	12	20	11	2,860 (16)
Argentina	11	16	19	3,344 (17)
Nigeria	10	17	20	3,400 (18)
Israel	20	19	9	3,420 (19)
S. Africa	16	18	18	4,184 (20)

conclusion is significantly reinforced for the near future when considering separate assessments of the soft power tools available to the United States and other countries in the West, and the leverage provided by these resources. The four BRIC countries and four of the five KISMET states complete the top thirteen powers. Only twentieth-ranked South Africa, the fifth BRIC, falls sharply out of position. G-20 countries from the Middle East are next, with twelfth-ranked Saudi Arabia leading the way, while oil-rich Nigeria closes the ranks, immediately ahead of Israel, whose military capabilities exceed its economic power and critical mass by such margins as to be in question should it fail to sustain its close alliances with and in the West.

States that set the pace in front of the peloton of Great Powers are there because of their core attributes. Score a first for the United States and its main counterpart in Europe. Yet entering the second decade of the twenty-first century a recast global system makes it abundantly clear that American power, alone or together with the rest of the West, is no longer enough to control the rest of the world; this alone is suggestive of relative American and Western decline in the face of the rise of new influentials elsewhere. But even united and in some areas adversarial and potentially hostile, the rest of the world remains insufficient to control American and Western power; this, too, is convincing evidence of continued American and Western superiority relative to new powers that are emerging but can hardly be said to have emerged yet. To that extent at least, this post-Western moment remains an American one as well.

NOTES

1. Timothy Garton Ash, *Free World: America, Europe, and the Surprising Future of the West* (New York: Random House, 2004), p. 55.

2. Fareed Zakaria, *The Post-American World, Release 2.0* (New York: W.W. Norton & Company, 2011), p. 1.

3. Francis Fukuyama, *The End of History and the Last Man* (New York: Free Press, 1992).

4. Edward Hallett Carr, *Conditions of Peace* (New York: Macmillan, 1942), p. vix.

5. Robert A. Pape, "Soft Balancing against the United States," *International Security* 30, no. 1 (2005): 36–37. Also, Keir A. Lieber and Gerard Alexander, "Waiting for Balancing," *International Security* (Summer 2005): 109–39.

6. Richard N. Haass, "The Age of Nonpolarity," *Foreign Affairs* 87, no. 3 (May/June 2008): 44–56. After 9/11, the wars in Afghanistan and Iraq led Krauthammer

to envision a unipolar "era" for "thirty to forty years." Charles Krauthammer, "The Unipolar Moment," in "America and the World," *Foreign Affairs* 70, no.1, supp. (1990/1991): 23–33 and "The Unipolar Moment Revisited," *National Interest* 70 (Winter 2002/2003): 17.

7. Anthony Lake, "Confronting Backlash States," *Foreign Affairs* 73, no. 2 (March/April 1994): 45–56.

8. Francis Fukuyama, *America at the Crossroads: Democracy, Power, and the Neoconservative Legacy* (New Haven and London: Yale University Press, 2006), p. 6.

9. Charles Krauthammer, *Democratic Realism: An American Foreign Policy for a Unipolar World* (Washington, DC: American Enterprise Institute, 2004), p. 6; Christopher Layne, "The Unipolar Illusion: Why New Great Powers Will Rise," *International Security* 17, no. 4 (Spring 1993): 7–10.

10. Stephen M. Walt, *Taming American Power: The Global Response to U.S. Primacy* (New York: W.W. Norton & Company, 2005), p. 80.

11. Henry Kissinger, *Diplomacy* (New York: Simon & Schuster, 1994), p. 85.

12. George F. Kennan, *Memoirs, 1925–1950* (Princeton, NJ: Princeton University Press, 1967), p. 241.

13. Hajo Holborn, *The Political Collapse of Europe* (New York: Alfred A. Knopf, 1951), p. 70; Anton de Porte, *Europe between the Superpowers* (New Haven, CT: Yale University Press, 1979), p. 10.

14. Raymond Aron, *The Century of Total War* (Garden City, NY: Doubleday, 1954), p. 305.

15. Kenneth Waltz, "The Stability of the Bipolar World," *Daedalus* 93, no. 3 (Summer 1964): 889.

16. "Internal soundness and permanence of movement need not yet be regarded as assured," wrote Kennan in a telegraphic message to the secretary of state on February 22, 1946. George F. Kennan, *Memoirs, 1925–1950*, p. 558. At first, Kennan predicted that "ten to fifteen years" would be enough for containment to succeed. John Lewis Gaddis, *George F. Kennan: An American Life* (New York: Penguin, 2011) p. 246.

17. Henry Kissinger, *White House Years* (Boston: Little, Brown, 1979), pp. 1201–3.

18. As secretary of state, Madeleine Albright often referred to the United States as "the indispensable" but not the "only responsible nation." Also, Josef Joffe, *Uberpower: The Imperial Temptation of America* (New York: W.W. Norton & Company, 2006); and Fareed Zakaria, *The Post-American World*.

19. Edward Luttwak, *The Grand Strategy of the Roman Empire: From the First Century A.D. to the Third* (Baltimore: Johns Hopkins University Press, 1976), p. 2. Luttwak's more recent study of Byzantium is *The Grand Strategy of the Byzantine Empire* (Cambridge, MA: Harvard University Press, 2009).

20. David Gelernter, "The Roots of European Appeasement," *Weekly Standard* 8, no. 2 (September 23, 2002).

21. Niall Ferguson, "A World without Power," *Foreign Policy*, no. 143 (July/August 2004).

22. Manpower in the German army increased by a factor of 7 (from less than 100,000 to 720,000) between 1930 and 1938, while the size of Britain's army remained the same (about 210,000) and that of France grew by less than one-third (from 520,000 to 690,000). John Mearsheimer, *Tragedy of Great Power Politics* (New York: W.W. Norton & Company, 2001), pp. 303, 317.

23. Lord Curzon is quoted in George Scott, *The Rise and Fall of the League of Nations* (New York: Macmillan, 1974), pp. 94–97. President Wilson is quoted in Selig Adler, *The Isolationist Impulse: Its Twentieth Century Reaction* (New York: Free Press, 1957), p. 144. Also, Simon Serfaty, *The Vital Partnership: Power and Order; America and Europe beyond Iraq* (Lanham, MD: Rowman & Littlefield, 2005), pp. 31–32.

24. Bootie Cosgrove-Mather, "Poll: Talk First, Fight Later" (CBS News public opinion survey, January 19–22, 2003) and "Poll: Americans Back Ultimatum," (CBS News public opinion survey, March 15–16, 2003), http://www.cbsnews.com/sec tions/opinion/polls/main500160.shtml.

25. Public opposition to the Korea and Vietnam wars also grew when casualties rose without evidence of success or credible expectation of a quick withdrawal. What was specific to Iraq, however, was how steadily the opposition grew with a relatively modest rate of casualties. John Mueller, "The Iraq Syndrome," *Foreign Affairs* 84, no. 6 (November/December 2005): 44–55.

26. "In terms of precedent, look at the Cuban missile crisis . . . where there was a decision made before the United States was attacked," it was argued. Simon Serfaty, *Architects of Delusion: Europe, America, and the Iraq War* (Philadelphia: University of Pennsylvania Press, 2008), pp. 70–71.

27. James D. Fearon, "Rationalist Explanations for War," *International Organization* 49, no. 3 (Summer 1995): 379–414.

28. Condoleezza Rice, *No Higher Honor: A Memoir of My Years in Washington* (New York: Crown Publishers, 2011), p. 210.

29. Glenn Kessler, "In 2003, U.S. Spurned Iran's Offer of Dialogue," *Washington Post*, June 18, 2006; David L. Phillips, *Losing Iraq: Inside the Postwar Reconstruction Fiasco* (Boulder, CO: Westview Press, 2005), p. 104.

30. Robert D. Kaplan, *The Coming Anarchy: Shattering the Dreams of the Post Cold War* (New York: Vintage, 2000), p. 24.

31. Joseph S. Nye, Jr., *The Future of Power* (New York: PublicAffairs, 2011), p. 11.

32. Winston S. Churchill, *Malborough: His Life and Times* (New York: Charles Scribners' Sons, 1953), vol. 1, p. 82. Quoted in Eugene V. Rostow, *A Breakfast for Bonaparte* (Washington, DC: National Defense University Press, 1995), p. 25.

33. Hans J. Morgenthau, *Politics among Nations: The Struggle for Power and Peace*, 4th ed. (New York: Alfred A. Knopf, 1966), p. 173; Gordon A. Craig and Alexander L. George, *Force and Statecraft: Diplomatic Problems of Our Time*, 3rd ed. (New York: Oxford University Press, 1995), p. 27.

34. John Lewis Gaddis, *We Now Know: Rethinking the Cold War* (New York: Oxford University Press, 1997), p. 15.

35. "Foreign Policy in an Age of Austerity," Conversation with Brent R. Scowcroft, *American Interest* (Winter [January/February] 2010): 35.

36. Raymond L. Garthoff, "Estimating Soviet Military Force Levels," *International Security* 14, no. 4 (Spring 1990): 93–116.

37. Robert S. McNamara, *Essence of Security: Reflections in Office* (New York: Harper & Row, 1968), pp. 57–58.

38. Cline's original equation reads: Power perceived = (military Capabilities + Economic capacity + critical Mass) x (Strategy + Will). Ray S. Cline, *World Power Assessment, 1977: A Calculus of Strategic Drift* (Boulder, CO: Westview Press, 1977), pp. 34, 173–74.

39. Kenneth W. Waltz, *Theory of International Politics* (Reading, MA: Addison-Wesley Publishing, 1979), pp. 129–31; Hans J. Morgenthau, *Politics among Nations*, pp. 80ff; Ivo Duchacek, with Kenneth W. Thompson, *Conflict and Cooperation among Nations* (New York: Rinehart and Winston, 1967), pp. 116ff; Raymond Aron, *Peace and War among Nations: A Theory of International Relations* (Garden City, NY: Doubleday & Company, 1967), pp. 52–55; Thierry de Montbrial, *L'action et le système du monde* (Paris: Presses Universitaires de France, 1992).

40. See also *CSIS Commission on Smart Power*, Richard L. Armitage and Joseph S. Nye, Jr. (Washington, DC: Center for Strategic & International Studies, 1997).

41. Data on military capabilities come from Global Firepower, *World Military Strength Ranking, 2011*, at http://globalpower.com/.

42. Joseph S. Nye, Jr., *Bound to Lead: The Changing Nature of American Power* (New York: Basic Books, 1990), p. 168.

43. James Baker, *The Politics of Diplomacy: Revolution, War & Peace, 1989–1992* (New York: G.P. Putnam & Sons, 1995), pp. 284–85, 288, and 194–95; George Bush and Brent Scowcroft, *A World Transformed* (New York: Vintage, 1999), p. 360.

44. Christopher Layne, "The Unbearable Lightness of Soft Power," in Iderjeet Parmar and Michael Cox, eds., *Soft Power and U.S. Foreign Policy: Theoretical, Historical and Contemporary Perspectives* (New York: Routledge, 2010).

45. Jonathan McClory, *The New Persuaders II: A Global Ranking of Soft Power* (Harvard University and the Institute for Government, 2011). The index relies on fifty metrics that "capture perceptions, policies, and outcomes." Notwithstanding an attempt to "normalize" the raw data for each indicator, their number may explain the dominance of the more established Western powers, relative to emerging powers like China and Brazil respectively ranked twentieth and twenty-first. Also, Andrey P. Tsygankov, "If Not by Tanks, Then by Banks? The Role of Soft Power in Putin's Foreign Policy," *Europe-Asia Studies* 7, no. 58 (2006): 1081; Sheng Ding, "Analyzing Rising Power from the Perspective of Soft Power: A New Look to China's Rise to the Status Quo Power," *Journal of Contemporary China* 19, no. 64 (2010): 255–72.

46. Angus Maddison, *The World Economy: A Millennial Perspective* (OECD: Development Center Studies, 2006), p. 263.

47. Kaushik Basu, et al., *The Evolving Dynamics of Economic Power in the Post Crisis World. Revelations from a New Index of Economic Power*, India's Ministry of Finance (2010), p. 5.

48. C. Fred Bergsten, "A Clear Route to Recovery: Exports," *Washington Post*, February 3, 2010.

49. Joe Leahy, "Drawn into an Ever Closer Embrace," *Financial Times*, Special Report, May 23, 2011. The CIA *World Factbook* for 2012 lists Argentina and Germany, as well as the Netherlands (exports) and Japan (imports) as Brazil's other main trade partners.

50. Global Investment Research, "Is This the 'BRICs Decade'?" May 2010, http://www2.goldmansachs.com/our-thinking/brics/brics-decade.html.

51. Soner Gagaptay, "The Empires Strike Back," *New York Times*, January 15, 2012; Satoru Mori, "Crisis Invigorates Japan-Europe Cooperation, But for How Long?" EuroFuture Project, German Marshall Fund of the United States (March 2012), p. 4; William Wallis, Andrew England, and Katrina Manson, "Ripe for Reappraisal), *Financial Times*, May 19, 2011.

52. Karl Deutsch, *The Nerves of Government* (San Francisco: W. H. Freeman and Company, 1963). Quoted in Bruce Russett and Harvey Starr, *World Politics: The Menu for Choice* (New York: Basic Books, 1981), p. 156.

53. Chester Wilmot, *The Struggle for Europe* (New York: Harper & Brothers, 1952), p. 578; Harry S Truman, *Memoirs*, vol. 1: *Year of Decision* (Garden City, NY: Doubleday, 1955), pp. 91ff.

54. Robert Gould-Adams, *John Foster Dulles: A Reappraisal* (New York: Appleton-Century-Crofts, 1962), p. 200.

55. Robert Mann, *A Grand Delusion: America's Descent into Vietnam* (New York: Basic Books, 2001), pp. 305–8.

56. John L. Harper, *The Cold War* (Oxford and New York: Oxford University Press, 2011), p. 246.

57. Anthony H. Cordesman, et al., *The Real Outcome of the Iraq War: US and Iranian Strategic Competition in Iraq* (Washington, DC: Center for Strategic & International Studies, December 21, 2011), p. 2.

58. Zhengyuan Fu, *Autocratic Tradition and Chinese Politics* (New York: Cambridge University Press, 1993), p. 7.

59. See Royal Society, *Knowledge, Networks, and Nations: Global Scientific Cooperation in the 21st Century* (London: March 2011).

60. Costs include direct damage and the economic impact of the attacks ($188 billion), homeland security and related costs ($588 billion), and the military costs of the wars in Iraq and Afghanistan ($1,205 billion) plus their related costs ($444 billion) as well as estimated future war funding (277 billion) and future care for veterans ($589 billion). Amanda Cox, "A 9/11 Tally," *New York Times*, September 11, 2011.

61. Thomas L. Friedman and Michael Mandelbaum, *That Used to Be Us: How America Fell Behind in the World It Invented and How We Can Come Back* (New York: Farrar, Straus and Giroux, 2011), p. 45.

62. Quoted in A. J. P. Taylor, *Bismarck: The Man and the Statesman* (New York: Vintage, 1967), p. 40.

63. Global Firepower, *World Military Strength Ranking*. Nigeria is not among the top fifty military powers. The EU is not ranked in this survey, but the estimate is based on related variables gathered from the CIA *World Factbook* for 2012.

64. Kaushik Basu, et al., *The Evolving Dynamics of Economic Power in the Post Crisis World*.

3

SIGHTS OF POWER

For much of the twentieth century, American power grew while other powers declined and ultimately collapsed. Along the way, the United States overcame Europe, the previous center of the Western world, which, quite simply, became the hostage of America's capabilities and intentions. This outcome was the logical result of all that had transpired before in and beyond the European continent, and even reaching back prior to the founding of the American Republic: decades of European preponderance and decline combined with American self-denial and ascendancy.

At first, the Founding Fathers had shown little taste for travel. Their journey across the Atlantic did not anticipate a return trip. Content in a Western Hemisphere that they declared to be outside the reach of rivals and adversaries alike, Americans stayed away from the "old" world, in opposition to which the New World was born. The grand history of interstate relations provides few examples, and theory accepts none, of a power's reluctance to seek, elevate, enforce, and sustain its rank and influence outside its boundaries. Seemingly, wars were the product of lesser people and smaller-minded countries; they were for others to start and wage, though elsewhere, even if it later became America's habit to join and conclude them, though belatedly. But with each conflict making its European protagonists weaker, and with every hegemonic pretender defeated by an unexpected input of American power and leadership, the United States was gradually tempted to make use of its strength earlier and more widely.

After 1945, the final transfer of power in the West took a dozen years. During that time, a transatlantic defense community that made room for a defeated Germany and provided for the first-ever peacetime deployment of American (and British) forces on the continent was organized, and a small European Economic Community was launched as the down payment for an "ever closer" and larger union. By that time, in 1957, the core of a Western institutional framework was in place; by that time, too, the European retreat from empires in much of the world was nearing completion. As the Cold War came to an end, in 1989, another global transition also lasted a dozen years, until 2001, but it was mostly wasted. The Clinton administration sat out the decade of the 1990s and failed to exploit the clear dominance of American power it enjoyed. Especially relative to Russia, the newly defeated state, there was neither an urge for punishment, as had been the case for Germany in the 1920s, nor a will for reconstruction, as happened after 1945. Instead, there was indifference and even disdain: too much history now stood between the two former protagonists, which was cause for mistrust, but too much geography also kept both countries apart. For nearly a full decade a contented West thus slept as a victorious America looked disengaged, a uniting Europe grew distracted, and a rebuilt Japan went astray. Elsewhere everyone seemed of limited significance: although there were short-lived bursts of U.S. concerns about Iraq and a sharp focus on NATO enlargement, there seemed to be no need to force the pace of events with an active foreign policy. At last, history had been vanquished and the world tamed—and America stood alone as its triumphant and unchallenged conqueror. The irony, as it was soon to be shown, is that America was so busy globalizing the world, and urging it to resemble its own image, that it failed to adapt to the globalizing world it was sponsoring.

Now, a dozen years after 9/11, the page is being turned at last on the short century behind and the post–Cold War moment of U.S. preponderance that followed. Calling the world ahead post-American and post-Western is premature, though; while some emerging trends are sufficiently clear to point to known new realities, much remains at best presumed and even unknown.

MORE POWERS ABOVE OTHERS

The end of the American unipolar moment modifies the Western strategic position in the world, but it need not change the world's strategic position relative to the West. For one, the reconfiguration of the global power structure will take time. As the process evolves, all power attributes—mass, force, and the economy—also evolve, and the course of events will change more than once—whether with a bad war, new acts of terror, another serious recession, unexpected political instabilities, unprepared leaders, or restless populations that rise against growing inequities within and between nations. Most simply, the ascending trajectories of one or more states targeted for "greatness" may be redirected because of intrinsic weaknesses they would not have been able to manage.

Japan's odyssey since the 1990s is worth remembering: it was not so long ago that Japan was projected as the most promising new Western pole in a global structure transformed by America's decline and Europe's insufficiencies, and challenged by Soviet ascendancy and China's resurgence. Instead, the evidence now points to Japan as a small island that is being turned into an economic afterthought relative to some of its larger and more populated Asian neighbors, and into a weak country that is fading into geopolitical irrelevance relative to the whole of Asia. Even before a God- and man-made calamity traumatized Japan in early 2011, an astounding 95 percent of all Japanese were "very worried" (50 percent) or "worried" (45 percent) about their future, while 85 percent found their nation incapable of assuming international leadership, including 62 percent who feared being overtaken by other countries.[1] Such conclusions come after a twenty-year period that coincided mainly with the post–Cold War era and during which the Japanese economy grew at a miniscule rate of 1.1 percent a year, the total value of its stock market collapsed by an estimated 75 percent in real terms, and its government net and gross debt vaulted from 13 and 68 percent of GDP in 1991 to an estimated 115 and 227 percent in 2010. All in all, Japan's share of global GDP has fallen from 14.3 percent to 8.9 percent, and its per capita ranking has fallen to the thirty-eighth place according to CIA data.[2]

After the global economic recession of 2008, Japan's economy declined by 6.3 percent in 2009, the weakest performance of any high-income G-7 country. The rebound in 2010 (below 4 percent) was one of the worst in the world (ranked 101st, but still better than the 193rd place held the previous year according to CIA statistics). In early 2011 Japan entered an unchartered political course with the end of fifty years of uninterrupted rule by the Liberal Democrats. Shortly thereafter, a catastrophic earthquake worsened by its nuclear overtones may have been the coup de grace. And for 2011, with a debt already more than twice the country's GDP, and on top of an economic contraction near 0.5 percent, Japan reported its first trade deficit since 1980. If the losers of the past two decades were to be ranked, for opportunities missed and expectations unmet, Japan would come out on top—no longer the leading Western state in Asia, but also no longer the leading Asian state in the West and no longer the most capable U.S. partner across the Pacific. This, in short, is a crippled country with weak prospects for anything better than a partial recovery from what it used to be and had hoped to become. Fatalist about their condition, 73 percent of the Japanese report to be "content" as a less affluent country with lesser social disparity and reduced global relevance—all of this while their population shrinks and ages more and faster than nearly anywhere else.[3] Compare Japan's views of its own condition to those held by China, where 97 percent of respondents have a "favorable" perception of their country, and 87 affirm their "satisfaction" with the direction it is taking. "The greatest problem in Japanese politics over the last two decades," declared Prime Minister Yoshihiko Noda in April 2012, on the eve of an official visit to the United States, "is that we put off what needed to be done."[4] This is hardly a problem limited to Japanese politics, and Japan's fate over the past two decades is likely to be repeated elsewhere over the next two decades: the uncertainty is over the identity of the next loser out of the current winners.

Even before 2011, the lessons of Japan's prolonged economic crisis and geopolitical decline were meaningful for other high-performance emerging economies. First, a slowdown after a long period of fast growth in a catch-up economy (which was Japan's case for twenty years beginning in the 1970s) is hard to reverse and even harder to manage politically. This is true whether the slowdown results from economic fundamentals, errors of governance, a public resistance to reforms, or manmade events. Second, a reversal of fortune in a reportedly ascending power is especially difficult to control after it is stalled and regresses: fraught with political and societal significance, a sense of decline, even if relative to expectations only, spreads like a terminal cancer for which the recommended cure causes irreparable harm with extra doses of austerity and retrenchment—a choice between the slow death of chemotherapy and the medieval scorching of radiation. And third, there is little that is ever preordained in the rise and fall of powers, and talk of an irresistible rise to the top can be, and is, no less premature than a parallel talk of irreversible decline.

China Goes Global

For China, this is its first opportunity to engage the world on its own terms in nearly two hundred years, which China lived mostly as a "victimized state"—an easy prey, that is, for Western powers eager to fragment and devour the country and its people. As shown in table 3.1, China accounted for one-third of the world's economic output in 1820, more than double that of Europe (23.6 percent) and much more than the thirteen states of the newly born American Union, whose share of world output barely reached 2 percent at the time. For the next 130 years and up to 1950, Chinese GDP remained virtually constant in real terms, but its collapse was calamitous during the first half of the twentieth century: still twice as large as that of the United States after the Civil War, China's GDP fell to only one-sixth of U.S. GDP after the Chinese revolution—about the same as for Western Europe, barely out of thirty years of devastating wars. By comparison, Japan's rise was steady: in 1870, Japan's GDP amounted to less than 15 percent of China's, and notwithstanding the dramatic interruption of World War II the Japanese economy began to surpass China in the 1970s. Meantime, India followed a comparable but slightly more robust trajectory from 1820 to 1950, by which time the Indian economy stood markedly above that of China.

But now, China is back—meaning the availability of ample measures of usable capabilities, deepening global interests, spreading universal saliency, and growing nationalist zeal. At home, China's motivational self-portrait as a victimized state is gradually replaced by the proud image of a great power-like-any-other, which includes a domineering mentality prepared to do anything on behalf of its ever-wider core interests. Abroad, it is greeted (but also feared) as the can't-miss superpower of the future. "China will . . . be the strongest Asian power by a considerable margin," noted a 2010 report by the Australian defense minister, notwithstanding his country's growing dependence on China as Australia's main trade partner and a primary source of foreign investments.[5] But why wait? Already, China's behavior is increasingly assertive and its discourse often truculent. Yet, as noted by leading American sinologist David Shambaugh, the Chinese remain "deeply conflicted" and their country's role in the world remains unsettled.[6] Like the "new Germany"

Table 3.1. Back on Top: Economic Growth in Perspective (Gross Domestic Product, Million 1990 International Dollars)

	1820	1870	1913	1950	1978	1998
West Europe	162,722	320,223	906,374	1,401,551	4,133,780	6,960,616
United States	18,548	98,374	517,383	1,455,916	3,536,622	7,394,598
Japan	20,739	25,393	71,663	160,966	1,242,932	2,581,576
China	228,600	189,740	241,344	239,903	740,048	3,873,352
India	111,417	134,882	204,241	222,222	494,843	1,707,712

Source: Angus Maddison, *The World Economy: A Millennial Perspective* (Paris: OECD Publishing, 2006), p. 261.

in Europe, China covets stability; but unlike what is the case for the Germans, stability is deemed too important to be left to any single power or institution, including the United States, a source of much grief and humiliation in the past—let alone the United Nations, whose flag once gave the U.S. war with China in Korea a universal seal of approval.

Thus, two decades after the Cold War, and ten years after 9/11, China questions the intent and sustainability of American power and the efficacy of its leadership. Fearing a vacuum, a modern "China first" doctrine supersedes an earlier interest in "keeping a low profile" for a few more decades, as urged by Deng Xiaoping thirty years ago. With the United States resented for its alleged attempts to undermine, disrupt, and even derail China's economic and military rise to primacy, China can no longer afford a time out from the world. Rather an expanding range of pressing "core national interests" drives its quest for power and influence commonly associated with imperial behavior, imperialist policies, and the facts of empire.[7] Most pointedly, an official 11 percent increase in defense spending scheduled in 2012 after a one-year reprieve from a decade of double-digit increases confirms China's commitment to reinforce its capabilities for global power projection even at a time when its projections for economic growth are reduced. This adds to the strategic distrust between the two states as each set of leaders responds to the other's alleged intent to usurp its number one position, or perforce compel it to remain number two.[8]

In recent years, India has overcome a prolonged period of sluggish "Hindu rate of growth" and emerged as the third largest economy in Asia with the world's second fastest growing economy. Now, India stands ahead of Japan as China's main rival in Asia and a strategic partner of choice for the United States and Europe. A lesser reliance on exports (approximately one-fifth of GDP) than China's (over two-fifths of GDP) provided protection from the global economic recession of 2008. Yet India's higher reliance on service-sector exports—meaning, outsourced jobs—will not suffice to create the million new jobs needed monthly in a country of 1.21 billion people with half the population under the age of twenty-five (and about 30 percent under age fifteen). Already, India is falling into a lower growth trajectory—below 7 percent for the balance of the 2010s. The need for structural reforms is stifled by the erratic compulsions of India's coalition politics in this large and highly fragmented country whose best years may be falling behind.

Moreover, although India shares land borders with relatively few countries it is dangerously exposed geopolitically. Since 1947, it has waged armed conflicts in and with Pakistan, Bangladesh, Sri Lanka, and the Maldives, as well as China. When China became a nuclear power shortly after it had humiliated India in a border war in 1962, India chose to go nuclear, too—a decision it came to regret after a hostile and unstable Pakistan soon became nuclear as well. Three other neighboring states (Myanmar, Nepal, and Sri Lanka) besides Pakistan also face internal instabilities that, in varying degrees, do or can spill over into India. Such turbulence is cause for concern and a catalyst for a significant rise in defense spending as well: in 2011, India passed China as the world's largest arms importer.[9] In 2012, India's successful missile test gave its dialogue with its main rival a decidedly nuclear tone as China's most important cities fell within the range of an Indian nuclear strike for the first time ever.

At home, meanwhile, India's population continues to grow, unlike China's: by over 180 million during the first decade of the century, and a projected increase of 671 million more people by the year 2050. As a result, poverty does not abate: according to the World Bank, an astounding three-fourths of India's population live on less than $2 a day (a significantly higher number than in China), which is far too many to meet even the most modest expectations.[10] Three main ethnic groups and fifteen official languages make India look like a heavy economic elephant moving on the delicate political legs of a panda—a weak country with a weak state, which belies predictions of its "irreversible" future as a global pole of power.[11] India's recognizable negative is that for many fundamental social objectives the Indians do not only fail to catch up, they are falling behind. That India's gaps with China would be widening in most areas can be understood—from life expectancy and infant mortality to education and health. More troubling, though, is India's inability to move decisively ahead of its poorer neighbors, which contradicts aggregate estimates of the size and performance of the Indian economy. Consider, for example, that on much of the social agenda, failing Bangladesh outperforms or keeps up with an ascending India. With a persistently lower GDP growth than India's (6.2, 6.0, and 5.6 percent in 2007–2009, compared to 9.0, 7.4, and 6.5 percent), Bangladesh's GDP per capita is much lower, too ($1,600 versus $3,100). But average citizens in Bangladesh, both male and female, nonetheless live longer and have a better chance to hold a job than citizens in India, while their chance to be born and go to school are close enough to be comparable.[12]

In short, while India is certainly an emerging economy and has many of the attributes needed to become a Great Power, it is nowhere near that point yet. Unlike or more than China or Russia, the attention it receives anticipates what it can later achieve as a counterweight for China, more than what it can already accomplish as a counterpart for the West.

The rise (too quick), scope (too intrusive), and style (increasingly com-
bative) of Chinese power, combined with the facts of Japanese decline
(too steep) and the pace (too slow) of India's emergence, restore ancient
geopolitical rivalries in Asia. With China too rich and too big to be ignored
by other states in the region, but also too strong and too near for them to
not seek input and protection from a more distant countervailing power,
closer security ties with the United States are no longer causing the public
controversies that were common during and after the Cold War. Unlike the
United States, which struggles to remain a power in Asia even though and
because it still lacks credibility as an Asian power, China is an Asian power
that is losing legitimacy as a power in Asia because its new imperial capabilities do not leave it historically adverse to becoming imperialist and building
an empire. That is not a matter of ideology, and it would be true regardless
of the ideological evolution of the Chinese government. A *revanchiste* zeal
fed by the country's memories of past wars and other externally induced
"humiliations" completes the picture of China's imperial temptation in Asia.

In Southeast Asia, Thailand and especially Vietnam (as well as the Philip-
pines) are torn between an interest in closer economic relations with their
largest neighbor and security concerns over China's political influence and
military power. Even as commercial exchanges expand and Chinese money
flows in, defense expenditures in these countries rise and Western weapons
are purchased. Vietnam's memories of the war with the United States have
faded, but memories of its subsequent war with China linger—on top of
what is remembered of Vietnam's older struggles with Imperial China in
the fourteenth and eighteenth centuries. Meantime in East Asia, China's
growing intimacy with Pakistan is cause for concern in India, especially
as Pakistan pursues a cooperative triangular relationship with Iran and
Afghanistan, and even with Nepal, feared by the Indians and the Chinese
alike as a transit route for Pakistan-trained terrorists and Tibet-linked human rights advocates respectively. At least up to the God-made events that
struck Japan in early 2011, the Japanese government too was reorienting its
defense policy away from Russia and toward China (and North Korea): both
are cited as the main threats to Japan, and thus a catalyst for a new interest
in closer cooperation and further integration with the U.S. military—as has
been happening gradually with India for the past decade. But unlike India,
Japan's geopolitical anxieties are muted by growing economic ties with its
rising neighbor: in 2010, China was Japan's biggest trade partner, like India
but without the same economic mass.

Increasingly, the range of China's imperial power expands beyond Asia.
When the Chinese went global after the Cold War, Africa was a first stop

for needed commodities (as in oil-rich Sudan) or for influence in the continent (as with commodities-rich South Africa), or for both (as with Nigeria).
The relative neglect of Africa by Western powers has eased China's entry
into the business of empires; and enormous Chinese slush funds that other
powers are lacking are welcomed by developing African states for their size
(multibillion dollar, multiyear low-cost loans or occasional no-cost grants)
and their terms (free of any political, human rights, or environmental
preconditions, with the explicit possibility that some loans will be written
off). The numbers are impressive. Chinese aid to Africa grew from a near-
zero level in 2002 (a miniscule $10 million) to an imposing $18 billion in
2008, with the near totality of Chinese aid invested in infrastructure and
public works.[13] Indeed, no other country has used "cash diplomacy" more
openly and more effectively since post-1945 dollar-rich America. Call this
soft power if you will, but it is meant to achieve the outcomes traditionally
sought with hard power—the latter by pushing and the former by pulling.[14]
Now, China is a source of funding more ample than the World Bank and
less constraining than the International Monetary Fund (IMF). Money is
the vehicle of choice, and it is especially prized because it can be justified
by recipient countries relative to other individual or multilateral donors said
to be historically compromised, without standing in the way of China's own
interests and gains—at least pending the birth of an "ugly Chinese" comparable to the label formerly carried by Americans and Japanese. Meantime,
Africa's demographic surge makes the continent look like an irresistible
market of two billion future consumers of Chinese goods—ironically reflective of the way Westerners used to view China: most of the roughly twenty
countries with a fertility rate over five children per woman are in Africa,
and nearly one-fourth of its forty-eight countries have shown a real economic growth over 6 percent for six or more successive years.[15]

Outside Africa, China's influence in Latin America and Europe, and the
choreography of China's bilateral relations with Germany and Brazil, are of
particular interest. Both countries are economic locomotives for their respective regions, with Brazil's economy growing at twice the pace of Mexico
(itself a high performer) and Germany far ahead of its low performing euro
partners (mostly low performers). According to UN figures, Chinese trade
with Latin America increased more than sixteen times between 1999 (a
mere $8 billion) and 2009 ($130 billion). Admittedly, this is still a fraction
of U.S. trade with Latin America, but as is the case elsewhere, it has been
growing at a faster rate. Between 2000 and 2009, Brazil's exports to China
increased eighteenfold, with a further 53 percent increase to $56 billion
in 2010, when China passed the United States as Brazil's biggest trade

partner. By comparison, the share of trade between the three signatories of the North American Free Trade Association (NAFTA) has fallen nearly 10 percent over the past decade, from 55 percent of the countries' global exports in 1999 to 46 percent in 2009.[16]

The same trend is visible in Europe. Like Brazil, Germany has become China's main EU trade partner, and the EU as a whole has moved ahead of the United States as well (close to $600 billion of total EU-Chinese trade in goods in 2011, compared to slightly over $500 billion for China's bilateral trade with the United States). Whether China's relentless commercial pressures might divert patterns of trade and investment between the United States and Europe but also within Europe remains doubtful, however. Trade flows within the EU and across the Atlantic dwarf those between individual EU states and China. For example, Germany's rising trade with China still looks rather small relative to the U.S. trade with China, not to mention Germany's and the U.S.'s trade with other EU members; and substantial trade deficits with China cannot be endlessly balanced by Germany's or the United States' trade surplus within or with the EU. But the trends are ominous. Bilateral trade in goods between the two countries is projected to reach $285 billion by 2015 (as compared to a paltry $109 billion in 2009).[17] And even under conditions of limited economic growth in Europe, great differences in per capita income within the EU (ranging from $7,000 to as much as $78,000) add to the appeal of an EU market worth $15,500 billion with an enormous potential demand for low-priced and technologically competitive Chinese goods.

No less significantly, direct investments have also started to flow from China into its main trade partners in the West. These reinforce the Chinese capacity to "re-innovate" Western technologies at lesser cost (but lower quality) and thus strengthen China's position as a formidable competitor in the mass markets of the main exporting countries. In 2010 the Chinese were on their way to becoming Brazil's largest direct investor. In Germany, too, relatively low Chinese investments are growing rapidly: in 2011, Chinese companies were the number one foreign investor in Germany, ahead of U.S. companies. Notwithstanding the Chinese reluctance to make massive purchases of unwanted bonds issued by EU states except Germany, the "American challenge" of the 1960s, when U.S. foreign direct investments (FDIs) to Europe first exploded, may prove to be pale by comparison with what may be coming from China in the 2010s. That would take the form of a global shopping spree worth as much as $2,000 billion for the acquisition of assets by the end of the decade while China redirects its economy away from its reliance on exports. For the United States, which gets only a sliver of Chinese foreign investments ($1.13 billion in 2011, compared to $4.6 billion in Europe and even $2.1 billion in Africa), China's preference for short-term U.S. financial assets accumulated as treasury bonds and other securities is hardly reassuring.[18]

Russia Stays Local

Among the leading bidders for great power status Russia stands rather small—the hole in the Euro-Atlantic doughnut. That Russia was a mess at the close of the Cold War is an understatement and its collapse, which remained possible, was feared. In the difficult post-Soviet years of the 1990s, a majority of Russians seemed to regret the communist model of a small but guaranteed income (from 45 percent in 1989 to 60 percent in 1999) at home, with the relative satisfaction of a powerful and assertive state abroad. During those years, too, only a very few seemed to prefer the advantages offered by a weak and humiliated state, like owning their own business, with all the risks and rewards that might entail (from 9 to 6 percent during that period).[19] Helpless, a majority of Russians concluded they had been better off in fact when they had felt worse off in theory. Even now, a generation later, a reportedly ascending Russia still struggles to recover from its Soviet past, whose inherited societal ailments appear to worsen—including a nationwide alcoholic binge, a wasteful oil-for-food grand barter, widespread corruption, and a rigid one-party rule based on the infallibility of unmovable and recyclable rulers.

After his first election as president in the spring of 2000, Vladimir Putin quickly sought to restore Russia's self-image with a vocal and often bitter criticism of a unipolar order organized, he complained, around "one center of authority, one center of force [and] one center of decision making" in the United States, whose triumph left the Russians in an unsettled state of bipolar funk.[20] While waging the Cold War against the Soviet Union, the United States and other Western countries had seemingly forgotten about Russia's other characteristics, deeply rooted in centuries of shared primacy in Europe. Still suffering from a historical addiction to imperial ambitions, Russia has enough military power left from its Soviet days to seek and assert influence on neighboring states liberated from Soviet domination only recently, or to claim and justify security concerns for newly independent states that used to pass as so-called republics of the defunct Soviet empire.

Undoubtedly, Russia is a power in Europe, which Russian analyst Dmitri Trenin calls "Pluto" in the Western solar system.[21] Yet Russia is not and cannot become a true European power-like-any-other. Neither of the two benchmarks for Europeanness—membership in NATO or the EU—is realistically a part of Russia's future. Even shorn of one-fourth of its Soviet territory, and after having dissipated much of its czarist legacy (in Ukraine, Kazakhstan, and Uzbekistan), Russia remains the biggest country in the world—1.7 to 1.8 times larger than the United States and China, and 5 times larger than EU-27. But there is more to a distinctive portrait of Russia than size alone. As a power obviously settled in Europe, Russia is also too near, too nuclear, and too well endowed with resources to be ignored, and it is too historically resentful, too geopolitically sensitive, and too nationally assertive to be provoked.

This profile of Russian power is the rationale for "re-setting" Western (American and European) relations with Moscow—for the recurring need "to apply brakes to the . . . relationship, pull over to the sides of the road, and study the map for a while," as President George H. W. Bush put it.[22] "Give them time," the postwar architect of containment, George Kennan, used to insist. "Let them be Russian; let them work out their internal problems in their own manner"; and Kennan added "not to rush to judgment" in assessing post-Soviet Russia, "Patience, patience—that's what we need."[23] Patience is, of course, what is needed—enough patience to neither provoke nor indulge.

Making of Europe a home for Russia, but also helping Russia feel at home in the West, is complicated by a tenacious Russian self-image that has defeated the realities of geography, withstood the trials of history, resisted repeated waves of inept and harsh authoritarian governance while rejecting the democratic and modernizing stimuli that its rulers occasionally sought to import from other countries. The historian Tim McDaniel has described the Russian idea as the certainty that Russia's distinctiveness and historical tradition set it apart from the West and guarantee its future as a great power—a country, observed Isaiah Berlin, so sure of its own unique laws that it dismisses "the experience of other countries [with] little or nothing to teach it."[24] There is a Russian soul after all, but this is not the soul that George W. Bush claimed to have uncovered after his first official meeting with Putin in June 2001 but rather, and still, that which the inspired Russian writer Fyodor Dostoyevsky liked to present as the "holy" character of a Russian people dangerously open to Western modernity. "And this is the civilization they wish to impose upon our people! Never will I give my consent to that! . . . Such transplantations always begin with luxury, fashions, scholarship, and art—and invariably end in sodomy and universal corruption."[25] The exalted idea Russians have traditionally had of their country and its role in Europe is a condition that often led the Russian state astray and ended badly. As Henry Kissinger put it, "Thwarted, Russia nurse[s] its grievances and bid[s] its time for revenge—against Great Britain through much of the nineteenth century, against Austria after the Crimean War, against Germany after the 1878 Congress of Berlin, and against the United States during the Cold War."[26] Long before he became the American ambassador to Moscow, Russian expert Michael McFaul diagnosed Putin's "paranoid nationalism" as the source of his prevailing fear of Western "plots" designed to undermine Russian sovereignty.[27]

After the Soviet unconditional surrender of its empire helped end the Cold War peacefully, the United States and the states of Europe seemed content to sit back and watch Russia fall precipitously while Russian citizens sank under the weight of their newly acquired democratic freedoms. During the post-Soviet decade going from 1989 to 1998, the Russian GDP fell by 44 percent in real terms, while industrial production and investments decreased two- and five-fold respectively. In just three years (1990–1993) during that period, exports dropped by more than 70 percent (from $280 to $60 billion) and imports fell from nearly $200 to a mere $44 billion.[28] Outside of Germany's cash paybacks for the liberation of East Germany there was little aid from the West, and resentment over such gross neglect lingers. But even in the context of this resentment, the idea of an imperial Russia "biding its time for revenge"—Kissinger's phrase—is an idea that has gone old and is outdated: the Russian state can no longer support it, the Russian people can no longer endure it, Europe can no longer afford it, America can no longer tolerate it, and the rest of the world can no longer accommodate it. For Russia to put that idea aside—and end thoughts that a payback for past misdeeds must be exacted from the West and the rest for Russia to regain its future—will test the recasting of Russia from a neo-imperial into a postimperial power. In August 2008, a short war in Georgia served as a forceful reminder of this Russian past: there is more to its military power than the remnants of the strategic arsenal that used to define the balance of terror with the United States, and there remains enough of a will to use it to motivate and justify the U.S. interest in resetting its bilateral relations with its former adversary.

Russia's bid for primary influence on the continent is enhanced by oil and gas resources that give it a hold on its energy-dependent neighbors, including the EU, which bought more than 80 percent of Russian oil exports in 2010 (about one-fourth of EU demand, which is also the level of EU dependence on Russian gas), but also many of the Community of Independent States for which the EU offers no credible prospects for membership any time soon. Yet the political leverage thereby gained by Russia may not be sustainable: it is ranked eighth in the world for oil reserves, but second after Saudi Arabia as oil producer and exporter. Already operating at or even beyond capacity because of the economy's needs for ever larger cash infusions, Russia has little room for political maneuvering: irrespective of market conditions to which it must respond more than it can shape, especially as new suppliers emerge in Canada, West Africa, and South America—all tempting for European markets where the demand for oil is in any case stagnating. With regard to gas, while Russian reserves are second to none, its capacity for gas delivery is hampered by a worn-out pipeline network that remains primarily directed toward its European clients and has been in need of improvements since the 1980s: a large percentage of the pipelines is older than thirty years, and ten years after the Cold War it was estimated that $2,000 billion was needed over twenty years for attending to past neglect in maintenance of what has become "a gigantic rust belt" that stands on "the edge of catastrophe."[29] Admittedly, new pipelines like the Nord Stream underwater facility will strengthen delivery capacity while bypassing Ukraine, which is a notoriously difficult transit state. But all plans for new gas pipelines, as well as for the exploration of new oil fields, usually depend on Western technologies and investments that ultimately reduce Russia's control and influence. Meantime, endemic corruption, worsened by the resource curse commonly found in failed states, makes Russia look more like Nigeria or Algeria than Norway or Britain. In October 2010, then-president Dmitry Medvedev estimated the theft of money from government contracts at a total of $33 billion or roughly 3 percent of GDP, while Transparency International ranked Russia as the 154th most corrupt country in the world, out of the 178 countries it reviewed.[30]

In short, the DNA of Russia shows troubling signs of a failing state more—or at least no less—than those of an ascending power. Signs of self-induced demographic genocide compromise further the inflated expectations of a renewed surge to primacy. These signs include one of the lowest fertility rates in the world (173rd worst) combined with very high infant mortality (150th worst). But unlike other low-fertility countries in Europe and in Japan or China, Russia's dismal birth rates are made worse by short life expectancy (160th worst) and high death rates (7th worst): aberrant individual behavior and insufficient state policies reduce the average life of Russian men by fifteen years relative to the West and even the like of Pakistan and Bangladesh. With high rates of abortion—reported to reach an average of 3.2 during a woman's child-bearing life—and large outflows of immigrants, Russia's population is projected to shrink to 135 million or less by 2025.[31]

Signs of Weaknesses

Daunting signs of weaknesses spare none of the most commonly identified emerging powers. Take China, today's most populated state but an increasingly "geriatric state" faced with difficult demographic trends that spill over to every other power attribute.[32] An estimated 250 to 400 million births have been suppressed since the adoption, so to speak, of the one-child policy in 1980—which balances the 200 to 400 million people reportedly taken out of poverty since the start of economic reforms in 1978. China's one-child policy has delivered one of the world's lowest fertility rates, down from 6 percent in 1949 after the Communist revolution, to 2.2 percent in 1982 after the Cultural Revolution, to 1.54 percent now—much below the normal replacement rate of slightly more than two children per woman. During the decade between 1995 and 2005 the population of working-age adults grew by 100 million; between 2025 and 2034, it is expected to fall by 79 million. This smaller and certainly older Chinese population is also showing meaningful gender imbalances. This is common for most low-fertility countries in Asia, where families favor male births at the expense of female fetuses or infants, aborted or killed after birth if the first child was not a male (as is increasingly the case in high-fertility India). But China's one-child policy is more pernicious because it encourages gender preselection prior to any birth since there can presumably be no second chance after the first child is born.

A sharp aging of the population caused by rising life expectancy worsens this demographic draught. China has 178 million elders (sixty years old and over) according to a recent government census. That number is expected to jump to 216 million, or 16.7 percent of the population, by 2015. By the mid-2020s, the elder population will grow annually by an estimated 10 million, while losing an estimated 7 million working-age adults, resulting in a mass of 438 million elderly people by 2050 (including more than 100 million people over the age of eighty). In other words, as is the case for most of Europe (but not the United States), China is getting older even more quickly than it is getting smaller. But while European states (including Russia), as well as some in Asia (like Japan), actively fight for higher birth rates with a wide range of family subsidies, China's one-child policy makes it far easier to age than to be born—unless, of course, that policy were to be reversed.

These demographic trends have broad consequences. First, even under conditions of sustained economic growth most Chinese citizens will age before they can become richer. As an aggregate, China is an economic superpower scheduled to surpass the U.S. economy as early as 2016 according to some IMF estimates, which place the Chinese share of world income (measured in purchasing power parity prices) at 18 percent by that time, as compared to 17.6 percent for the United States.[33] However, on a per capita basis, its "emergence" remains slow: in 2010 China ranked 126th out of 229 countries for per capita GDP (in purchasing power parity), and while the average standard of living in Shanghai approximates that found in Portugal, it remains closer to Rwanda's in the rural provinces. Prospects for affluence among the young is kept elusive by an education system that gets a higher rating in the United States and other Western countries, where there is much admiration for the performance of young Chinese (or Chinese-born) students in local schools and colleges, than in China where schooling is not widely and evenly spread among the populace. Thus, while 55 percent of China's adult population graduate from high school (as compared to less than 10 percent in India), only 5 percent of all adults gain more advanced degrees. In other words, what Chinese education produces is a large pool of cheap and unskilled labor with a highly worldwide competitive primary education in mathematics and English, readily available for low-paying manufacturing jobs upon graduating from elementary or high school, and a much smaller group of managers and executives (many of them trained elsewhere).[34]

China's rising median age is especially significant because of a culture that is respectful of age and is imposing on small family core units of three (including one child) the care of as many as four grandparents who have little access to income (lower for the elderly than the national average) and often lack minimal social and welfare coverage. No matter how fast the Chinese economy grows, poverty is therefore likely to remain unimaginable by Western standards for years and decades to come, although it might look relatively enviable in India and some other countries in Asia. As recently as 2004, 170 million Chinese were reported to live on less than $1 a day, and 99 percent of the Chinese had per capita income below the U.S. average. Even at current growth rates, it would take about three decades for China to catch up with, and overtake, income levels in Mexico.[35]

Low income and the need for savings also keep China's per capita consumption very weak. In 2009, savings rates amounted to 40 percent of all household incomes. Kept low, wages are a small percentage of GDP (only 40 percent that year, as opposed to 60 to 70 percent in the West), which reduces internal demand accordingly. Household consumption amounted to 40 percent of GDP in 2000, and fell to 36 percent at the end of the decade. This meant an average yearly consumption of about $2,500, compared to an estimated $30,000 in the United States. It also points to a vast transfer of household wealth designed to facilitate the investment explosion that fuels the country's economic growth, with persistently low interest rates paid by the state for household savings (about half of the rising inflation rate in late 2011).[36] The problem is not that Chinese citizens do not "like" to consume. Consider the reported 1.2 million Chinese tourists in the United States—admittedly the wealthier share of the population—who spent an estimated $6,000 each during their stay: this is 50 percent more than the average Western tourist whose wealth is at least five times higher than the average Chinese.[37] But for the huge majority of Chinese, consumption is a luxury they cannot afford because they are too poor and too unsure of their future to not maximize savings, even at an inflation-induced loss. As a result they purchase few of the goods they assemble and which they manufacture mostly for the world—not because they have enough or more than enough but because they cannot get more of what they need, let alone what they want. To a Western consumer, everything seems to have been made in China, and although it may not always be, look, or work better and longer it is always cheaper—most of the world's toys, more than half of its bikes and half the shoes, but also half the world's microwave ovens, one-third of its television and air conditioners, and so forth. Yet with World Bank forecasts of an increase in China's middle class from 56 million in 2010 to 360 million people by 2030—the total population in the United States—expectations of a larger internal demand invite foreign investments, notwithstanding the difficulty to compete with local companies, on top of the obstacles raised by the Chinese bureaucracy.[38]

A logic born out of historical precedents dictates that China's phenomenal economic growth of the past decade will end or slow down. The most recent five-year plan called for annual growth of 7 percent from 2011 to 2015, down from 11.2 percent for the previous plan, and official growth estimates for 2012 were set at 7.5 percent down from 9.2 percent in 2011. Meantime, China's huge current account surplus with other countries, which rose steadily from 2001 (1.3 percent of GDP) to 2007 (10.1 percent) has fallen sharply since 2012, with a low estimated by the IMF at 2.4 percent in 2012.[39] In February 2012, a World Bank report, "China 2030," cowritten by one of China's main government research units also emphasized the imperative of extensive changes that can create "equality of opportunity" and a shift to high income status—which Premier Wen Jiabao implicitly endorsed with a call, the following month, for an end to the monopoly of state-owned banks to increase capital flows through private hands.[40] Lacking such reforms, the second and next generations of Chinese citizens born under the 1980 one-child policy will get poorer faster than they get older while a larger privileged class becomes increasingly wealthier earlier. With many of the reforms likely to cause strong resistance from entrenched ideological, bureaucratic, and business interests, China may be racing time as its new president attempts to buy more political stability with more economic growth.

The so-called China price is the gold standard of competitiveness but it is exacting a price of its own, which has to do with the deflated expectations of citizens whose work is not appropriately rewarded. As was seen with Japan and elsewhere in the 1980s, low wages and high productivity economies that outperform high productivity and high wages economies are eventually exposed to the competition of lower wages economies that achieve high productivity with the redeployment of productive assets in search of higher revenues.[41] In other words, it takes Third World wages and practices to build a First World economy, but the virtuous process ends when the labor supply and public tolerance needed to sustain Third World wages and endure harsh working practices are depleted and can no longer be controlled, possibly before a truly competitive First World economy has emerged.

Entering the 2010s, China is also showing signs of labor shortages. For some priority sectors, these cause wage and inflationary pressures that will be difficult to control, let alone reverse. Thus, with the number of people under age fourteen down by about one-third during the first decade of the century, first-time workers between the age of fifteen and twenty-four, which peaked at 227 million in 2005, are expected to fall to 150 million in 2025. Meantime, real wage increases that averaged 12.5 percent a year from 2000 to 2009 already make Chinese workers several times more costly than in other Asian countries like Vietnam, even though there, too, wages are rising quickly.

Nor are wages the sole indicator of falling productivity and eroding competitiveness. Other indicators include ever more resistance to working long hours and agreeing to seasonal migration or long commutes for work; lesser savings encouraged by a galloping thirst for consumption; growing social and political resentment of a better educated skilled labor class over rising inequalities; and conjectural conditions like input prices for commodities and shortages in vital natural resources such as water. Where else the new economic upstarts will be found is not clear—in Asia or in yet-to-emerge economies elsewhere, including Africa, or even among mature economies in reclaimed technology- and innovation-driven sectors that require few but highly skilled workers. More than in India, the vulnerability of the export-driven Chinese economy was exposed in 2009 and 2010 when the global recession forced the internal repatriation of tens of millions of workers who had left their villages for "good" manufacturing jobs in urban hubs close-by or far away. Back to being peasants and poor again, these migrants remember all too well the short-lived affluence promised too readily, gained too hastily, and lost too suddenly. This is not a recipe for stability: expectations rise because they are expected to be met, and denying them is often a determining cause for serious instabilities.

Finally, unless the government prioritizes domestic social issues over growth and other issues, Chinese citizens are likely to become sicker as they get older and before they become richer. According to the World Bank, 71 percent of the people in China had access to state health facilities in 1981, but only an astounding low 21 percent did twelve years later with a reported level of household spending on health care above 8 percent, including 41 percent of all expenses spent on high-priced drugs.[42] Numbers have improved since, but they remain below needs. For a country with huge sovereign funds this is obviously not the austerity confronted in Western countries. But still, it is an issue that will determine not only what sort of great power China wants to become but also, and more pressingly, what sort of a country it wants to be.

In sum, the risks of difficult-to-serious societal disruptions in China during the coming decade are real, along demographic (young-poor), regional (urban-rural), professional (white collar–labor), and gender lines (men-women)—not to mention over political issues of ideology and governance (including corruption). There are no prospects of a prodemocracy "Chinese spring" but any such disruptions would still have significant consequences for the region, including a risk of foreign adventurism as a distraction from local misadventures and a rallying point for some unfinished territorial business in Taiwan, for example, or for the protection of core interests in the Persian Gulf (like Iran) or the Middle East (like South Sudan).

NEW INFLUENTIALS

Entering the second decade of the twenty-first century, Russia, India, and China form a geostrategic troika that challenges the primacy of the Western powers. Both Asian countries are ascending powers, with one—which is China—rising faster than the other—India, that is. Both states are also fragile powers exposed to internal instabilities and external shocks—though more so for India than China (and Russia). Neither China nor India can be indifferent to the other: what each is and does, and what each becomes and plans. Together, they lead an economic locomotive that is pulling the

East ahead of the West, even though each aims at different directions. Meantime, Russia, which would welcome a special partnership with either, though India ahead of China, finds both unreceptive to its advances. There is more to a recast world than this troika of emerging powers, however. Also surging ahead are many new influentials and a few pivot states whose failure, should it occur, would have significant consequences for their region and the totality of the international system.

Going South

Nearly twenty years after the Cold War, the Western-inspired recession of 2008 has exposed the fragility of the developed economies and featured the new dynamism of developing economies. Even assuming the capacity of the United States and Europe (as a union) to regain their economic balance and financial solvency, and assuming the elevation of China as the world's second biggest economy, the push of other powers to global influence introduces additional changes. Early in the 1970s, Zbigniew Brzezinski envisioned a world order at "$2\frac{1}{2} + x + y + z$."[43] The half-a-role then given to China has expanded, and Europe has the capacity to replace Russia as a complete pole of power if the European states prove able to sustain their union. What is emerging now, then, is a world at "$3\frac{1}{2}$" or more "$+ \ldots + x + y + z + \ldots$"—with the first few dots pointing to the remaining gaps between the top three and a half global powers (the United States, China, and Russia plus a uniting and thus unfinished Europe) and two of their pursuers (India and also a tired Japan). The second set of dots describes an evolving number of new poles of influence that are going global or whose regional reach is globally consequential (especially Brazil and Turkey respectively) modified by a group of failed states (like North Korea and Pakistan) and an expanding list of applicants for failure, including more and more states in the Middle East, but also others like Nigeria. This is not a recipe for order but it can be a stage for anarchy, especially in the absence of rules and regulations that can be widely accepted and readily enforced.

On the southern part of the Western Hemisphere (and the southern shores of the Euro-Atlantic area), Brazil has had a long career as an emerging power, but its most recent rise as a new influential looks more convincing than ever before in the country's history.

For much of the twentieth century, Brazil was a reliable (though occasionally reluctant) follower of the United States. In 1917, this was the only large country in South America that entered World War I, and during

World War II no other country from the region sent troops to Europe—for which Roosevelt briefly sought to reward Brazil with a permanent seat at the UN Security Council he envisioned for the postwar world. Through these wars, but also for most of the Cold War, Brazil's relations with the United States prevailed over any other, especially in the context of its vulnerability to, and dependence on, trade. In 1960, nearly 45 percent of Brazil's exports went to the United States, with about 25 percent shipped to a nascent European Common Market—and very little elsewhere.

That dependence is gone now, and what passed for a doctrine named after President Monroe is dead and beyond resurrection. In 2008, the U.S. market for booming Brazilian exports already ranked behind Asia (15 percent for the former, and over 25 percent for the latter), as well as behind a commercially more integrated Latin America and an increasingly present European Union. After China surpassed the United States as Brazil's biggest trading partner in 2009, exports to China continued to increase—by more than 43 percent in 2011 relative to the previous year.[44] No less and even more significantly, the U.S. share in foreign direct investments in Brazil has also declined sharply over the years, from about one-half in the 1990s, when FDI flows in Brazil were below $1 billion, to barely one-fifth in the 2000s, when Brazil became one of the world's top fifteen recipients of foreign investments, second only to China among the emerging economies.[45]

Like several other new influentials, Brazil is a locomotive for global economic growth. Remember: less than thirty years ago, in 1993, the Brazilian rate of inflation exceeded 2,000 percent a year. But now, after an Asia-like growth rate of 7.5 percent in 2010, the Brazilian economy is expected to average about 4.5 percent a year during the period 2011–2013 (higher than the 4.1 percent average recorded during Lula da Silva's defining presidency, from 2003 to 2010). The most populated country in Latin America (193 million in 2010, a third of its total) with a strong demographic curve, Brazil's GDP represents two-fifths of Latin America's total economic output, which makes Brazil the seventh largest economy in the world, ahead of Italy, as well as of Russia, India, and South Korea. Together with a modern, efficient, diversified, and innovative agriculture that covers one-fourth of the world's arable land and may top the world in a matter of years, Brazil enjoys natural resources second to few and immediately relevant to most vital areas of the world's economy. These include oil, for which Brazil has become a leading U.S. supplier, with deepwater reserves that should move it from the fifteenth to the fifth rank of national reserves and production.

In short, Brazil is a regional hegemon—meaning, a state that surpasses the power, influence, and reach of its neighbors, including historical rivals and G-20 members Argentina and Mexico.[46] With defense spending up from $13.6 billion in 2006 to 33.1 billion in 2010 (more than all of Latin America),[47] Brazil is a counterweight for a small cluster of self-styled, post-Castro revolutionary states led by Hugo Chavez's Venezuela and Daniel Ortega's Nicaragua. But for a region that is now open for business with the rest of the world, Brazil is also a reassuring counterpart of the domineering power up North. In recent years, Brazil's influence has gone global. In a moment of reduced European interest and influence in Africa, Brazil looks like a plausible example of development for a struggling continent, for which it is rewarded with diplomatic support at the UN and elsewhere: in 2010, for example, Brazil's role in manufacturing Portugal's election to the UN Security Council at the expense of Canada's more relevant bid enhanced Brazil's influence on the significant global issues that crowded the agenda next, like economic sanctions on Iran and military intervention against Libya (over which it abstained together with its three main BRIC partners). Outside the UN, as a leading and influential member of the BRICS, at G-20 meetings when urging the European powers to put their house in order; at open-ended summits when negotiating UN-sponsored climate change treaties, or standing up to Euro-Atlantic pressures for a new WTO-managed trade agreement, Brazil enjoys quasi parity with more mature great powers, assumes central stage on global issues that transcend its traditional interests and surpasses its potential, and pursues openly autonomous policies from the United States to which Latin America has never mattered as much as it does now.

Turkey, too, stands out as an unfinished but rising power with actionable expectations of regional influence and global reach. This is a new influential that is not a member of the BRIC group but stands atop a grouping of second-tier new influentials we called the KISMET states (including South Korea—which is also a dependent Western derivative—as well as Indonesia, Saudi Arabia, and Mexico). A big, dynamic, and heavily populated Muslim country in an affluent but stagnant and aging Europe, but also a poor European country situated between an unstable Middle East and the unsettled Muslim periphery of the former Soviet empire, Turkey is a key to Western relations with Islam in and outside Europe—a credible and even compelling example of secular governance, Islamic modernity, and economic dynamism for the Arab world where it is reintroducing itself as a non-Western state without fear that the West might dismiss it as a Muslim country.

Compared to Brazil, Turkey's restored influence has come quickly after an extended descent from primacy and even relevance. Entering the twenty-first century a mere decade ago, the contrast with its arch-rival Greece was striking. While Greece was allegedly showing its European maturity when it qualified for euro zone membership in January 2001, Turkey suffered from Third World disarray with a budget deficit of 16 percent of GDP, a 72 percent rate of inflation, a growth rate that lagged far behind its robust demographic growth, and an army-dominated mode of governance. One decade later, amid the euro-ic ruins of the Greek state, Turkey is closer to meeting the criteria for the euro than many of the seventeen euro zone countries. Increasingly, Turkey emerges as an appealing example for countries like Egypt, launched on an arduous democratic trajectory, but also as a partner of Muslim states that remain firmly theocratic, including Iran, or are threatened with postrevolutionary failure, like Libya. This, then, is a defining moment for Turkey as it completes at last a revolution that was launched nearly ninety years ago, discards the awkward dependence of its imperfect democratic institutions on the army without succumbing to some new religious dependence, and returns to a status lost two centuries ago when it still stood as the most formidable power in Europe.

The risk with Turkey's growing expectations and global stature is a degradation of its relations with traditional Western allies as the price of its upgraded relations with countries in the Middle East, Caucasus, and Central Asia. That would be a significant change of course from the previous century, when Turkey's choices repeatedly favored the West: after World War I with a conversion to secularism in 1922 inspired from the top down but often questioned from the bottom up; after World War II when this now-secular Muslim country chose to mature within the Atlantic Alliance it entered in 1952 after its important military contribution during the war in Korea; and after the Cold War when once again the Turkish government chose to follow the West in Iraq during the 1991 Gulf War. But now, after 9/11 and a second war in Iraq that caused much public discontent in Turkey, pro-Western choices can no longer be expected as readily. Combined with the reduced benefits associated with NATO membership since the Cold War, Turkey's inability to gain EU membership is redirecting its interests outside the West: the EU accounted for 41 percent of Turkish trade in 2011, down from 56 percent in 1999; during this same period, Islam's share of Turkish trade climbed to 20 percent from 12 percent.[48]

Thus recast with but not in the West, and kept outside Europe but not irreversibly sunk into its more broadly defined Muslim neighborhood, Turkey transcends an oversimplified debate of secularism versus modernity.

Led by an Islamist-inspired political party that ended decades of secular dominance often enforced at its expense, Turkey's rise teaches its Muslim neighbors a religion of faith and law: that the hold on politics is strengthened with a participatory government that binds together the state and the mosque by consent rather than force.[49] As argued by a prominent Turkish scholar, somewhat abusively but regretfully typically and in tones that resonate well in the Middle East: "We don't want trouble [in our neighborhood]. The Americans create havoc, and we are left holding the bag."[50] Yet Turkey's lack of alternatives endures: if not in and with the West, including its institutions of choice, where and how?

There are other new influentials, arguably less visible and active than Brazil and Turkey but moving closer to center stage because of their geopolitical position, because of their access to vital commodities, or because of the reach of their political leadership: possibly a dozen of countries extended from Australia to South Africa (the fifth wheel of the BRIC quartet), and including the five KISMET countries, each of which could have easily qualified as a BRIC state as well. These are heard and cultivated by emerging powers and weaker neighbors alike, bilaterally and through the multilateral institutions to which they belong. With an impact on world order that remains uneven and fragmented, these states have little to do with the nonaligned countries of the past era of bipolarity. For them to form a bloc is neither an ambition nor a vocation. While competing for market shares the new influentials impact levels of wages, prices, interest rates, and profits in developed economies, as well as affect commodity prices (including but not limited to energy) and scarce resources (food, water, and more). Already, their influence extends to global peacemaking and peacekeeping: acting alone, at two, or at many, the new influentials can launch initiatives that separate them from more mature Great Powers to which they can lend their weight and legitimacy to steer multilateral institutions like the UN Security Council or the Group of Twenty, and redirect global negotiations over trade, climate change, or even arms control to their liking.

Right of Interference

According to historian Eric Hobsbawm, the imperial world of the past no longer exists, and the age of empire is dead.[51] This somewhat wishful conclusion could prove premature. Admittedly, there is more to power than force, which diminishes the temptation of empire; but there is also more to order than justice, which restores the context of a renewed right of interference. After half a century of imperial rollback and exaggerated warnings of neoimperialist resurgence, postcolonial sovereignty ceases to be a historical entitlement: it must be earned again—and again and again by "quasi" or "contingent" states that the former imperial powers "created in error" for their own gains and convenience, and around a religion, a clan, a tribe, a dynasty, or even for an army. Lacking legitimacy at birth, these "fractured" countries are at the mercy of centrifugal forces that pull them apart and which the state cannot manage or fix.[52] Torn by internal violence, occasionally inspired or encouraged by other countries, and no longer able to provide for the welfare and security of their citizens because of an intrinsic shortage of administrative and coercive capacity, these states can gradually lose their capacity to control territory and borders.[53] As a result, they are turned into "incubators of terror" and threatened with "decertification" as might-be producers of genocide and would-be exporters of instabilities.[54] Thus, a reformulated right of interference grows out of a need for self-preservation dressed in the fancy clothes of self-abnegation (a compassionate commitment to aid and, allegedly, a will to share) that cover the Emperor's clothes (the greed to grab and ultimately the temptation to own).[55]

A "resource curse" gives a number of such states something especially valuable to fight over, from within as well as from without. Resources that can be accessed and transported easily, like diamonds or drugs, are cause for civil wars and foreign conflicts. In Mexico, a surging economic power, a war between local drug cartels yielded at least 29,000 casualties during the five years after President Felipe Calderón took office in late 2006—a period during which a violence akin to outright war spread to Central America and the Caribbean.[56] When these resources are not easily transportable, as is the case for oil and gas or various minerals, they build "rent economies" that invite internal strife over huge revenues that can be distributed to families, tribes, and cronies.[57]

The proliferation of failed states, which resurrects the logic of empires and imperialism and can incite power grabs by non-Western states, adds to the lack of conceptual clarity about a new multipolar world order. A so-called rescue of a failed or failing state from collapse can be costly. States are worth that cost when their location and resources are of strategic consequence for their neighbors or other global powers. A triage is accordingly needed—meaning a hierarchy of states and priorities.[58] How that triage comes out depends on an ambiguous balance between power, interests, and purpose. It produces little policy consistency from country to country, region to region, and even moment to moment. The oratory is absolute, as it anticipates a generalized doctrine of humanitarian intervention: "national sovereignty is not a license to slaughter your own people," insisted

Obama in late April 2012. But its execution remains inconsistent because, as noted by Hillary Clinton a few months earlier, "our choices also reflect other interests . . . and there will be times when not all [of them] align."[59] These comments echo Henry Kissinger's reflections on U.S. policies toward Eastern Europe after World War II and later during the Cold War: "Our sin was less betrayal than the raising of expectations we could not possibly fulfill" thus imposing an "overall calculus of forces" that was not an act of cowardice but one of elementary prudence.[60]

The map of state failure is littered with dozens of countries that do or might qualify soon. They threaten a return to the dark ages of pre-Westphalian anarchy. Consider Nigeria, otherwise a possible new influential endowed with many decisive attributes for power, including size, population, capabilities, and resources: the reality below the aggregate data unveils a galloping demographic explosion with more births every year than in the entire European Union—which adds to the burden of a state already faced with one of the world's worst levels of infant mortality and, with the third highest level of people living with HIV/AIDS, a life expectancy at birth barely above forty-seven years. With 70 percent of the population below the poverty line, Nigeria's average GDP per capita also ranks among the lowest in the world, reflective of its distorted oil-generated rent economy that justifies its world-leading reputation for corruption. With more than 250 ethnic groups spread in an imperially constructed territory, and a nearly even split between Muslims (50 percent) and Christians (40 percent), Nigeria is a failed state-in-waiting—arguably too important to fail but too big to save.

The wait for failure may be shorter for Pakistan, whose worsening condition stands out because of its position as a geopolitical "shatterbelt"—a convergence point for Central, South, and East Asia with the Middle East.[61] This is the only Islamic country with nuclear weapons and it is also the only certified nuclear country without a stable central government (although it is likely to remain more rational than the unmovable North Korean regime). The threat of failure was a birth condition for a state that was said to have been devised for an army rather than the other way around. Indeed, the army's defeats provide the narrative for the country's failure: during the first twenty-five years of Pakistani independence, wars waged by its army caused a loss of territories inhabited by half of the country's initial population.[62]

Even without the ongoing war in neighboring Afghanistan, Pakistan's geopolitical milieu would be rich in drama, with two and a half other nuclear powers (China and India, but also Iran)—plus an erratic and nuclear North Korea farther away but very close to China. To the east, India, Pakistan's arch adversary, shares its longest border with Afghanistan (also a neighbor of China) and stands next to Iran (bidding for a leading regional role). China (Pakistan's main geopolitical partner) also shares borders with India (Pakistan's traditional adversary) and Iran (a main oil supplier). These are the main actors of a nuclear quartet for which there is no choreography but which cannot leave any state indifferent: the United States relative to Pakistan (and Iran) with consequences for its bilateral relations with India (and China); China relative to India (and Iran, too) with consequences for its bilateral relations with Pakistan (and North Korea); India relative to Pakistan (and Afghanistan) with consequences for its bilateral relations with China (and the United States)—and so forth, including Europe, greatly concerned about Iran (and, to an extent, about Pakistan, too) with consequences for its relations with the United States (and also India), or Russia, concerned about China (and Afghanistan) with consequences for its relations with India (and Europe).

Relations among these states are influenced by the war in Afghanistan, the second foreign war in this country in less than a generation. Pakistan, India, and China are all nuclear powers with barely enough electricity to cover their growing needs: each views Afghanistan as a vital bridge to Central Asia's vast gas and oil reserves—including Iran's, which is also a major oil exporter without enough refined oil for its domestic needs. In a post-America, post-NATO but not postwar Afghanistan these countries' struggle for influence will condition not only the next regional conflict but also other alignments in the area. Already, closer U.S. relations with India, combined with growing tensions with Pakistan, have motivated closer strategic ties between Pakistan and China, thus adding to the historic tensions between the three Asian states. The goal for China in Pakistan is not to gain a partner for its dialogue with India. As will be seen, on the whole China does not think it needs help to balance or divert Indian power. Rather, it reflects Chinese concerns about a pivotal neighbor that would go astray or fall apart in a radical surge of Islamic fervor or in the counterrevolutionary takeover of a nationalist army.

However differently, North Korea is nearly as significant to China as Pakistan is to India. Desperately isolated, the North Korea government is a complete supplicant. Its options are few: an unlikely suicide with an apocalyptic nuclear strike aimed at archrival South Korea or even Japan (as a proxy for the United States), an economic takeover by neighboring China, or the regime's abdication through a reunification engineered by the South Korean government. Among these three options, China looks best. This is after all how life began for the North Korean state in 1950, with a war launched from the North against South Korea, but soon joined by China against the United States. As to the Chinese, involvement with such an erratic government would be explained by an alleged desire to influence the North Koreans to denuclearize in the context of liberating six-party talks hosted by China and used for a diplomatic display of the U.S. marginalization in Asia. In sum, if any country is going to have a finger on the nuclear trigger, the Chinese hope to keep that hand in their pocket rather than an American pocket or that of the United Nations. Whether dealing with North Korea or Pakistan, China has little interest in a nuclear exchange that would be initiated by either country against its most immediate neighbors, and to which China could not remain indifferent.[63]

How much power is enough, or rather, how much power is needed during a zero-polar intermission to be found sufficient for keeping up with others or even moving ahead of them? All too often the answer is kept to one word—"more"—for no level might ever be found enough for a rising power to be satisfied and for a dominant power to feel safe. "The Soviet build-up" of strategic forces in the 1960s, wrote former defense secretary Robert McNamara, was "in part a reaction to our own." It was, added McNamara, a "miscalculation during a period of tension."[64] The miscalculation proved costly and quite dangerous, and nearly caused the bipolar confrontation that was feared by the two superpowers. Absent a transparent understanding of power sufficiency, and with its measurement insufficiently accurate to live for long with a credible sense of parity, realist theorists claim that hegemonic preponderance is the ultimate goal of all great powers—"a constant incentive to change [the current distribution of power] in their favor."[65] This claim, too, is neither convincing nor satisfying—and probably no longer within reach, assuming it ever was. The perception of power often prevails over the facts of power—so much so that in March 2012, the U.S. president found it necessary to insist that "I don't bluff" as an attempt to intimidate Iran and reassure Israel. More power is sought by one state over the other because more power is thought to be needed by each state relative to the other. But how much power is thought to be needed also depends on which state holds it, and whom it is aimed to accordingly. For reputations, too, linger, and history makes some powers look more benign and less dangerous than others.

In sum, all powers were born dangerously alike but not all have matured and aged in ways that keeps them equally dangerous in the eyes of their neighbors or distant rivals. In much of Europe, Russia's expansionist past lingers more than Germany's, and so does China's past for much of Asia relative to Japan's. But then, few states have been historically spared by, or innocent of, inhumane brutality imposed by or on their neighbors. During the Thirty Years' War, casualties in Prussia reached genocidal proportions—maybe as much as 40 percent of the total population: Sweden was the chief culprit then, but since that time it has become a country with an impeccable reputation as a peacemaker. For given enough time history, too, moves on, and as most of the past is forgotten much is seemingly forgiven—much of it, that is, but not all, and most of the time, too, but not always.[66]

For much of the twentieth century Americans who waged wars started by other countries in Europe and the rest of the world were asked to understand the history of the nations and people they were about to defeat, as well as that of the nations and people they were expected to save. Entering the twenty-first century, as other countries were called upon to help respond to a "war" launched against America, it was their turn to be asked to understand American history. For it is only in the context of that history that the rest of the world, including the rest of the West, can fully understand the depth of emotions caused by the attacks of September 11, 2001. These events will dominate the nation's emotions for much of the decade to come. Allies and adversaries did, and will again, dismiss the U.S. response to the horrors of such violence on its territory as excessive and possibly self-defeating. They will say these are the tragic ways of history. That may well be true. But what happened on September 11 had little to do with the American way of history—distant from war and invulnerable to attacks. On their own, these events might not have changed the world. Lived by the United States they did because for the preponderant power to assert that the world was changed by those events is in fact enough to make it so.

In the 2010s, the definition of a Great Power must still insist on the availability of many capabilities in large quantities; and even more than ever the fuller and more complete the state's access to such capabilities and the greater its power. But for a while at least, a Great Power can now reach out to the world through other mechanisms that have gained relevance during the past century: it can gain de facto recognition as a Great Power in a formal organization of leading states (like the Group of Twenty) or with an upgrade in an organization to which it already belongs (like permanent membership in the UN Security Council), or by asserting leadership for, or volunteering to, peacemaking diplomacy or peacekeeping operations on an issue and in an area of global interest (like the Quartet for the Middle East).

Western states that are still left with more power relative to others are limited nonetheless to a more confined role in a world they can no longer control alone; non-Western states with less power relative to the West want a more significant contribution to a world they can at last influence; failed or failing states with no power except that of nuisance fluctuate between them as both tragic victims and *agents provocateurs*. This adds up to many states able to bid for a major role on all sorts of issues to which they can often contribute only small capabilities and over which, therefore, even the most powerful among them are doomed to cooperate. That such conditions restraint the strong may be good news—a possible triumph of order and justice over power; that these conditions may also make the weak more assertive can also be bad news—a possible call on power to restore order irrespective of justice.

NOTES

1. "Asahi Shimbun Poll—Security," June 14, 2010, at http://newpacificinstitute .org/jsw/?p=1332; Pew Research Center, http://pewglobal.org/database/?indicator =24&country=45.

2. The CIA *World Factbook*, 2012. Simon Tilford, "Turning Japanese?" Center for European Reform, *Insight*, April 30, 2010; Michiyo Nakamoto, "Government Sets Out to Lure Foreign Investors," *Financial Times*, September 8, 2010, and "Need to Tap Fresh Sources of Dynamism," February 25, 2011; Martin Wolf, "What We Can Learn from Japan," *Financial Times*, January 13, 2010; "Japan's Debt Woes Are Overstated," *Financial Times*, February 9, 2010.

3. In 2010 Japan's fertility rate was ranked 219th (with 1.21 children born per woman) and life expectancy at birth was ranked 5th, at 82.25 years. CIA *World Factbook*, 2012.

4. Chico Harlan, "Japan Can No Longer Delay Making 'Tough Decisions,' Noda Says," *Washington Post*, April 20, 2012.

5. John Pomfret, "Australia Welcomes China's Investment, If Not Its Influence," *Washington Post*, February 14, 2010.

6. David Shambaugh, "Coping with a Conflicted China," *Washington Quarterly* (Winter 2011): 7–27.

7. Lichal He, "Ready to Become a Great Power? The Recent Nationalist Movement and China's Evolving National Identity," *Journal of International Affairs and Area Studies* 16, no. 2 (2009): 62.

8. Kenneth Lieberthal and Wang Jisi, *Addressing U.S.-China Strategic Distrust*, John C. Thornton China Center, Brookings Institution, Monograph Series, no. 4, March 2012, p. 23.

9. Simon Denyer, "Border Spat Reignites India-China Tensions," *Washington Post*, February 29, 2012.

10. Rama Lakshmi, "India Reports 17% Increase in Population," *Washington Post*, April 1, 2011.

11. "A Tale of the Future," writes Fareed Zakaria, *Post-American World* (New York: W.W. Norton, 2008), p. 148.

12. Amartya Sen, "Quality of Life: India vs. China," *New York Review of Books*, May 12, 2011, pp. 44–46. According to the CIA *World Factbook*, 2012, the data are: infant mortality rate (47.57/1,000 in India versus 50.73 in Bangladesh), life expectancy at birth (66.8 versus 69.75 years), people living with HIV/AIDS (ranked 4th in the world versus 117th), school life expectancy (10 years versus 8), and unemployment (10.8 percent in 2010 versus 4.8).

13. Thomas Lam, et al., *China's Foreign Aid Activities in Africa, Latin America, and Southeast Asia*, Congressional Research Service, 7–5700, R40361 (February 25, 2009), p. 8.

14. Joseph S. Nye, Jr., *The Future of Power* (New York: PublicAffairs, 2011), p. 20.

15. William Wallis, Andrew England, and Katrina Manson, "Ripe for Reappraisal," *Financial Times*, May 19, 2011.

16. Thomas Lum, et al., *China's Foreign Aid Activities*, p. 14; Anthony Faiola, "Germany Rustles Up Big Business in Germany," *New York Times*, September 18, 2010; Geoff Dyer, "The China Cycle," *Financial Times*, September 13, 2010; John Paul Rathbone, "China Is Now the Region's Biggest Partner," *Financial Times*, April 26, 2011; Joe Leahy, "Drawn into an Ever Closer Embrace," *Financial Times*, May 23, 2011; Matthew Kennard, "Backyard Increases Its Global Importance," *Financial Times*, April 26, 2011.

17. Judy Dempsey, "Chinese Leaders' Visit to Germany Ends with Large Trade Deals," *New York Times*, June 28, 2011.

18. Richard McGregor, "Chinese Poised to Amass Over $1,000 bn of Foreign Assets," *Financial Times*, May 5, 2011; Keith B. Richburg, "Bad Perceptions Holding Up Chinese Investments in U.S.," *Washington Post*, February 11, 2012; Paul Gettner, "China, Amid Uncertainty of Home and Europe, Looks to Germany," *New York Times*, April 23, 2012.

19. Hryhoriy Nemyria, "Civil Society in Russia," in Janusz Bugajski with Marek Michalewski, eds., *Toward an Understanding of Russia: New European Perspectives* (Washington, DC: Council on Foreign Relations, 2002), p. 18.

20. Vladimir Putin, Speech at the 43rd Munich Conference on Security Policy, Germany, February 10, 2007.

21. Dmitri Trenin, "Russia Leaves the West," *Foreign Affairs* 85, no. 4 (July/August 2006): 87.

22. George Bush and Brent Scowcroft, *A World Transformed* (New York: Vintage, 1999).

23. Quoted in Strobe Talbott, *The Russia Hand: A Memoir of Presidential Diplomacy* (New York: Random House, 2002), p. 401.

24. Tim McDaniel, *The Agony of the Russian Idea* (Princeton, NJ: Princeton University Press, 1996); Isaiah Berlin, "The Silence in Russian Culture," *Foreign Affairs* 36, no. 1 (October 1957): 2.

25. Geir Kjetsaa, *Fyodor Dostoyevsky: A Writer's Life*, translated from the Norwegian by Siri Hustvedt and David McDuff (New York: Viking Penguin, 1987), p. 283.

26. Henry Kissinger, *Diplomacy* (New York: Simon & Schuster, 1994), p. 173.

27. Michael McFaul and Kathryn Stoner-Weiss, "The Myth of the Authoritarian Model: How Putin's Crackdown Holds Russia Back," *Foreign Affairs* 87, no. 1 (February/March 2008): 73.

28. Tassos E. Fakiolas and Efstathios T. Fakiolas, "Domestic Sources of Russia's Resurgence as a Global Great Power," *Journal of International and Area Studies* 16, no. 2 (2009): 92.

29. Keith Bush, *Russian Economic Survey* (Washington, DC: U.S.-Russia Business Council, May 2007), pp. 26–27.

30. Dmitry Medvedev, "Forward Russia," September 10, 2010; Julia Joffe, "Net Impact," *New Yorker*, April 4, 2011, p. 26.

31. See Anders Aslund and Andrew Kuchins, *The Russia Balance Sheet* (Washington, DC: Peter G. Peterson Institute for International Economics and the Center for Strategic & International Studies, 2009); also, Zbigniew Brzezinski, *The Geostrategic Triad: Living with China, Europe, and Russia* (Washington, DC: CSIS Press, 2001), pp. 58ff; Julie DaVanzo and Clifford Grammick, *Dire Demographics: Population Trends in the Russia Federation* (Santa Monica, CA: Rand Press, 2001).

32. The discussion that follows relies on data borrowed from Mark Haas, "A Geriatric Peace: The Future of U.S. Power in a World of Aging Populations," *International Security* 32, no. 1 (Summer 2007): 131; Matt Isler, "Graying Panda, Shrinking Dragon: The Impact of Chinese Demographic Changes on Northeast Asian Security," *JFQ* 55 (4th quarter 2009): 101–3; Richard Jackson, Keisuke Nakashima, and Neil Howe, *China's Long March to Retirement Reform* (Washington, DC: Center for Strategic & International Studies, 2009), p. 7; and Keith B. Richburg, "China's Birth Policy Contributes to New Year's Strife," *Washington Post*, January 18, 2012.

33. Gideon Rachman, *Zero-Sum World: American Power in an Age of Anxiety* (New York: Simon & Schuster, 2011).

34. Bobo Lo, *China and the Global Financial Crisis*, CER Essays (London: Center for European Reform, April 2010), p. 25.

35. According to prominent economist Roberto Newell, as quoted by Damien Cave, "For Mexicans, home is now an option," *International Herald Tribune*, July 2011.

36. Jacques Mistral, "La réorientation de la croissance chinoise: Sa logique, ses enjeux et ses conséquences," Centre des études économiques, Institut français des relations internationales (March 2011), p. 14; also, "China Seeks Orderly Shift to Consumption," *New York Times*, November 27, 2010; and Michael Pettis, "China Must Bridge the Growth Gap," *Financial Times*, March 15, 2011.

37. Stephanie Clifford, "Luxury Stores Pull Out Mandarin Phrase Books to Make the Sale," *New York Times*, April 14, 2012.

38. Joseph Quinlan, *The Rise of China: A Brief Review of the Implications on the Transatlantic Partnership* (Washington, DC: German Marshall Fund, 2006).

39. Howard Schneider, "China Takes 'Promising' Steps to Free Up Currency and Trade," *Washington Post*, April 19, 2012.

40. Keith B. Richburg, "Report: China's Growth Requires Extensive Change," *Washington Post*, February 28, 2012.

41. Paul Krugman, *Pop Internationalism* (Cambridge, MA: MIT Press, 1997), p. 50; Howard Schneider, "For China's Workforce, Growth Is Over," *New York Times*, June 1, 2011; Kevin Brown, "China's Rising Wage Bill Poses Risk of Relocation," *Financial Times*, February 16, 2011.

42. Sharon Lafraniere, "In China, Patients Turn on Doctors," *International Herald Tribune*, August 10, 2010.

43. Zbigniew Brzezinski, "Delusions of Balance," *Foreign Policy* (Summer 1972): 54–59.

44. Exports to China in 2011 hit $44.3 billion, and Brazil's total trade for that year amounted to $256 billion, for a trade surplus of nearly $30 billion. *Washington Post*, January 3, 2012.

45. Carlos Gustavo Poggio Teixeira, "Brazil and United States: Fading Interdependence," *Orbis* (Winter 2010): 156–57.

46. Shannon K. O'Neil, *U.S.-Latin America Relations: A New Direction for a New Reality*, Independent Task Force, no. 60 (New York: Council on Foreign Relations, 2008).

47. *Comparative Atlas of Defense in Latin America and the Caribbean* (Buenos Aires: Red de Seguridad y Defensa de América Latina, 2010).

48. Saner Gagaptay, "The Empires Strike Back," *New York Times*, January 15, 2012.

49. Charles Kupchan, "Be Careful What You Wish For," *International Herald Tribune*, February 24, 2011.

50. Quoted in Stephen J. Flanagan, "Misplaced Priorities: Turkish Assessments of U.S. Power," in Craig S. Cohen, ed., *Capacity and Resolve: Foreign Assessments of U.S. Power* (Washington, DC: Center for Strategic & International Studies, June 2011), p. 98.

51. See Eric Hobsbawm, *The New Century: In Conversation with Antonio Polito*, trans. Allan Cameron (London: Abacus, 2001).

52. Robert H. Jackson, *Quasi States Sovereignty, International Relations, and the Third World* (New York: Cambridge University Press, 1990), p. 81; Gérard Kreijen, *State Failure, Sovereignty and Effectiveness* (Leiden: Koninklijke, 2004), p. 141; John Herbst, in Robert I. Rotberg, ed., *When States Fail: Causes and Consequences* (Princeton, NJ: Princeton University Press, 2004), p. 304.

53. Robert I. Rotberg, "Failed States, Collapsed States, Weak States: Causes and Indicators," in Robert I. Rotberg, ed., *State Failure and State Weaknesses in a Time of Terror* (Washington, DC: Brookings, 2003), p. 3.

54. James A. Piazza, "Incubators of Terror: Do Failed and Failing States Promote Transnational Terrorism?" *International Studies Quarterly* 52, no. 3 (2008): 470.

55. Francis Fukuyama, *State-building: Governance and World Order in the 21st Century* (Ithaca, NY: Cornell University Press, 2004), p. 93.

56. U.S. Department of State, "Background Note: Mexico," http://www.state.gov/r/pa/ei/bgn/35749.htm (accessed October 28, 2011); Randal C. Archibold and Damien Cave, "Drug Wars Push Deeper into Central America," *New York Times*, March 23, 2011.

57. Stephen D. Krasner and Carlos Pascual, "Addressing State Failure," *Foreign Affairs* (July/August 2005): 153–63.

58. Robert Dorff, "Responding to the Failed State: The Need for Strategy," *Small Wars and Insurgencies* 10, no. 3 (1999): 68–69.

59. President Obama's speech to the National Democratic Institute, Washington, DC, November 7, 2011; Karen DeYoung, "Clinton Defends U.S. Stance on Syria, Bahrain," *Washington Post*, November 8, 2011.

60. Henry Kissinger, *White House Years* (Boston: Little, Brown, 1979), p. 156.

61. Saul Bernard Cohen, *Geopolitics: The Geography of International Relations* (Lanham, MD: Rowman & Littlefield, 2009), p. 44.

62. Stanley Wolpert, *India and Pakistan: Conflict or Cooperation?* (Berkeley: California University Press, 2010), p. 45.

63. Jing-Dong Yuan, "The Dragon and the Elephant: Chinese-Indian Relations in the 21st Century," *Washington Quarterly* (Summer 2007): 131–44.

64. Robert S. McNamara, *Essence of Security*, pp. 60, 81.

65. John L. Mearsheimer, *The Tragedy of Great Power Politics* (New York: W.W. Norton, 2001), p. 3.

66. To this day, for example, neither Germany nor Britain has truly forgotten about the air war that each state waged on the other after June 1941, mostly aimed at civilian targets.

4

A LONE SUPERPOWER

Few "ideas" are more fashionable than the idea of American decline. It is used by critics as ammunition against policies in disfavor, or as a partisan indictment of a president in disrepute. Both uses converged during the "Johnson War" in Vietnam, and they converged again during the "Bush War" in Iraq. Never mind that a reliable public opinion survey found the United States ranked as the leading world power by 81 percent of all worldwide respondents in 2006, arguably the worst of the bad years for a then-worsening Iraq war; China, viewed as America's nearest competitor, came second, significantly behind. Yet the same poll also showed a 24 percentage point drop for the projected U.S. status in 2020, with a score (57 percent) barely above China (55 percent).[1]

Imagine such forecasts in 1910 for the year 1920, when the United States would not even have been listed among the powers offered to hypothetical respondents for possible ranking: the results would have seemed strange, quite strange, before too long. But there seems to be little doubt about the current century. As early as September 2001, it was proclaimed an "age of terror" and an Asian century: farewell to the United States and the rest of the West, and hello to China and the rest of the East, including Japan (which was ranked just behind China by 32 percent of the respondents) and India (with 24 percent, after the EU at 30 percent, and Russia at 26 percent). Indeed, the declinist feeling grew so deep that a noted French analyst devised a so-called geopolitics of emotions that maps the world around each region's expectations about its future—described, *noblesse oblige*, as helpless and resigned in the West (especially the United States but also Europe), but hopeful and domineering in the East (especially China, but also India), and resentful and even vengeful in the South (especially the Middle East, but also everywhere else).[2]

This sort of analysis is not useful. All too often it betrays an irresistible submission to the fashionable idea of the moment, as well as an abusive exaggeration of recent setbacks that history might later show to have been inconsequential. The consensual wagons thus formed stifle the imagination and condition the "surprises" that follow. Between the surprising Revolutions of 1989 and the no less surprising Arab Spring of 2011, the wars in the former Yugoslavia, the attacks of September 11, the wars in Iraq and in Afghanistan, the financial debacle of 2008, and the euro crisis were also surprising system-changing events about which experts who should have known better and earlier, said little and forecast even less. Everything else, it seems, was deemed so self-evident as to not require much attention and debate: that the Cold War would never end, that America was beyond the reach of inept Third World terrorists, that the military mission in Iraq could be accomplished on the quick, that economic cycles were a thing of the past, that Western democracies had become immune to populist forces. The few who were right ahead of their time mattered less than those who were wrong until it was too late to matter: as ambitions take precedence over convictions, to not agree with the self-evident truth of the moment is almost perverse. Back to decline, then, which, writes Adam Gopnik, "has the same fascination for historians that love has for lyrical poets." Often announced but repeatedly postponed, it forces every new wave of declinist historians to explain why their colleagues were wrong and why "the previous era was actually a peak rather than the valley" it was made to be.[3]

AN IMPERIAL POWER LIKE NO OTHER

The relative safety of its milieu and a providential endowment in natural resources, together with a visionary leadership continuously renewed by a people of character, combined to make the United States a nation that was born and grew like no other. Most of the country's early life was lived during an era of relative international stability and with a luxury of distance that other powers never enjoyed to a comparable extent—a luxury, that is, which gave America the ability to stay away from "over there." That permitted the new republic to keep a distant relationship with history, which

Americans explored with little baggage and with enough leisure time to grow confident in their own future as a nation (if only by comparison with the travails of others).

At first, the new country had few interests in the world. America had a "destiny" but it was "manifest" that it was to be lived "over here" where the "pursuit of happiness" motivated the earliest settlers to ensure for their New World the "inalienable rights" they had been denied in the Old World. In short, the Founding Fathers did not make of power the central idea of the nation to which they aspired. But they believed in the power of the ideas that inspired it, not because these ideas were new but because founding a government and raising a society on the principle of natural rights was new. To this extent, the principles that guided America's rise to preponderance made the United States "dangerous" and the Declaration of Independence, which was its birth certificate, was also its first foreign policy document. A decade later, the American Constitution was a best seller in Europe, notwithstanding its foreign readers' haughty dismissal of its authors as "provincials, borderland people."[4]

Nor did a quest for superiority motivate America's ascendancy. On the contrary, the new nation lived its early life in self-denial, happy to stay behind a "meridian of partition"—Jefferson's phrase—across the Atlantic. Later on, the Civil War served as a dress rehearsal for half a century of total wars in Europe. It also was a tragic demonstration of the nation's enormous power potential. In the mid-1860s, the re-United States had the largest standing army in the world, and its five hundred–ship navy was second to none; but it could also rely on an industrial capacity second only to Britain, an agricultural productivity superior to all, and a growing entrepreneurial population that was soon to show that it, too, was above any other. Indeed, the neglect of the Civil War as an unexpected opportunity to derail the American Union and end what the London *Times* called the "nightmare" of an "American colossus" was later viewed in Germany as an "unpardonable blunder" for which the Germans were to pay a very heavy price twice, in 1917 first and in 1941 next.[5]

Yet after the Civil War the United States quickly dismantled its military forces and again turned inward for reconstruction and reconciliation. To Europe's relief, this decision reaffirmed an American resistance to becoming all of the world power it could otherwise be because of the scope of its resources, the range of its ideas, and the disposition of its people. The Old World that stood on the other side of the Atlantic was far removed from the new nation's concerns, and its trials and tribulations seemed of little immediate relevance to U.S. interests. And even after America began to move into the world, its leadership was not asserted because of the power it acquired and could seemingly increase at will but because of the power its competitors wasted and could no longer renew. Thus, Europe's suicidal death march in the twentieth century passed through two connected and global conflicts that ended only with a tardy investment of American power. That investment was made after the strength of the states that had started, welcomed, and waged these conflicts had been exhausted. That, wrote historian Arthur Schlesinger, left the United States "a virtual prisoner of its client states," first in Europe and soon elsewhere in the world.[6] In short, the reduction of the Western world into an American world was not a goal explicitly sought in the United States, but the emergence of a post-Western world as an anti-American world would not be an outcome readily acceptable either.

Imperial America

An imperial power is more than a great power; it is a power that stands above all others. As a matter of facts, this status entails capabilities second to few in any area, but superior to all in their totality; global interests, with many deemed sufficiently vital to warrant intervention; and universal saliency, which provides for at least some measure of legitimacy. As a matter of intent, it is designed to shape its rivals' behavior by means that include the threat or the use of force, the manipulation of economic inducements or sanctions and political pressures, and even personal ties or inspiration— all with the goal to compel, intimidate, or otherwise influence others. Thus, an imperial power can be coercive, compensatory, and remunerative or even seductive; it can act unilaterally or through a coalition in which the followership of the weaker state does not require prior consultation since the action of the stronger state does not demand third party contributions.

An imperial power need not be imperialist by definition, but it often succumbs to an imperialist temptation if and when circumstances, real or imagined, give it the "zeal" it might have lacked otherwise.[7] It is after a "little glorious war" with Spain in 1898 that "a tidal wave of imperialist sentiment" in the United States grew out of widespread public perceptions of an increasingly powerful country whose enlightened and benevolent progressivism could be exported abroad.[8] This war, boasted President McKinley, meant that America "in a few short weeks . . . has become a world power." A short life rather than a short while is what the U.S. president meant: born as a world power because of its unquestioned attributes America was destined to rise as a power in the world by virtue of its character. Only its own ambivalence and self-denial stood in the way. McKinley shied away from the "I" word, but the nation's drift to imperialism, and its sharpened taste for empire, had been growing during the previous decade, when, wrote historian Thomas Bailey, the United States decisively faced Germany over the Samoa scramble in 1889, Italy over the New Orleans lynching bee in 1891, and Great Britain over the Venezuela boundary question in 1896. In each case, serious trouble was avoided and there was no significant military confrontation. Instead, the European powers sought accommodation, including and especially Britain whose government hoped to rely on U.S. power to balance a European security order that had already outgrown the Westphalian state system.[9] But even at a time of imperial ascent, America, while responsive to Britain's gestures of unilateral restraint, was not ready to join the continent in opposition to which the republic had been born. Indeed, the U.S. failure to accept Europe's invitations to enter the maelstrom of world affairs was such that in August 1914 war erupted in Europe without any debate in the main European capitals about a possible U.S. role.[10]

The Old World caught up with the New in 1917 but the American mistrust of an unprincipled Europe endured. As narrated by historian Margaret Macmillan, Wilson brought to Versailles the best available experts he could find in government and out of the universities with "crates of reference material and special studies" to make of this war the war to end all wars.[11] But the other European powers had no need for such expertise. The history they knew best was the history they had lived, and they feared America's peacetime intentions no less than they had welcomed its power in wartime: this odd country across the Atlantic was a Great Power like no other, or, at the least, unlike any of them. Now that there seemed to be a lesser need for American power, Wilson's oratorical discourse was not enough, therefore, to overcome Europe's passionate inhumanity and desperate lack of common sense. For the victorious European powers, there could be absolution from the atrocities of the previous five years only if the defeated states assumed a war guilt that meant the innocence of the victorious protagonists. Even the League of Nations, which Wilson had envisioned as the caretaker and enforcer of the new "principles" for world order, was made an intrinsic part of the punitive peace signed in 1919. A former political science professor at Princeton University, Wilson should have known better: everything taught by history about the nature of international relations argued that the international organization constructed by the League's Covenant and explicitly attached to a vengeful peace treaty, could not work and was bound to fail.[12]

As the league was institutionally constructed but also as it was emotionally understood: with the peace thus kept retroactive by the explicit intent to punish rather than reconcile, the war soon resumed and the United States, too, returned to Europe, once again with much reluctance and only after Hitler declared war in anticipation of the U.S. response to the Japanese attack on December 7, 1941. But even after World War II, President Truman still feared an isolationist surge that would keep the United States away from Europe and the rest of the world. It is in fact with an emphasis on America's "responsibilities" and its obligation to restore stability in Europe and, next, the de-Europeanized and de-imperialized periphery, that the United States could explain, admittedly conveniently, occasional imperial outcomes that betrayed its initial anti-imperial intentions. As Dean Acheson was fond of saying, the world knew of America's "good intentions" and its hubris alone was thought to be enough to forgive bad results.[13]

So remembered, the rise of American power provides for a narrative other Great Powers that have lived history and its tragedies more intimately do not follow readily. Elsewhere, the narrative is mostly one of war—a narrative that relies on repetitive and horrific stories of provocation, mobilization, invasion, subjugation, occupation, and humiliation. In the United States, emphasis is placed on heroic postwar tales of liberation, reconstruction, rehabilitation, reconciliation, and valor. These narratives are not only different but also incompatible. They clash most dramatically over the harsh accounting of the killing and maiming—the 120,000 U.S. combat deaths during World War I, which seem horrifically few relative to Britain's 885,000 deaths, or France's 1.4 million and Germany's 2 million; and the 420,000 U.S. combat deaths during World War II, compared to 2.1 million for Japan, 3.8 million for China, 5.3 million for Germany, and about 11 million for the Soviet Union; or the U.S. combat deaths in Korea and Vietnam, or Iraq (twice) and Afghanistan relative to those suffered by enemy losses in combat or so-called collateral casualties among civilians.[14] "They have not had their Verdun," pointedly said Joschka Fischer, at the time Germany's foreign minister, about the 3,000 deaths caused by the terror attacks of September 11, 2001: Verdun was the battle waged in 1916 over a few kilometers of French land during which more than 300,000 combatants were killed in about eight months.[15]

The bland banality of statistics does not lessen the unspeakable tragedy of each death. The difference between zero and one is infinity, and even if that single casualty remains unknown the largest numbers grow exponentially one casualty at a time.[16] But together with the memories that sustain their reality, these aggregate numbers have produced an American "philosophy of international relations"—Henry Kissinger's one-phrase causal assessment of the Vietnam War[17]—that is fundamentally different from other countries, not because of an early submission to militarism, as in Russia or China, or because of a late conversion to pacifism, as in Europe or Japan, but because of different historical experiences with the meaning and the relevance of force as a solvent of interstate differences. As Walter Lippmann eloquently wrote in December 1941, U.S. presidents "announce, proclaim, disclaim, exhort, appeal, and argue. But they do not unbend and tell the story, and say what they did, and what they think about it, and how they feel about it."[18]

Looking back, the first postwar years midway through the twentieth century betrayed America's immaturity as a world power—what European-born political scientist Stanley Hoffmann called a condition of "perpetually renewed historical virginity."[19] With the Western world left bankrupt by Europe's geopolitical madness and moral betrayals, the Truman administration took responsibility for its reconstruction and ultimate rehabilitation with brilliant insights and visionary policies but also some glaring misunderstanding and disturbing omissions. For example, associating occupied Germany to Europe's reconstruction a few months after its unconditional surrender was bold and constructive, but calling even more quickly for its rearmament was not as constructive even if it may have looked no less bold. The call, initially made by the then secretary of state James Byrnes in Stuttgart, Germany, in the fall of 1946, caused predictable concerns throughout a continent that had just fought the second of two tragic wars with that country in slightly more than a generation. As noted by George Kennan, the past and its relevance to the future were dismissed too readily and contemptuously: only America's own history seemed to matter, which, warned Kennan, betrayed colossal conceit.[20] Indeed, so satisfied was the United States at the close of the war that no discussion of U.S. interests seemed necessary; so superior was American power, militarily and economically, that no assessment of U.S. priorities was seriously attempted; and so supremely confident in its capacity to act anywhere in the world that no specific prescription was convincingly offered. If there was a vision, it only came later—a post facto reminder of anything worth remembering after every failure or setback has been forgotten (see table 4.1).

Objections to U.S. leadership, which reflected the different perceptions held abroad about the threat of Germany's rearmament and the risks of Soviet expansion, were dismissed by a narcissistic America as "neurotic"—the "instinctive" responses of failed states to their flawed history. When dimly heard at home, too, these objections were rejected as misguided voices of

Table 4.1.   Empire by Solicitation: Building a Western Community

An Evolving U.S. View	Views in Europe
1945–1948: Cooperative, Dominant	**1945–1948: Divided, Aligned**
Perspective: Interwar Events (post-1919)	Perspective: World War II (post-1933)
Manage Europe's retirement from the world	Arrange America's entanglement in Europe
Mood: America Noon	Mood: Europe Midnight
Weary, confident, cautious	Postwar history of silences and divisions
Assumptions: Some Risks, Few Threats	Assumptions: Many Threats, Few Risks
Soviet expansion without Stalin having to lift a finger (Communist parties)	Germany, the empires, Communist parties, Russia, and the United States
Interests: Economic, Political	Interests: Reconstruction, Security
Right of interference: sovereignty not allowed at U.S. expense	The Cold War was as much an outside as an internal problem
Formula: European Integration	Formula: Back to the Future
Selling the American vision at home was not easy	France-Russia Alliance, Anglo-French Treaty, Brussels Pact
1948–1951: Intrusive, Assertive	**1948–1951: Supportive**
Perspective: Postwar Events	Perspective: Postwar events
What does Stalin want?	What will Truman do?
Mood: Fearful, Urgent	Mood: Fearful, Confused
Stabilization, reconstruction, rehabilitation, reconciliation	Foreign wars, domestic political wars, transatlantic tensions
Assumptions: Growing Risks, Threats	Assumptions: Growing Threats, Risks
A collective defense alliance to guarantee the U.S. commitment	German *revanchisme*, Soviet expansionism, imperial collapse
Interests: Strategic →USSR	Interests: Security →Germany/USSR
Conditional support for integration: Will Europe follow?	Followership based on some expectations: Will the United States listen?
Formula: European/North Atlantic	Formula: North Atlantic/European
Restore Europe's autonomy with temporary U.S. engagement	Lock America in permanently
1951–1957: Containing the USSR	**1951–1957: Engaging Germany**
Perspective: Interwar?	Perspective: Hopes Betrayed
The Korean War as a decisive incident	The Korean War as a successful test of U.S. credibility
Mood: Combative, Even Bellicose	Mood: Ambivalent
The rise to globalism (Indochina, China, Nonalignment)	Protection from U.S. good intentions and Soviet ambitions
Assumptions: Global Military Threat	Assumptions: Threat Elsewhere
Rearmament/strategic buildup; brinksmanship	The Suez crisis: U.S. immaturity, Europe's impotence
Interests: Economic, Political, Strategic	Interests: Political/Strategic Status Quo
The United States as a power in Europe: deployment of U.S. forces	over Germany and with the United States: a clash of perspectives
Formula: Trans-Atlantic	Formula: Euro-Atlantic
Germany down, USSR out, and the United States in: agenda misunderstood?	Germany in, USSR down, and United States out: hidden agenda?

alleged communist-inspired fellow travelers or worse. In short, putting the American vision together took much time and flexibility, and selling it was no easy task. Yet, what is remarkable in retrospect is that the American ahistorical approach to Cold War bipolarity worked well and with relatively few tears, notwithstanding the relentless criticism it received for being "too naïve, too calculating, too violent, too isolationist, too universalist, too unilateral, too moralistic, too immoral" and worse.[21] In the end, the stability and prosperity of Europe's widening democratic peace put in place by American leadership, power, and purpose stood in sharp contrast with the atrocities and dislocations that had taken place during the first half of the century. Self-determination with a strong bill of rights and territorial consolidation with a constrained state were intrinsic parts of the good life that had been instituted in the New World, and were exported to that "half of the world" that lacked the capacity to proceed alone. Led by the United States a restored Western world thus ended the twentieth century the way it had started—on top.

This broad description does not fit the traditional idea of empire, which political scientist Michael Doyle has described as "a system of interaction between two political actors, one of which . . . asserts political control over the internal and external policy . . . of the other."[22] Nor does it have much to do with historical patterns of imperialism, which posits a controlling core over the controlled periphery.[23] Absent a coercive will to control its allies' domestic or foreign policies, let alone both, no empire was intended. And if an American empire emerged nevertheless, it did so by invitation rather than by coercion, and as a series of improvisations rather than as the result of a grand design. In Europe specifically, the United States was urged to enter into a powerful and cohesive alliance that was promptly given an organization (NATO) that provided the alliance with the tools it needed to satisfy its members' goals. Left without the ability to assume the heavy price of empire, the European states themselves agreed, more or less reluctantly and peacefully, to withdraw from those parts of the world where they had given the West a bad name. And in response to explicit U.S. pressures, they also committed to building a united and strong community among them, which became ultimately a "union"—one step and one state at a time.

The facts of U.S. superiority were beyond doubt long before the Soviet collapse left the United States without any credible or willing competitor. But even after the United States was left as the century's last power standing— a "lonely superpower," wrote Harvard professor Samuel Huntington—the American preponderance appeared to be of little concern to other states.

References to an American empire—or to American imperialism or to America's imperial power—were discounted with an apologetically soothing word that pictured the United States as an empire, to be sure, but one that was reassuringly "lite" or "benevolent" and even (but less convincingly) "oblivious" and "inadvertent." In any case, it was fated to remain "final" due to the characteristics of America's identity, so unrepeatable as to signify the end of empires.[24] In short, leaving the twentieth century, the United States was the first anti-imperial imperial power—imperial by position and anti-imperial by intent since the American creed is an "imperialism of anti-imperialism."[25] Yet in a world of emerging powers that might have their own imperial temptations that, too, makes U.S. preponderant power dangerous as a rampart against the changes they might seek or wish to impose.

Structural Meanderings

A preference for unipolarity comes naturally to the United States, both by instinct and by tradition—every moment is an "American moment," and every century, an "American century." The facts of superiority are easy to grasp and even easier to justify, as some sort of divine entitlement—a right of birth that empowers the nation to act on behalf of others because of physical and moral attributes that give it power over others. By comparison, self-limiting goals like "parity" or "sufficiency" are abstract concepts made more confusing by foreign words like *equilibrium, raison d'état*, and *realpolitik*, which are all words that lose their historical meaning in translation—meaning, away from their European context. Superiority makes it possible to act alone with an agenda that prevails over that of others and permits action where and when deemed necessary, regardless of others. Unipolarity has little need of diplomacy, which is said to be conducive to wasteful delays and self-defeating appeasement. Instead, priority is placed on power of the "hard" sort, and unilateral action is permissible without the constraints of coalitions whose members, whether they are willing or not, remain of marginal relevance to the mission anyway.

In a unipolar world, power talks but rarely listens. There is little need for consultation before decisions are made, and even less need to defer action after the decision has been made. In the end "willing" partners can do for the preponderant power less than what it can do for and to them. Unipolarity also enables the preponderant power to maintain an ever-available option to withdraw at will when expectations are not met and the costs of intervention become too steep. Nothing is wrong in hoping for a zero-casualty war from which there is an ability to withdraw by a date certain, however unlikely such goals remain in practice—the triumph of Western technology and expediency at the expense of adversaries that have access to lesser and fewer capabilities but have the time to take their time.

Unipolarity is predictably exhausting, though. In a moment of primacy a recognized need for prudence is distorted by a zealous urge for engagement. Each issue is turned into a test, and each test is said to be decisive, with failure feared to be fatal although no test is ever expected to be final. For the preponderant state to declare a war won is not enough unless success is recognized by other states in the region and elsewhere; for its adversaries or allies to perceive retreat may be enough to imagine new opportunities or risks that must be defeated or corrected. Lived in near-Sisyphean terms unipolarity has the preponderant power to haul the boulder on top of the mythical hill only to see it roll down time and again. There is little satisfaction with such a condition. In life or in death, as a man or a state, Sisyphus cannot be imagined happy.

Bipolarity is the structural godfather of unipolarity, to which it gives birth after either superpower runs out of capabilities, interests, and will—unless they first strike a deal, which the French used to call a *condominium* (another "foreign" word that escapes translation in American English). The United States learned how to manage a bipolar structure after 1945, though awkwardly at first, when trying to understand the Soviet beast before attempting to contain it. Bipolarity produces entangling alliances, the original scourge of American history but an efficient way to deny the other power gradual expansion and final preponderance until it is rolled back and brought down. In a bipolar power structure, confrontation threatens to turn global, and so do the alliances that define it. As a result, geography appears to prevail over history: moving East–West or North–South, a bipolar world keeps power broadly indifferent to diplomacy, not only because of each superpower's dominance over its respective allies but also because of a stalemate that invites them to mutually exclusive and dangerously confrontational zero-sum games. With bipolarity, power informs but rarely consults, and it asserts more than negotiates. It is as if two unipolar worlds had been juxtaposed, and what each superpower does for and to its allies usually matters more than the other way around—so long, that is, as the allies, willing or coerced, find life without the superpower worse than life under its patronage: meaning less safe, less affluent, less stable, and even less predictable.

Whether in terms of adversary relations (U.S.-Soviet) or alliance cooperation (U.S.-European), the Cuban Missile Crisis in the fall of 1962 is an especially good example of bipolar conditions: a "hell of a gamble" for

Moscow to make, but also for Washington to follow with a risky bet of its own. Played out in the Caribbean the gamble nonetheless used Europe as its main stake, for it is there that the nuclear confrontation would have taken place had neither superpower blinked—raising the possibility of a war Kennedy viewed at one critical point as a 50–50 proposition, and about which the Europeans were not consulted but merely informed.

Perhaps more than with any other structure, bipolarity compels the two main protagonists to oscillate between the extremes of force and appeasement. In the nuclear age, a balance of terror relying on the credibility of a threat that is fundamentally in-credible makes these opposite options hard to assess: to this day it is not possible to tell whether President Kennedy would have ordered a nuclear strike had Moscow refused to end its attempt to deploy most of its available strategic capabilities in Cuba. But whether Kennedy himself knew what he would do is moot, although he surely sounded casual about the "the couple [of atomic bombs the Soviets can get] over on us anyway."[26] What mattered more during the crisis is what the Soviet leaders perceived, for it is on the basis of their perceptions that they ultimately accepted Kennedy's demands. Thus, a bipolar structure is made even more dangerous when acting first is understood as an advantage. But that in turn leaves the smaller powers at risk. Taking a chance on annihilation should qualify for a right of consultation before the decision is made. That, however, is not a right either superpower is likely to grant easily to lesser allies caught between them in a bipolar structure.

Already in the 1960s, and soon after the Cuban Missile Crisis, a multipolar diffusion of power was openly sighted. According to Defense Secretary Robert McNamara, it is then that "the bipolarity we knew in the post–World War II period began to disintegrate," thus announcing "a more pluralistic world."[27] Paradoxically, the Soviet and American acquiescence to China and France's elevated status confirmed the relative stability of a bipolar order that was so well balanced as to leave each superpower feel it was not decisively threatened by such a change or, in the case of China, the early signs of an emerging power with a potential to challenge either and both of them. But since the Cold War, the sights of a new multipolarity are not as clear and cause for more concern. At two, the other key actor was always identifiable, and other countries mattered less; at one only, the rise of others might matter more but seemed less likely. But in an emerging multipolar structure, would new powers (but which) rise on their own (but how) or by invitation (but whose); would they act as "responsible" stakeholders (but to whom) with a shared sense of what these responsibilities can entail (but where) and with a common understanding of what the stakes are (but at what cost)? In all cases, there is ambiguity in intent, ambivalence in policy, and contradictions in interests—all of which add to the confusion of the geopolitical transition to more than one or two preponderant powers or, conversely, from one or two to many.

Unlike the bipolar and unipolar models of the past sixty years, multipolarity cannot neglect diplomacy given the inability of any one pole to surpass, equal, control, or even influence all the others. On most issues, trade-offs are difficult to evaluate and execute: do not ask what you can do for your ally, but reflect on what cannot be done without or against it, and thus ask what you must do with it and even on its behalf. Power combinations in an anarchical, dangerous, and possibly hostile but not hierarchical world are different from the cooperative or adversarial arrangements in a unipolar or bipolar structure. For the former, ad hoc "coalitions" are preferred, but for the latter the focus is on "entangling" alliances and for neither is balance an urgent concern. In a multipolar structure, the shifting nature of alliance and adversary relationships for the preservation of an all-important balance is especially challenging and even unpleasant for a power like the United States, which shows a predilection for harmony and institutional order. Multipolar alignments also follow too closely the substantive realities of power, which Americans like to have in abundance and even to an excess, to guarantee a control they do not generally like to share, and to respond to self-interests that are often hidden behind a self-serving rhetoric of ideals and principles. That is a source of confusion, especially for a democratic political system in which values can be voiced on the cheap from the bottom up but self-interests must be preserved at a cost from the top down. "This is not a game," thundered Obama in early 2012 in reference to "those folks" without "a lot of responsibilities" who "talk about war" with Iran with "casualness."[28]

Each power configuration thus breeds its own challenges: the delicate expectations of multipolar flexibility when allies, rivals, and adversaries are interchangeable; the dangerous risks of bipolar rigidity when each agreement and each confrontation can be played out as a zero-sum game between the two superpowers and their allies; the exhausting demands for unipolar omnipresence when the preponderant state assumes it cannot ignore any conflict anywhere without risking the rise of challengers that might question its resilience or efficacy—and hence, its durability, too; and in all cases, a demanding need for transparency between and within states, to permit credible threat assessment and lasting national consensus. Every response by uni-, bi-, or multipolar powers to new challenges is open to criticism and limits: a lack of staying power and capable allies if the instruments of power are deemed too robust or onerous; inadequate attention to the uses and benefits of soft power if the action lacks the nonmilitary dimensions of peacekeeping; and insufficient belief in harmonious end games if principles are said to condition the need to prevail.

DECISIVE DECADE

There is something oddly decisive about the second decade of centuries past. Thus, memories of the eighteenth-century start with the Treaty of Utrecht in 1713, which ended the War of the Spanish Succession, for both European and colonial possessions, with an explicit recognition of territorial compensations as the most effective way to sustain an orderly balance among the European powers. The treaty followed the death of Emperor Joseph I (1711) and preceded that of his arch-adversary Louis XIV (1715); it completed a reorganization of the international system started some sixty-five years earlier, after the Treaty of Westphalia (1648) had ended the religious wars and asserted the nation-state, set within a sovereign territorial framework of shared beliefs and common values, as the cornerstone of the modern state system. Thus began a "short" century during which interstate relations were "a sport of kings . . . played for strictly limited stakes" with relatively small wars that were waged prudently until the French Revolution of 1789 started the century that followed, under the guarded eyes of an infant American Republic determined to keep the unprincipled Old World at a distance.[29]

Memories of the nineteenth century also begin in the 1810s with the French invasion of Russia in 1811, Britain's war with the newly united states of America in 1812, Napoleon's final defeat in Waterloo, and the Congress of Vienna in 1815. After that, a rather "long" century, which had started in violence with the French hegemonic bid that followed the revolution of 1789, proved relatively stable, though eventful, for the next ninety-nine years until a burst of uncontrolled intra-European brutality in August 1914 escalated into a world war.

A lot happened during the opening decade of the twentieth century—including the failed Russian Revolution of 1905, a historic Anglo-French reconciliation into a so-called Entente Cordiale, and the spread of Great Powers' conflicts outside Europe: Russia with Japan, Spain and the United States, Britain in South Africa, and nearly everyone in China. However, it is what came next that proved decisive, including the Great War in 1914, the American intervention and the Soviet revolution in 1917, and the failed peace of 1919. These events were also the prelude for what occurred subsequently—until another suicidal war, in 1939, turned the delusions that had defined Europe at the turn of the century into what an inconsolable Stefan Zweig, the great European humanist, called "retrogression and gloom."[30]

Most likely, the same will be said about the twenty-first century, one hundred years from now. Notwithstanding the dramatic events that opened the new millennium in September 2001, and granted the system-changing events that followed, the decade ahead will be decisive, and standing still is not an option. During the coming years, and earlier rather than later, conditions within and among states will become much better or much worse, but they will not remain the same. How change evolves will most likely be shaped by what America does, and how well. Even in an emerging post-Western order this is still America's time because now as before it remains a country with the largest and most capable military forces, and the largest and most enticing economy, as well as the country with the most legitimate claim to the most central role in global governance. In short, it is still a power without peers, and thus indispensable, even if it can no longer be decisive and thus exclusive.

Anxieties of Decline

The durability of American power was often questioned in a bipolar world that threatened to end in a war that neither superpower wanted or thought the other able to wage. After 1945, Stalin was cautiously respectful of American power, but he bet against the will of the American people to remain involved in a world they did not know well and did not like much. Convinced that time was on his side, Stalin was prepared to take his time—a prudent geopolitical logic that paralleled Japan's earlier but less patient calculation that its superior adversary would not endure the pain of war long enough to defeat a more resilient though admittedly weaker enemy. Similarly, the Soviet leader expected that Truman and his successors would gradually lose patience with a world that, to them, was more a hobby than a lasting interest, and more a burden than an opportunity.

For the Cold War at least history has now returned a final verdict that leaves little room for appeal. Like Germany on two previous occasions, and also like Japan, the Soviet Union was not competitive after all. On occasions, America's will seemed to bend, as Stalin had gambled, but it never broke; and whenever American power appeared to be running short, it was always replenished. In this sense, too, America was not an imperial power like any other, for none before had shown such eagerness to go home, as well as such capacity for renewal: from an unexpectedly bold Truman after an allegedly irreplaceable Roosevelt, to a predictably strong Reagan after a reportedly weak Carter. Thus confronted with relentless American presence, the Soviet regime collapsed after an imperial war in Afghanistan brought Moscow's own overstretch to the breaking point.

To be sure, getting to that point was not easy. For the United States to prove Stalin wrong and remain in an interventionist mode some emotion about "them"—adversaries but also allies—was needed. Across the Atlantic the American emotion was readily felt: Europe was family, however estranged the family had become. Farther away, across and beyond the European continent, there was less spontaneous emotion. But the risks raised by the former allies, now adversaries, were sufficiently real to justify "scaring the hell out of the American people," in the urgent words of Senator Vandenberg, the Republican godfather of bipartisanship during the Truman administration. Exaggerations followed. "They eat children in Russia, don't they," a U.S. congressman anxiously inquired at a House hearing from his nodding witness, a one-time ambassador to Moscow.[31] Thus provided with demonic "Others," an angelic "us" embraced a credible Manichean view of the world, which traditionalist Cold War historians helped sustain with a self-serving emphasis on the purity of U.S. actions—"in design, in fact or in temper."[32] That condition lasted until a new school of revisionist history uncovered how much of "them" there was in "us" even though little of us could be found in them. With the United States and Russia lacking comparable geographic perspectives and historical narratives, their conflict lacked grounding, and both superpowers behaved against nature: by staying in Europe for the United States, a country born away from and against Europe; and by moving far into the world for Russia, a country whose pre-Soviet imperial instincts for expansion had never been lived globally before.

The past century has defined America well enough to not allow the first post-9/11 wars to deny the nation's credibility for the new century. To think otherwise would repeat the mistake made by the Soviet Union in a bipolar world with new questions about the U.S. capacity to prepare for the subtleties of a multipolar structure America has not known historically and which Americans abhor culturally. Entering the twenty-first century on a unipolar high, the wars in Afghanistan and, especially, in Iraq confirmed that preponderance is not quite the same as omnipotence. Imperial states, which know plenty about power, must also know their limits. "Reality is a very good teacher" on both accounts, explained Robert Gates shortly before he stepped down as defense secretary while warning his successors of the "folly" to engage in wars of choice.[33] Exposing the illusion of omnipotence need not alter the facts of preponderance, and preponderance does not demand for every issue to be a do-or-die test with a never-give-up, failure-is-not-an-option, with-me-or-against-me strategy.

Moving from one period of decline to the next throughout the Cold War, the United States remained markedly superior. There was no imperial overstretch because there always remained enough unused capacity for a strategic reset that restored American primacy, as shown decisively by the Reagan administration for military power, and no less convincingly by the Clinton administration for economic power. By comparison, the Soviet dash to military parity, or better, was exhausting and suffered from, and eventually destroyed, the country's third-rate economy, not to mention an aberrant system of governance that had burdened the Russian state long before the Soviet revolution. Now, fresh out of another costly and divisive war in Iraq, American power faces new pressures that are especially felt from an ascending China, also an imperial state like no other: not a Western nation-state but a civilization-state founded on the Confucian "emphasis on moral virtue, on the supreme importance of government in human affairs, and on the overriding priority of stability and unity." That emphasis, coupled with traditional Han Chinese beliefs in their own cultural superiority and "destiny" bodes poorly for a regulated world of multipolar balances and negotiated compromises rather than a hierarchical world of limited conflicts and self-induced cooperation between the would-be owners of a new global order.[34]

That being the case, austerity looms like the Achilles' heel of American power: how long, and how, can the world's biggest borrower compete for primacy with the world's biggest creditor? Remember: after World War I, the pound sterling collapsed in a single decade, during which the weight of the British debt proved too heavy for Britain to maintain its hegemonic role—as was acknowledged twenty years later (which also came twenty years too late). Since fiscal year 2009, four successive annual deficits in excess of $1,000 billion, which surpass the budget of most other countries in the world, have taken their toll.[35] If kept unchecked the U.S. debt level might equal or exceed the full size of the U.S. economy by 2020. With defense spending representing more than half of all U.S. discretionary spending, the cash-strapped politics of scarcity threaten to take precedence over the geopolitics of security.[36] "We will be smaller," acknowledges a newly appointed chairman of the Joint Chiefs of Staff.[37] Being smaller has consequences—like, said Robert Gates shortly before his retirement, "going to fewer places and . . . doing fewer things," or, added his successor, Leon Panetta, a "hollow force . . . incapable of sustaining the mission it is assigned" and, concludes the 2012 Pentagon's strategic guidance, unable "to conduct large-scale, prolonged stability operations."[38] Coming after a decade of contested wars fought at high costs, austerity also worsens a general public fatigue with the world, which a majority of Americans would now like to keep away again. In 2010, an overwhelming 91 percent of the public found it more important for the United States "to fix problems at home" than to "address challenges" from abroad (9 percent), while 69 percent thought the rise of such new influentials as Brazil and Turkey "mostly good" because "then they do not rely on the U.S. so much."[39]

In the end, though, the durability of American power cannot be doubted—"I mean," Vice President Joseph Biden said succinctly, "it's ridiculous."[40] To forecast a collapse of American power is to forecast the collapse of everyone else. That conclusion goes for any dimension of American power, including its military force and the will to use it, its currency and the totality of its economy, and its people and their willingness to stay involved in the world. In other words, what is good for the United States need not be good for the rest of the world: that is or should be obvious; but what is bad for the United States is likely to prove to be bad for the rest of the world, too: although that may not be as obvious it is certainly true nonetheless.

Leading from Behind

In 2009, President Obama's apprenticeship of power showed how difficult it is to translate a language of principles into an actionable strategy.[41] "The first question," he said during his first year in office, "is whether we're doing the right thing."[42] Maybe—although doing it well, too, is another "first question" that should not go without saying. That Obama's leadership wanted to be pragmatic by shedding the nation's illusion of omnipotence most recently displayed in a war in Iraq that the new president had opposed from the start, satisfies neither the academic guardians of realism nor the persistent mandarins of a discredited neoconservatism.[43] "To be blunt," noted Obama in 2011 to explain his opposition to the direct involvement of American troops to forcibly remove Colonel Qaddafi from power, "we went down that road in Iraq" and "that is not something we can afford to repeat."[44] A few months later, Hillary Clinton's Wilsonian instincts, which praised "democratic advancement" in but also beyond Syria as "not just possible but a necessary part of preparing for the future" took a clearly differentiated tone when she insisted nonetheless that the diverse nature of U.S. interests makes "situations vary dramatically from country to country" thus confirming the U.S. intention to stay away from any "one-size-fits-all approach" that would "barrel forward regardless of circumstances."[45]

There is cynicism in such pragmatism but that need not be a mortal sin either. Cynicism, wrote George Santayana, is "the chastity of the intellect, and it is shameful to surrender it too soon or to the first comer."[46] "My ideal for foreign policy," said Bismarck, the German master of *realpolitik*, "is freedom from prejudice, the independence of our decisions from impressions of dislike or affection for foreign states and their governments."[47] In practice there is morality in pragmatism because its final test is about efficacy, hardly in evidence during the past three U.S. presidencies. On May 1, 2011, killing Osama bin Laden in Pakistan, less than forty-eight hours after a U.S.-sponsored NATO strike had killed one of Qaddafi's sons in Libya, might not have made Wilson proud but it would have pleased Bismarck.

The delicate military operation that killed bin Laden was a risky bet, which Obama viewed as a "55/45" proposition, notwithstanding the "outstanding job" of U.S. intelligence. But these relatively weak odds did not deter Obama from taking the bet: winning the wager, he calculated, meant gains that justified the risks of failure.[48] There have been many such bets before, and there will be many more in the future: every strategic decision is a bet on the future, and while measuring the odds is hardly scientific it is oddly reassuring. Remember General Douglas MacArthur displaying God-like confidence in a "5000-to-1 gamble" that required "a combination of perfect timing, perfect luck, precise coordination, complete surprise, and extreme gallantry."[49] In September 1950 the amphibious landing at Inchon succeeded and changed the course of the Korean War (and possibly that of the Cold War, too). A decade later, in the fall of 1962, the two superpowers went to the brink of war: "Mr. President," noted the then defense secretary Robert McNamara at the start of the thirteen-day crisis opened by the Soviet deployment of strategic weapons in Cuba, "there are a number of unknowns in this situation," which "we ought to accept as foundations for our future thinking." Nonetheless, President Kennedy threatened military action because he feared the consequences of doing nothing more than Secretary of State Dean Rusk's own fears of "a general nuclear war."[50]

Not all "bets" work, predictably, and some threatened to bring the house down. Vietnam is an especially compelling example. The air campaign that defined the Johnson years was decided with numerical estimates that would be, with insight, comical if they did not prove so tragic in real time. For a senior advisor to McNamara, the U.S. goals were "70 pct.—To avoid a humiliating U.S. defeat. . . . 20 pct.—To keep [South Vietnam] SVN (and then adjacent) territory from Chinese hands. 10 pct.—To permit the people of SVN to enjoy a better, freer way of life." The odds were meant to make the decision look authoritative. In fact, they hid the uncertainties that kept all decisions about the war tentative. As confirmed eventually, a bombing campaign was not the best way "to demonstrate the will and the ability of the United States to have its way in foreign affairs"—said to be the ultimate U.S. goal.[51] According to Leslie Gelb, who later became president of the powerful Council on Foreign Relations, policymakers who gambled on the air campaign did not believe that "their decisions would provide victory," but "at best they hoped they might be lucky" although "they did not expect to be."[52]

Praying for luck can work but it is not a strategy: even God, reportedly said Albert Einstein, does not play dice. In working toward foreign policy goals that can be achieved, the first task of the pragmatist is to define priorities that are compatible with the nation's interests, capabilities, and purpose. That is not because of a lack of interest in what ought to be done over time, but because of a lack of capability for what must be done first. Goethe said it best when he warned against the urge to do it all at once. "Man," he wrote, "is not born to solve all the problems in the world, but to search for the starting point of the problem and then remain within the limits of what he can comprehend."[53] Not only what can be comprehended but also what can be accomplished.

If anything, the post-Western moment is likely to remain quite messy a bit longer. Periodically, states will engage in single-issue cooperative-adversarial-competitive relationships based on odd but self-serving inconsistencies. For example, in the spring of 2010, Brazil and Turkey, two leading new influentials, hoped to mediate the Western confrontation with Iran by offering to store some of Iran's enriched uranium. Criticized by the United States and Europe, the proposal was applauded by China and Russia, which nevertheless sided with the Western powers to agree to the tougher Iran sanctions Brazil and Turkey had sought to avoid. A few months later, in January 2011, Brazil and Turkey endorsed actively the democratic changes in Tunisia and Egypt; but when the UN Security Council voted on military intervention in Libya, Brazil abstained and Turkey approved. These instances do not point to a cohesive BRIC grouping, or to special bilateral partnerships between China and Russia, or between Brazil and Turkey. But they do point to a need for inclusiveness as a condition of international legitimacy, which clashes with the need for selectiveness as a condition for efficacy. In a zero-polar environment, the contradiction is especially glaring and occasionally consequential, but it does not hint, as will be seen, to any new patterns of alliances and rivalries in a future structure of power.

To balance such state-to-state and multilateral confusion, there is little prospect of a "concert" remotely comparable to what emerged in Europe after the Napoleonic Wars, and what was briefly hoped for when World War I took a time out with the armistice of November 1918. There is too little consensus about the permissibility and directions of global changes. Institutions matter more than before, and the need for accommodation is also higher now than ever, but national interests still prevail over multilateral governance. The main powers are sucked into a web of shared positive interests that invite them to cooperation and even some form of integration, but they also remain sunk into a quagmire of negative interests that impose competition and even some risk of confrontation.[54] To that extent, which states outside the United States, or even what entities beyond traditional nation-states, are or will become most decisive or most relevant in a new global structure of power is unclear.

Europe's legendary nineteenth-century diplomats—Talleyrand and Metternich, Bismarck and Palmerston—would nod approvingly. No "permanent" alliance or rivalry will suffice to define and manage the new global order—not even a sturdy Euro-Atlantic alliance that has not closed its door on Russia, and into which Japan may still find some small place, nor a budding competition between the United States and China or between China and India, or a so-called clash of civilizations for which no cohesive lineup is discernible. The risk is that with time some of the rivalries inherited from past global or regional conditions may reveal a lasting quality that will soon take an air of permanency, though not necessarily by design. Attending to that risk is not the least dimension of a post-Western world. This conclusion would give Woodrow Wilson some satisfaction—at least for a Western world that still remembers enough from the "organized insanity" it learned to defeat during much of the past century.[55]

An American Moment

As America's first full-time post–Cold War president, Bill Clinton bears some responsibility for wasting the unipolar moment. For the most part, he lived the future in the past tense.[56] The little he remembered conditioned the little interest he showed in the new world inherited from a Cold War he had mostly ignored, with the exception of Vietnam, which distorted his assessment of America's power. Clinton assumed that lesser was better, and he paradoxically hoped to retain America's influence in the world by keeping his distance from it. The best way for America to enjoy its hard-earned peace dividends was in a comfortable semi-retirement guaranteed by substantial returns on its earlier investments in Europe and elsewhere, which he reinvested globally in the new economy after the Cold War. Except when economic interests were at stake, American power stood mostly idle—neither used well nor shared or even saved constructively. The time was already half past Clinton when the war in Bosnia served as a reminder that American leadership was still indispensable, which Clinton belatedly acknowledged with a painless NATO intervention that ended the war without a single American casualty, ahead of another quick military intervention in Kosovo that also reasserted the U.S. capacity to assert the primacy of its power on the cheap.

Throughout, Clinton's strategic vision looked like a nostalgic visitation of Truman's bold leadership—celebrating the fortieth anniversary of the Marshall Plan with an announcement in 1997 that NATO would be enlarged to the East, or wishing a happy fiftieth to the North Atlantic Treaty by welcoming three new alliance members in April 1999, or even, evoking the fiftieth anniversary of Truman's recognition of Israel with a stage-managed handshake between the Palestinians and the Israelis at the White House in 1998. But these reminders of America's forceful leadership were not enough, especially in the absence of a clear policy toward Russia, a relative neglect of China (notwithstanding an opening to India), a broad indifference to Latin America, and the lack of a conclusive agreement in the Middle East, the new geopolitical pivot of future disorders.

With the United States viewed like a benign superpower, the rise of other great powers remained vague and distant. Forecasts of a new multipolarity intensified after 9/11, but they were dismissed as an anti-American aberration that prevailed mainly in an allegedly Old Europe led by France (with an assist from Germany) and joined by China (with half an assist from Russia). Like his father, George W. Bush was prepared to fight an alien concept for which he obviously did not care much and about which he knew even less. Said the then national secretary advisor Condoleezza Rice in London in June 2003, multipolarity is "a theory of rivalry, of competing interests" that "led to the Great War—which cascaded into the Good War, which gave way to the Cold War." Building up on the distorting simplicity of this narrative, Rice dismissed multipolarity as a "nostalgic" memory that was no longer a "necessary evil" and could satisfy only "the enemies of freedom." Other states—described as the "friends" of freedom—were said to favor the unipolar moment, at least pending some better knowledge of how the world should be recast—how many powers that matter, some more decisively than others, some more constructively than others, and some more permanently than others.[57] Yet that post-American but also post-Western moment was bound to come—a moment, that is, when the United States would expect more from the rest of the West, but also when the West could impose less on the rest and the rising rest could demand more. That moment was accelerated by the events of 9/11, but it would have emerged in any case, though, admittedly, later and arguably at a lesser cost.

The need for allies and partners that are not only willing but also capable and affluent is the agonizing "discipline" required to respond to a moment during which "no one nation can meet the challenges of the 21st century alone" because, Obama insisted in his inaugural address, "everywhere we look there is work to be done."[58] Even in the specific context of America's postwar history such a pledge is hardly unusual. "American assistance can be effective when it is the missing component in a situation which might otherwise be solved," noted the then secretary of state Dean Acheson when reviewing U.S. policies during the civil war in China.[59] Becoming a Lone Ranger was not America's ambition for the second half of the past century, but becoming Tonto is not America's new fate for the first half of this century either. After the war, Truman hoped to rely on the alliance with Britain, which lacked the power needed to satisfy America's expectation. For a short while, France was picked as a substitute partner of choice—the key to building the more united and stronger Europe the United States favored. But that, too, did not get enough response from a French Fourth Republic that soon collapsed amid the ruins of a fallen empire. In the 1970s Japan's economic surge elevated its status in a trilateral partnership with the United States and Europe, which was to regulate the then bipolar order against the Soviet Union. Such entente between the three leading world economies was also expected to keep an emerging Third World at bay at a time when it was challenging the West over the supply and prices of vital commodities, including but not limited to oil and gas. After the Cold War, George H. W. Bush offered a reunited and rehabilitated Germany "co-leadership" of a new world order. Finally, ten years later, George W. Bush responded to Vladimir Putin's "soul" during their first meeting in June 2001 with expectations of his availability as America's main partner for the post 9/11 wars.

In coming years, a "reluctant sheriff" who helps organize and joins a punishing posse can effectively shape an American moment during which a growing number of rising powers and new influentials shape the emerging post-Western order.[60] One such posse was formed for Libya at the initiative of a few European states, with the support of the Arab League and following passage of a UN Security Council resolution that no state dared oppose beyond a meaningless abstention. "This," Obama declared on March 18, 2011, "is precisely how the international community should work, as more nations bear both the responsibility and cost of upholding international law." Defensible for its geopolitical logic, the Obama approach also makes budgetary sense at a time when America cannot afford every war its allies might wish to wage or prefer to avoid. Unlike Bush's post-9/11 claim, it is not America but the world that is or risks being at war. The post-Iraq American discourse on behalf of leadership-from-behind thus also echoes the limitationist discourse of Richard M. Nixon during the waning years of the Vietnam War rather than Kennedy's interventionist exuberance ten years earlier, and it suits Clinton's America-first priorities ("It's the economy, stupid") better than Bush's siege mentality ("Bring them on"). After Korea, the doctrine that carried Truman's name and served as reference for much of the Cold War was a whole doctrine designed for only half the world, in Acheson's own words: goals were set, capabilities sought, and sacrifices acknowledged. But since coming to office Obama has offered only half a doctrine for the whole world: goals are asserted firmly and they are made explicitly compatible with American values and interests, but there is little acknowledgment of the capabilities and sacrifices required to fulfill them.

NOTES

1. *Who Rules the World? Conclusion from and Results of a Representative Survey in Brazil, China, France, Germany, India, Japan, Russia, the United Kingdom, and the United States* (Brussels: Bertelsmann Stiftung, 2005).

2. Dominique Moisi, *The Geopolitics of Emotion* (Baltimore: Johns Hopkins University Press, 2009).

3. Adam Gopnik, "Decline, Fall, Rinse, Repeat: Is America Going Down?" *New Yorker*, September 12, 2011, p. 40.

4. Robert Kagan, *Dangerous Nation: America's Place in the World from Its Earliest Days to the Dawn of the Twentieth Century* (New York: Alfred A. Knopf, 2006), p. 41; Bernard Bailyn, *To Begin the World Anew: The Genius and Ambiguities of the American Founders* (New York: Alfred A. Knopf, 2003), p. ix.

5. Thomas A. Bailey, "America's Emergence as a World Power," *Pacific Historical Review* 30, no. 1 (February 1961): 1–16. Up to the Emancipation Declaration of January 1, 1863, Britain was tempted to intervene: this concerned Lincoln who thought that one war was enough. It became even more of a concern when France joined Britain to force a mediation that, for all purposes, would have ended the "united" states with the independence of the Confederation. James M. McPherson, "What Drove the Terrible War," *New York Review of Books*, July 11, 2011, pp. 33–34.

6. Arthur Schlesinger, Jr., "The Making of a Mess," *New York Review of Books* 51, no. 14 (September 23, 2004).

7. George Liska, *Imperial America: The International Politics of Primacy* (Baltimore: Johns Hopkins University Press, 1967), p. 9.

8. Max Boot, *The Savage Wars of Peace: Small Wars and the Rise of American Power* (New York: Basic Books, 2002), p. 106; Ernest R. May, *Imperial Democracy: The Emergence of America as a Great Power* (Chicago: Imprint Publications, 1991), p. 7; also, Simon Serfaty, *The Elusive Enemy* (Boston: Little, Brown, 1972), p. 7.

9. Charles A. Kupchan, *How Enemies Become Friends: The Sources of Stable Conflict* (Princeton, NJ: Princeton University Press, 2010), p. 74.

10. America's indifference reinforced Britain's interest in an Entente Cordiale with France: there was no one else, and the rise of German power, including naval power, gave Britain ample motivation for accommodation with its historic enemy. Robert Tombs and Isabelle Tombs, *That Sweet Enemy: The French and the British from the Sun King to the Present* (New York: Alfred A. Knopf, 2007), p. 449.

11. Margaret Macmillan, *Paris, 1919* (New York: Random House, 2003), p. 3.

12. F. H. Hinsley, *Power and the Pursuit of Peace* (London: Cambridge University Press, 1963), p. 309.

13. Dean Acheson, Address to the University of California, Berkeley, March 16, 1950. *Department of State Bulletin*, vol. 22, p. 477. Quoted in Simon Serfaty, *The Elusive Enemy*, p. 29.

14. Tony Judt, "What Have We Learned, If Anything?" *New York Review of Books,* May 1, 2008, p. 18.

15. Interview with Joschka Fischer, "Amerika hatte kein Verdun," *Der Spiegel,* March 24, 2003; Hanson W. Baldwin, *World War I* (New York: Grove Press, 1962), pp. 74–80. That same year, in July 1916, British total casualties during the first day of the Somme Battle exceeded 60,000 in one single day.

16. Timothy Snyder, "Hitler vs. Stalin: Who Killed More," *New York Review of Books,* March 10, 2011, p. 35.

17. Richard M. Pfeffer, ed., *No More Vietnams? The War and the Future of American Foreign Policy* (New York: Harper & Row, 1968), p. 13.

18. Walter Lippmann's column, written on January 29, 1943, appears in Clinton Rossiter and James Lare, eds., *The Essential Walter Lippmann* (New York: Random House, 1963), p. 470.

19. Stanley Hoffmann, *Gulliver's Troubles, or The Setting of American Foreign Policy* (New York: McGraw-Hill, 1968), p. 110.

20. See John Lewis Gaddis, *George F. Kennan: An American Life* (New York: Penguin, 2011).

21. Walter Russell Mead, *Special Providence: American Foreign Policy and How It Changed the World* (New York: Alfred A. Knopf, 2001), p. 30.

22. Michael W. Doyle, *Empires* (New York: Cornell University Press, 1986), pp. 12–13. Quoted in Carlos Gustavo Poggio Teixeira, *Brazil, the United States,*

and the South American Subsystem: Regional Politics and the Absent Empire (Lanham, MD: Lexington Books, 2012).

23. Alexander J. Motyl, "Why Empires Re-emerge: Imperial Collapse and Imperial Revival in Comparative Perspective," *Comparative Politics* 31, no. 2 (January 199): 128.

24. Michael Ignatieff, *Empire Lite: Nation-Building in Bosnia, Kosovo, and Afghanistan* (New York: Penguin, 2003); Robert Kagan, "The Benevolent Empire," *Foreign Policy*, no. 112 (Summer 1998): 24–35; Mark Herstgaard, *The Eagle's Shadow: Why America Fascinates and Infuriates the World* (New York: Farrar, Straus and Giroux, 2002), pp. 66ff; William E. Odom and Robert Dujaric, *America's Inadvertent Empire* (New Haven, CT: Yale University Press, 2004); Jim Garrison, *America as Empire, Global Leader or Rogue Power* (San Francisco: Berrett-Koeler, 2002), p. 166. Simon Serfaty, *The Vital Partnership: Power and Order* (Lanham, MD: Rowman & Littlefield, 2005), pp. 17ff.

25. Niall Ferguson, *Colossus: The Price of American Empire* (New York: Penguin, 2004), p. 78.

26. Ernest R. May and Philip D. Zelikow, *The Kennedy Tapes: Inside the White House during the Cuban Missile Crisis* (Cambridge, MA: Belknap Press of Harvard University Press, 1997), p. 150.

27. Robert S. McNamara, *The Essence of Security: Reflections in Office* (New York: Harper & Row, 1968), p. 10.

28. Jacquie Calmes and Mark Landler, "Obama Scolds G.O.P. Critics of Iran Policy," *New York Times*, March 8, 2012.

29. Hans J. Morgenthau, *Politics among Nations: The Struggle for Power and Peace*, 4th ed. (New York, Alfred A. Knopf, 1966), pp. 173, 264.

30. Stefan Zweig, *Memories of Yesteryear* (Lincoln: University of Nebraska Press, 1964).

31. Quoted in James Aronson, *The Press and the Cold War* (New York: Bobbs-Merrill, 1970), p. 32.

32. Herbert Feis, "Is the United States Imperialist?" *Yale Review* (September 1951): 13.

33. Greg Jaffe, "Gates Envisions a New Game Plan for the Army," *Washington Post*, February 26, 2011; Thom Shanker and Elisabeth Bumiller, "Gates Says He Has Grown Wary of 'Wars of Choice,'" *New York Times*, June 20, 2011.

34. Martin Jacques, *When China Rules the World: The End of the Western World and the Birth of a New World Order* (New York: Penguin, 2010). Quoted in Christian Caryl, "Unveiling Hidden China," *New York Review of Books*, December 9, 2010, p. 33.

35. In 2009 only six countries had budgets in excess of the projected U.S. deficit for 2012—Japan, Germany, France, China, Italy, and the United Kingdom.

36. Michael Mandelbaum, *The Frugal Superpower: America's Global Leadership in a Cash-Strapped Era* (New York: PublicAffairs, 2010), p. 65.

37. General Martin E. Dempsey is quoted in Thom Shanker, "Economics Crash Course for New Military Chief," *New York Times*, October 3, 2011.

38. Edward Luce and Daniel Dombey, "U.S. Military Chief Warns on Budget," *Financial Times*, September 15, 2010; Leon Panetta testimony for the House Armed Services Committee, November 21, 2011.

39. The Chicago Council on Global Affairs, *Constrained Internationalism: Adapting to New Realities*, results of a 2010 National Survey of American Public Opinion (Global Views, 2010), pp. 14–17.

40. Quoted in E. J. Dionne, Jr., "Biden Off Message and Spot-on," *Washington Post*, April 4, 2010.

41. Simon Serfaty, "The Limits of Audacity," *Washington Quarterly* 33, no. 1 (January 2010): 99–110.

42. "Obama: Economy Won't Produce Jobs till 2010," CNN.com, September 20, 2009.

43. Paul Wolfowitz, "Realism," *Foreign Policy* (September/October 2009): 66–72; and comments in "Is Paul Wolfowitz for Real?": Stephen M. Walt, "Just Because He Walks Like a Realist . . ."; David J. Rothkopf, "A Neocon in Realist's Clothing"; Daniel W. Drezner, "Capitalization Matters"; and Steve Clemons, "Failing to Note the Difference When the U.S. Power Tank Is Full or Near Empty," http://www.foreignpolicy.com/articles/2009/08/27/why_paul_wolfowitz_should_get_real?page=0,0.

44. Helene Cooper, "Defending Strikes, Obama Says He Refused to Wait," *New York Times*, March 28, 2011.

45. Karen DeYoung, "Clinton Defends U.S. Stance on Syria, Bahrain," *Washington Post*, November 8, 2011.

46. George Santayana, *Skepticism and Abnormal Faith* (New York: Scribner, 1923), p. 69.

47. Quoted in A. J. P. Taylor, *Bismarck: The Man and the Statesman* (New York: Vintage Books, 1967), p. 40.

48. David Bauder, "Special: Experts Doubted Bin Laden Raid," *Washington Post*, September 1, 2011.

49. Matthew B. Ridgway, *The Korean War* (Garden City, NY: Doubleday, 1967), pp. 38–40.

50. Ernest R. May and Philip D. Zelikow, *The Kennedy Tapes*, pp. 57–59. Robert S. McNamara, *The Essence of Security*, pp. 58, 60, 81.

51. *The Pentagon Papers*, based on investigative reporting by Neil Sheehan (New York: Bantam Books, 1972), p. 255.

52. Leslie H. Gelb with Richard K. Betts, *The Irony of Vietnam: The System Worked* (Washington, DC: Brookings Institution Press, 1979), p. 3. Reflecting on his Vietnam decisions, former defense secretary Robert S. McNamara could only admit, however terribly late—"I was wrong, terribly wrong." *In Retrospect: The Tragedy and Lessons of Vietnam*, with Brian VanDeMark (New York: Random House, 1995), p. x.

53. Quoted in Hans J. Morgenthau, *Scientific Man versus Power Politics* (Chicago: University of Chicago, 1948), p. 207.

54. Richard N. Haass, "The Age of Nonpolarity," *Foreign Affairs* 87, no. 3 (May/June 2008): 44–56; Giovanni Grevi, *The Interpolar World: A New Scenario*, Occasional Paper, no. 79 (Paris: European Union Institute for Security Studies, June 2009).

55. G. John Ikenberry, Thomas J. Knock, Anne-Marie Slaughter, Tony Smith, *The Crisis of American Foreign Policy: Wilsonianism in the Twenty-First Century* (Princeton, NJ: Princeton University Press, 2010), p. 5; also, Zbigniew Brzezinski, *Out of Control: Global Turmoil on the Eve of the 21st century* (New York: Charles Scribner's Sons, 1991).

56. Simon Serfaty, "Memories of Leadership," *Brown Journal of International Affairs* 5, no. 2 (Summer/Fall 1998): 3–16.

57. Remarks by Dr. Condoleezza Rice, Institute for Strategic Studies, London, June 26, 2003.

58. Remarks of the President at the U.S.-China Strategic and Economic Dialogue, Washington, DC, July 27, 2009; Barack Obama's Inaugural Address, January 20, 2009.

59. From Dean Acheson's Remarks to the National Press Club, January 12, 1950, *Department of State Bulletin*, vol. XXII, p. 114.

60. Richard N. Haass, *The Reluctant Sheriff: The United States after the Cold War* (New York: Council on Foreign Relations, 1997).

5

CHOOSING ALLIES

The passing of the unipolar moment ends a Western era that was extended during the second half of the twentieth century after the United States took over for an exhausted group of fallen European powers. Moving from one era to the next will take some time, however—a moment during which American power remains superior and thus indispensable, but no longer decisive; Western power is still on top and thus inescapable, though no longer exclusive; and the power of the rest—meaning a large cluster of emerging powers and new influentials—is gaining broadly in stature and reach, and thus in influence and relevance, though not to the point of gaining global preponderance (see table 5.1).

The ride toward the post-Western world will be more stable if its passengers feel that the emerging new world order is in part their own. There is therefore no contradiction between striving to keep the West ahead of the rest while acquiescing to a larger role and more influence for the rest without the West. In fact, it is because the reverse is true that there is no need for the West to either provoke or indulge the rest, or for "the rest" to not do the same and engage but not follow the West. Standing in the way of the aspirations of the rest of the world after a long period of Western dominance would be of little benefit and might even encourage other states to exact revenge from the past era of subordination to Western preferences. Now, power is most effective when used with rather than over and at the expense of others.

Table 5.1.   Road Map to the Post-Western World

Struggling for Preponderance	*Struggling for Relevance*
The West above the rest	**Expectations and options**
The United States remains the only complete world power	Even a power without peers cannot remain without allies
The EU is not a world power but it is a power in the world	The United States is not a European power but it is a power in Europe
The United States and the EU form the only credible and fully capable G2	The rest of the West adds to the Western lead on the rest
The rest without the West	**Do not provoke, but no need to indulge**
China/India more interested in the West than in each other	India and China form a cautious and fractured relationship
No Russian card for China, or China card for Russia in the West	Russia: not a Western power but its future still with the West
The rest of the rest	**Doomed to cooperate**
In the Greater Middle East, the post-Western world has arrived, and there is no time for a time out	A tricontinental enlargement of the North Atlantic area that includes Turkey in the EU and Brazil with the United States.

THE WEST ABOVE THE REST

Forecasts of a declining West and an ascending East in a restored multipolar world are exaggerated. Abusively declared both irresistible and irreversible, these forecasts deceptively suggest ill-founded resignation and ill-conceived submission: deception for lack of conclusive evidence, resignation to what is accepted too readily as a fact certain, and submission to a sort of reverse colonization of the West that would be a historical revenge of the imperialized states over their former imperial masters.

The end of history announced at the close of the Cold War was said to complete a long process that had brought the best of the West to the rest of the world. As the historian Henry Steele Commager had observed, "being an American was a complex business" long before it became the nation's fate, no less complex, to lead this new breed of Western pilgrims to the "end point of mankind's ideological evolution," in the words of Francis Fukuyama.[1] Admittedly, with the Western model thus made-in-America not applicable to all states yet, history will take a while longer to end. All that is envisioned now is an end to geography, imposed by globalization and delivering an aged, wary, and timid West to the rest of the world.

A few significant realities still stand in the way of a Western surrender, however. One is the continued superiority of American power and the potential of the European Union as a superpower on its own. Also significant is the rest of the Western world: not only Canada but a wider arc of democracies that includes Australia and New Zealand at the far side of what used to be the British Empire, but also, on the Asian side of America's imperial reach, the like of Japan and South Korea whose Western vocation is reinforced by the threatening rise of China and a suicide watch for North Korea. As shown in table 5.2, the aggregate power of the West—the United States, the EU, and their derivatives—exceeds largely that of its main challengers, assessed one at a time, beginning with China, or as clusters of states like the ASEAN (Association of Southeast Asian Nations) or the BRIC countries—with both of these groupings and their respective members still substantially open to American and European influence.

Table 5.2. Measuring the West without the Rest and the Rest without the West

	The West without the Rest			
2010	EU 27	U.S.	U.S. + EU	Rest of the West*
GDP (PPP)	$14,820 billion	$14,560 bn	$29,480 bn	$8,099 billion
% World GDP	19.88%	19.67%	39.55%	10.87%
% World trade	12.10%	10.71%	22.81%	11.80%
% World FDIs	43.47%	14.34%	57.72%	7.70%
Population (2010)	492.4 million	313.2 mn	805.6 mn	235.3 mn
Per capita GDP (2009)	$32,700	$47,200	$36,593	$34,418
Area (km²)	4,325,000	9,827,000	14,151,000	18,471,000

	The Rest without the West			
2009	Rest of the World	China	ASEAN	BRICS**
GDP (PPP)	$37,896 billion	$10,090 bn	$3,094 bn	$19,069 bn
% World GDP	50.84%	13.54%	4.15%	25.58%
% World trade	65.39%	9.66%	6.58%	15.59%
% World FDIs	34.54%	3.65%	3.79%	9.05%
Population	5,867 billion	1,337 bn	613,766 mn	2,917 bn
Per capita GDP	$6,278	$7,600	$3,774	$6,537
Area (km²)	477,449	9,597	4,148	39,716

Source: Compiled from *The World Factbook 2011* (Washington, DC: Central Intelligence Agency, 2011), https://www.cia.gov/library/publications/the-world-factbook.
 * Australia, Canada, New Zealand, Japan, South Korea
** Brazil, Russia, China, India, South Africa

Axis of Stability

The unipolar moment was not a "fantasy" during which the United States emerged as "the leading disturber of peace," as argued by Johns Hopkins University professor David Calleo; but it was not either an opportunity for the enforcement of an American "benign, peaceful, and democratic world order," as forecast by neoconservative analysts William Kristol and Robert Kagan.[2] Standing short of these two extreme interpretations, the United States will likely remain the most complete power in the world during the coming decade. Its military superiority is far beyond the reach of other powers, and the lack of viable alternatives should keep even a weaker U.S. dollar dominant for years to come—until the mid-2020s according to the World Bank.[3] But recognizing the superiority of America's unmatched power, as well as the resilience of its people, falls short of suggesting a capacity and will for the United States to reassert its unipolar preponderance and act alone.

For Harvard political scientist Andrew Moravcsik, two global superpowers still prevail: "one is the United States; the other is Europe . . . the only other region . . . besides the United States, to exert global influence across the full spectrum from 'hard' to 'soft' power." Earlier, before 9/11 but after the Cold War, other analysts went so far as to envision Europe as the lead candidate to substitute for the United States as the West's last "best hope" to manage an unsafe world in the twenty-first century.[4] Consider: as an aggregate, the EU surpasses the United States in many areas, including size and population but also gross domestic product (though not per capita), two-way trade, and foreign direct investments; Europe's aggregate defense expenditures are several times larger than those of Russia and all other emerging powers including China, and its nuclear capabilities are second only to the former two superpowers. Around the world, Europe's contributions to peacekeeping and peacemaking operations exceed those of any country except the United States—with EU deployment in close to thirty civilian and military missions across three different continents—while its influence in multilateral organizations is magnified by its representation as states and as a union of states.[5]

Whether Europe's founding fathers knew, or even imagined, what they were starting when they signed the Rome treaties in 1957 is questionable. Their intent was not to bury the nation-state but to save it.[6] Pooling their national sovereignties looked like the best of the bad choices available. Over time, though, the more the new European institutions did for their members the more their members did through these institutions. In the process, cooperation grew into a habit, peace became a way of life, and the continent prospered as an increasingly integrated European community of centrist republics that disentangled themselves from their past ideological clashes at home and conflicts abroad. Initially endorsed as *indispensable*, and managed from the top down only, the process became *inevitable* from the bottom up as well. And why not: seemingly at little cost, "Europe" proved to be a remarkable producer of security, stability, and affluence—giving the new Europeans renewed pride in an identity that no longer carried the stigmas of its bellicose, nationalist, and imperialist past. Now, Europe is a "region-state" that merges the sovereign "I" of each EU member into the collective "We" of their institutions on an increasingly large number of significant issues.[7] For these issues at least, the European Union matters as much as, and often more than, any of its members—as if, in effect, the EU itself was a virtual member of the union. Note that even when the Europeans turn gloomy about the short-term outlook for their union, they still tend to show a more bullish view of its long-term prospects, thus confirming a basic understanding that however bad union may seem to be, it would probably be better than its alternative. Thus a relative majority of the Europeans surveyed in September 2006 still believed that the European constitution that had just been rejected by France and the Netherlands would soon reemerge, and even in a moment of rising Euro-skepticism that forces EU leaders to call for a time out for reflection and consolidation, decisive public majorities still viewed membership in the euro zone as an inescapable condition of their countries' recovery.[8] Five years later, in 2011, in the midst of a brutal euro crisis, more than half of the people surveyed in the seventeen euro states (53 percent) thought that using the single currency had been bad for their national economy, and yet there was little desire in most of them to seek a return to their national currency.[9]

Deeply motivated by a resolutely antimilitary character acquired by the Europeans since 1945, the EU has grown into a historically distinctive power designed for a "post-modern world" that breaks down the distinction between domestic and foreign affairs, condones mutual interference, rejects the use of force for the resolution of conflicts, asserts the growing irrelevance of borders, and simply rejects, according to diplomat-scholar Richard Cooper, "the morality of Machiavelli's theories of statecraft."[10] As a "civilian power," Europe is a power in the world that can pull other powers along the way, but it is not a world power that can forcefully impose its ways on others. Its role, adds German political scientist Hanns Maull, is "to civilize relations between states" with a new conception of a postmodern normal enforced "collectively

[and] with international legitimacy."[11] However, unlike the American union whose thirteen original states started their quest for a more perfect union with a shared understanding of what a more perfect world might be, including a clearly stated declaration of human rights that was intended to be universal, the EU lacks a common policy for the more perfect world to which their ever closer union and its members claim to aspire. It also lacks the capabilities needed to enforce it, or at least protect its members from those forces in the world that might threaten them. In other words, an unfinished Europe remains at the mercy of "uncivilized" events that are too significant to be ignored but which the EU is too weak to prevent, too timid to address, too divided to assume, and insufficiently motivated to defeat.

Paradoxically, it is this blend of power and weaknesses that makes the EU an especially sound partner of the United States whose unparalleled hard power is completed by Europe's "soft" capabilities, which the United States lacks or does not use well. Whether in the transatlantic context of NATO or through a European context with the EU, the United States (and Canada) and the states of Europe have learned to accommodate each other well: if not with each other, with whom? If not as a union and as an alliance, how? If not now, when?[12] France, which used to define itself in opposition to NATO, has returned to the Atlantic fold to stay; Poland, which voiced its skepticism of the EU after it joined, now teaches the gospel of European integration; Britain, which worried about the compatibility of the EU and NATO, now embraces a comprehensive strategy that praises their complementary potential; and the United States, once tempted by the commanding pleasures of unilateralism, now welcomes its allies' initiatives, which it claims to lead from behind and for which it contributes the needed assets, military and otherwise. For American neoconservative Robert Kagan, who used to locate Europe on the planet Venus far away from U.S.-dominated planet Mars, the case against Europe can be closed at last: "Even with its economic crisis," writes Kagan, Europe "is a mega-superpower and a very fine ally to have, indeed."[13]

Driven by an unsurpassed and relentless flow of investments, the Euro-Atlantic economy has grown bigger (and faster) than most nations, with over $4,000 billion of commercial sales and more than 14 million good "on-shored" jobs evenly distributed on both sides of the Atlantic. For the United States, this is a well-earned return on past speculative investments: first with the postwar Marshall Plan as a down payment for Europe's recovery, and next with the inflow of FDIs from the United States as the price of admission into an admittedly protectionist Common Market poised for growth.[14] For the states of Europe, too, these are substantial earnings that result from the risky strategic bets made after the war. In recent years, neither the brutal transatlantic and intra-European political clash over Iraq or the severe financial crisis of 2008, nor the disruptive volatility of the currency markets or the explosive crises in the Middle East in 2011 slowed the pace of transatlantic economic relations. By comparison, U.S. and European relations with China and other emerging economies are more like a speculation. In 2008 and 2009, under difficult economic conditions, the U.S. capital position in Europe continued to grow, but there was disinvestment from China, relative to 2007 and 2008, though not in 2010 relative to the previous year.[15]

Perceptions of a restrictive American ambivalence about a more united and gradually stronger Europe always were exaggerated. In April 1949, America agreed to its first peacetime alliance outside the Western Hemisphere only after six of its European members had signed the Brussels Pact as confirmation of their will to end Europe's divided, nationalist, and *revanchiste* past. In the early 1950s, U.S. warnings of an "agonizing reappraisal" of the North Atlantic Treaty were designed to encourage, not weaken, Europe's drive toward more unity—which was then aimed at the making of a European Defense Community. After that project collapsed in August 1954, it was an initiative of the Eisenhower administration (with an assist from Britain) that quickly locked a divided Germany into the West with an offer of NATO membership (May 1955) that served as a down payment for German membership in a small European Economic Community hastily launched in January 1958. Later on, Eisenhower and his successor urged Britain to join the emerging European Common Market rather than fight it with a narrower Free Trade Association. Still later, Kennedy's Grand Design boldly called on "our European friends to go forward in forming the more perfect union which will someday make [our Atlantic] partnership possible." In 1973, Kissinger's Year of Europe sought "a fresh act of creation" after Europe's first enlargement to Britain (plus Denmark and Ireland) and as a call to an ascending European Community to colead the Western Alliance.[16]

And so it went: if anything the case against the case against Europe grew steadily stronger as Europe grew steadily bigger and closer.[17] In the 1980s, the Reagan administration regained control of the Cold War in Europe by insisting on the need for transatlantic cooperation on urgent strategic issues like the deployment of new Soviet missiles in Eastern Europe, rather than on returning to faded political debates like the return of the Communist party in a newly elected French socialist government. After the Cold War, George H. W. Bush's call for a reunified German state to cochair a new world order was meant to involve all of a uniting Europe, which the United States also urged to expand to the former Soviet allies in the East. In short, as Europe has expanded in size, wealth, and stature the U.S. intent has not been to preserve an imperial control with policies meant to divide and weaken the European allies. Instead, U.S. invitations to colead the Western alliance became increasingly credible and even insistent as the prospects of a European Union with the capacity and the will to play a role commensurate with its influence grew.

Neither the rise of China nor its hypothetical role as a benevolent benefactor for Europe, or a resurgence of Russia as a substitute for the United States and a benign guarantor of European security, can seriously recast the Euro-Atlantic community and challenge its future as the world's most reliable axis of stability for the coming decade. After a century of shared history, the European Union and the United States show compatible interests, common goals, and overlapping values that make of them the world's only sustainable and most complete G-2—the most credible axis of stability in the post-Western world.[18] Admittedly, with Europe facing potentially catastrophic risks of cascading default, bank runs, and populist explosions that can quickly spread everywhere, both Europe and the United States might look at China as a possible lender of last resort with cash-and-carry transactions designed to transfer huge amounts of liquidities not readily available anywhere else—a case of a "new" East coming to the "old" West to save it, like the New World did for the Old halfway through the twentieth century. But such prospects remain unwanted by any of the parties involved, and there is little prospect of a change in their perspectives any time soon—meaning the views of the United States and Europe relative to China and to each other, as well as the views of China relative to the United States and Europe, as well as to both together.

Most pointedly, there is also occasionally talk of a Sino-American Group of Two that would combine the world's sole remaining military superpower and its drift as a Pacific power, and the world's fastest rising economic power and its rise as a redefined Western power. This vision is different from the U.S.-Soviet "condominium" formerly anticipated as the final outcome of a bipolar world. Then, the effect of such a condominium would have been to divide and share Europe, the main stake of superpower conflict. Now, it is said, the United States and China would shape a sort of inter-bipolarity that could change the world without dividing it, as a whole or around regional spheres of interest, but by pooling resources that no other country or group of countries can match one dimension at a time or in their totality.[19] Yet strategic intimacy between the United States and China has even less credibility than a Cold War strategic deal between the two superpowers. Most generally, the Chinese vision of its role remains rather passive—a critical follower more than a proactive leader—and there is little evidence of an impending change. To be sure, China has the temperament, let alone the capabilities, to be a dominant power: consider its lectures to the West about fiscal and social discipline, and consider, too, its bid to assert co-ownership of the seas, or co-managerial direction of the IMF and other such institutions. Yet, and at least for some more time, China is still a no-problem sort of Great Power that requires stability and would rather confine itself to polite inaction whenever forced to act, or asked to help, on specific issues of national or shared concern: to stop or at least moderate the manipulation of its currency, end or at least stall rogue nuclear programs (in Iran and North Korea), embrace or at least not block multilateral sanctions against gross human rights violations, defuse emerging civil or foreign wars (in Syria and Sudan), or help manage global issues (from climate change and the wasteful use of water to the free flow of earth and other precious minerals). As part of a multilateral process, the most, but also the best, that can be expected from China is polite acquiescence to, followed by a checkered participation in, institutional decisions made or inspired by other powers—a reluctant nod to blurry visions of multilateralism.

In any case, a G-2 with China based on U.S. "strategic reassurances" would bet that restraint will nudge China further into being a "responsible stake holder." Such a strategic bet is reminiscent of Kissinger's initial embrace of détente, which aimed at bringing Moscow into an entangling web of shared interests and formal agreements. What followed instead proved to be a surge of Soviet ambitions, which the Carter administration was unable to contain, and a window of vulnerability, which the Reagan administration was committed to close. Unlike mere normalization, which accepts confrontation when necessary but seeks accommodation when possible, a strategy of reassurance seems to assume that now is never a good time to insist and always a better time to retreat. It is a strategy of postponement, seemingly based on a rosy assumption that time is on the side of the peaceful party, and that all things good come to those who wait. This approach is a misreading of Chinese extreme realism: understood as further evidence of decline and dependence, every concession confirms the facts of China's ascendancy while encouraging the case for more assertiveness. In short, every display of oratorical appeasement or actual dependence threatens to weaken America's position relative to China's, with consequences for their respective interlocutors, including Europe and even Russia for the United States, and other Asian states and even other new influentials for China.

So achieved, a U.S. special partnership with China might be profitable in the short term but it would be costly in the medium to long term. History gives states a reputation that matters, and historically the United States has been a generally trusted power in the world, and a broadly reliable world power. Even at the peak of the debate over 9/11 and its aftermath the most exasperated critics of what America does kept their faith about who Americans are. That such would be the case has to do with the fact that on the whole American intentions are less feared than those of most historical alternatives—whether the aging European imperial powers before the world wars, the Soviet version of Russia during the Cold War, and now China, whose image deteriorates nearly as quickly as its power grows, its influence expands, and its resonance increases.

Thus, where there was neglect a few years ago there is now mounting concern about China—including in the United States (up from 45 percent in 2005 to 54 percent in 2010) and Germany (up from 44 to 53 percent). Nor are China's neighbors in Asia indifferent either, notwithstanding, and to an extent because of, their growing ties with its booming economy. The Chinese share of Japanese exports grew threefold in percentage terms between 2000 and 2010, but Japan's negative views of China rose to 88 percent in 2010, up from 78 percent five years earlier. The same trend appears in South Korea, where concerns about China moved up from 58 percent to 76 percent over the same period of time, from 2005 to 2010. As a result, even those with an unfavorable view of the United States now embrace closer bilateral ties across the Pacific (72 percent in South Korea, for example). In India, which expects the United States to stay ahead of China over the next decade, a drop in pro-Chinese sentiments, from 56 percent in 2005 to 46 percent in 2010, came together with a surge in pro-American sentiments that peaked at 76 percent after Obama's election—a 20 percentage points surge since 2006.[20]

A Euro-Atlantic G-2 will not be sufficient on its own, however: as was argued in the early post–Cold War days of NATO enlargement, "out of area or out of business." During the latter part of the nineteenth century, family ties between a newly unified Germany and a weak Austro-Hungarian Empire were extended to Russia with a *Dreikaiser Bund* that isolated archrivals Britain and France until the Entente Cordiale of 1905 produced a dramatic reversal of alliances. Although responding to different motivations, this is also what occurred in the 1930s when the Western democracies, including the United States, were not enough to defeat a totalitarian coalition between Nazi Germany, Imperial Japan, and the Soviet Union, thus forcing an alliance of convenience between the three democratic powers and one of the more distasteful states, which proved to be the USSR after both Germany and Japan overplayed their hands in Europe and the Pacific. In a world at five, six, and more, India already looks like a more credible third partner for the United States and Europe than an ascending and increasingly assertive China, a declining but ever more demanding Russia, and a willing but small and crippled Japan. Meantime, however, a Euro-Atlantic G-2 will find its best candidates for geopolitical enlargement among rebellious but recoverable new influentials like Turkey, whose EU membership has been delayed far too long, and Brazil, as the down payment of a tricontinental initiative designed to extend the "North" Atlantic area to the southern parts of the Atlantic, in and between Latin America (from Argentina to Mexico) and Africa (from South Africa through Nigeria and Angola and to Morocco).

THE REST WITHOUT THE WEST

Early in the 1970s, the economic recovery of Western Europe and Japan, a surge of Soviet military power, the early signs of an emerging China, and a growing presence of newly independent Third World states combined with a sizeable hijack of Western wealth during the first oil crisis to give a preview of a multipolar world that might eventually leave the West at the mercy of the rest—or at least their good will. "Four potential economic powers," noted President Nixon, now had "the capacity [to] challenge [the United States] on every front." Yet, "with a strong, healthy United States," Nixon reasoned, such a "new world order" could reduce the intensity of the U.S.-Soviet confrontation without inducing new conflicts outside their settled spheres of influence and at no cost to U.S. interests and commitments. China was placed at the center of a geopolitical triangulation that was expected to weaken Soviet Russia and favor the United States and the rest of the West.[21] As strategic compensation for America's post-Vietnam retrenchment, Nixon also hoped to recruit states like Iran, Nigeria, and Saudi Arabia as the viceroys of a new balance between interests, capabilities, and purpose. These were newly influential states whose geopolitical relevance, historical aspirations, and growing capabilities were moving the Cold War world out of its bipolar cage. With hindsight, such announcements of a changed multipolar structure were premature—relative to the end of bipolarity and the unipolar moment that followed. Yet past the current zero-polar transition, multipolarity remains the most likely future configuration of power in a post-Western world. It is not in place yet, but it is coming.

In a multipolar configuration, any power can in theory align with any other power. In fact, some face "handicaps, in the sense of being unwilling or unable to align with one or more states with which its relations are relatively more hostile."[22] As a result, choices of capable allies and partners can be limited or at least get complicated. Built over specific issues or even values, alliance handicaps can be set aside with tacit agreements that usually do not last long. Yet handicaps that seem historically insurmountable are ultimately overcome for good. Enemies stop being enemies even if they remain rivals and fail to become friends. As the legendary diplomat Palmerston argued while steering Britain's preponderance during the latter part of the nineteenth century, only interests are "permanent."[23] Consider the dynamics of bilateral relations between the three major EU powers during the second half of the twentieth century. The French and the Germans "learned" to be friends and even came to like each other; the British and the French became allies without ever trusting each other; and the Germans and the British still show historic scars that have not healed while wartime memories continue to linger.[24] By comparison, Americans usually tend to normalize relations with their past enemies relatively quickly—as happened with Germany during the decade after World War II, and with the People's Republic of China and Vietnam a mere twenty years after brutal but futile wars in Korea and Southeast Asia.

Entering the twenty-first century, unprecedented levels of interdependence make the international system structurally less anarchical, organizationally less hierarchical, and generally more self-disciplined but also more confusing. Now, globalization dooms the world to cooperation even for states whose interests are minimally and unevenly shared. Every enemy must be a bit of a friend but every friend can also become a bit of an enemy; rivals are occasional partners and partners occasionally return to being adversaries or even enemies. Wherever adversarial relationships are found they, too, have evolved: they are less conflictual now, and more conciliatory. Altogether, the past century of total wars is over: the use of military force between the main powers—meaning, the strong against the strong—is potentially too costly relative to possible gains. This does not mean that the threat and the use of force have become obsolete. But it does suggest that the risks of military conflicts are elsewhere—namely, between and within the weaker states, with or without the active or tacit involvement of stronger powers; but also from the weak to the strong, with or without provocation from the latter at the expense of the former.

Faking Convergence

A geostrategic troika consisting of Russia, China, and India evolves in the shadow of the United States and its alliance with Europe. All three states in this troika can only fake special partnerships between them: Russia is a postimperial power that holds no "China card," China is a preimperial power with no "Russia card" to play against the West, and India has little interest in playing any "card" with either state at the expense of the United States and Europe or the rest of the West. In all cases, America offers these states a better and more profitable game, and so does Europe, although to a lesser extent.

In the 1990s, Russia came out of the Cold War as a bitter country whose populace resented the humiliation of a double betrayal, first by its leaders who surrendered the Soviet empire without a fight, like Germany in November 1918, and next by the other superpower that did not welcome it in the victorious alliance, unlike what was done for Germany after May 1945. For most of the 1990s Russia stood on the verge of collapse—historically defeated, politically recast, and geographically reconfigured. In 2000, however, an abrasive Vladimir Putin appeared to resurrect a Russian tradition of pride and embodied the idea of a nation determined to matter again. Putin brought Russia back, so to speak, and in March 2012, Russia brought him back after Dmitry Medvedev's short presidential transition: among the BRIC countries, Russia shows the highest per capita GDP both in dollars and purchasing power parity (PPP) terms.

Whether Russia is a retired, postimperial superpower rather than a convalescent power in remission, or still an imperial power on a momentary leave of absence while it gets well, is not clear yet.[25] Pending full recovery an imperial relapse is possible, with a burst of nationalist sentiments at home and another expansionist outburst abroad. What is apparent, though, is that Russia is only beginning its post-Soviet journey, with its past a heavy baggage and its future still a risky speculation: a shrinking population, nonrenewable and falling oil reserves, worn-out military capabilities, and dwindling security space give Russia little time to assert the dominant status it has enjoyed historically and to which it continues to aspire emotionally— "for Russia to be secure and for our partners to listen carefully to what our country has to say," ominously wrote Putin in the spring of 2012, on the eve of his reelection and while recommending new defense expenditures of about $775 billion by the year 2022 for additional armaments and a more professional army.[26]

"We see zones of instability," continued Putin, "and artificially maintained, managed chaos emerging . . . in the immediate vicinity of Russia's borders." Geography, which has served Russian history unevenly, now seems to offer less protection. In the "near abroad" in Europe, a major chunk of the former Soviet security space, Russia's influence remains admittedly decisive. In 2008, the war with Georgia confirmed that there is more to Russia than a fading memory of what its power used to be. It also confirmed that Western powers, including both the United States and Europe, have no taste for a military confrontation with their neighbor in the east. But elsewhere little looks geopolitically safe. In Siberia and farther, a populous and rich China infiltrates Russia's least populated territories, which no one else seems able or willing to enter and assist, but in which China's growing influence looks contentious and even provocative: Russia eyes warily the cross-border movements of the 110 million Chinese massed next to the vast, resource-rich but underpopulated Far Eastern federal district, where live less than 8 million Russians, with a density below one person per square kilometer, and where the Soviet Union used to deploy as many as forty divisions—just in case. To the west, the EU and its image of affluence, as well as NATO and its Article 5 security guarantees seduce the former Soviet republics as an escape from their historic poverty and dependence on their former imperial master. To the south, Russia borders a rising Iran and a cluster of Muslim republics in North Caucasus with a dangerous radical potential, which is compounded by the growing influence of Turkey, a historical adversary.[27]

To view Russia as a European power like any other is historically wrong and geopolitically complacent.[28] "This famous space from Vancouver to Vladivostok," is still dismissed by the Russian leaders as an idea, if not a plot, of "Americans . . . who emigrated [from Europe] westward, and was spread . . . by the Russians eastward."[29] At best, Russia is a power in Europe: too close to be ignored and too powerful to be offended, but also too distinctive to be assimilated and too big to be integrated. Unlike any other bidder for global primacy, Russia is a *demandeur* state with a pressing need for the power attributes it lacks, cannot sustain when it has or acquires them, and cannot regain whenever it loses them: people because of its shrinking population, capabilities because of its aging arsenal, and resources because of its finite oil reserves. There should be no question in Russia that the Western powers are willing to make room for Russia: that would be a sound strategic investment so long, that is, as Russian leaders, too, end convincingly all remaining questions in the West about their own willingness to make space for Western powers in Russia.

For a moment after the Cold War, it looked as if Russia might look at China as a privileged partner of choice and a convenient alternative to unsatisfactory relations with a U.S.-led NATO or a Germany-led EU. Indeed, neither state can find another available likeminded partner. A common 2,600-mile border might have been cause for concern, but there is no territorial dispute left between the two countries and neither needs fear the other militarily—Russia because of its strategic superiority and China because of its conventional mass. Russia and China both rely on strong and assertive states that show little sensitivity to human rights, favor an authoritarian form of capitalism, and tolerate or even invite corruptive practices; they are both oddly mistrustful of and attracted by the West, which makes them prudent revisionist powers willing to change the status quo peacefully but not derail it forcefully; they are both regional powers that are increasingly sighted in areas outside their traditional core priorities; and they both share a stake in reforming global governance, whether the WTO, which remained closed to Russia for too long, or the Western-dominated IMF and World Bank. The Russian and Chinese narratives converge because their recent histories also converge, although for opposite reasons. Watching the Soviet collapse in the 1980s taught China what not to do, which the country's leaders have managed rather well since: effective economic reforms must precede any semblance of political perestroika. Meanwhile, watching the rise of China in the 1990s taught Russia how to do it, too, although three Russian presidents since Mikhail Gorbachev have been less effective than their counterparts in China in initiating and enforcing internal reforms.

A strategic partnership that would link a renewed bid for Russian primacy in Europe and the expected bid of China for primacy in Asia would be alarming for the West and China's neighbors. Yet prospects of Sino-Russian strategic intimacy are dim, and neither country can realistically hope to use the other as a trump card against the West or in Asia. Russia's negative views of Chinese power reached 88 percent in 2010, from 59 percent five years earlier. Notwithstanding Putin's aggressive oratory, Russia's future will be better served with rather than against the United States and the West: as a convenient counterweight to a rising and potentially domineering China, Russia's most distinct Asian neighbor. Nor does a triangular partnership with France and Germany show much promise: in the end, a re-nationalized and de-Americanized Europe would not serve Russian interests any better now than it has in the past. In retrospect, the Grand Alliance with the United States was Russia's most successful geopolitical experience in the twentieth century—the only time when Russia ended up on the side of the winners, and certainly better than the Triple Entente before

World War I or the Sino-Soviet alliance during the Cold War. Closer ties with the West will similarly serve a post-Soviet Russia better than moving away from the West, like Soviet Russia did in the 1920s.

History lingers and keeps Russia away from China. Whether in the mid-1920s at the start of their civil war, or in the early 1950s during their difficult war with the United States, or after that when they struggled to define their cultural revolution, the Chinese had ample opportunities to learn that they cannot expect much from Russia. More to the point, they know how much they have gained since the normalization of their relations with the United States and the rest of the West. Now, Chinese collusion with Moscow would be even less beneficial than it was during the Cold War, and collision with the West would occur at an even higher cost even in the absence of a highly unlikely war. Russia offers little that China wants and may be worth fighting for or about—including trade, cutting-edge technologies, arms and even energy: whatever remains of Russian ambitions in South Asia is of little immediate concern for China, relative to such other concerns as India, which motivates Chinese policies toward Pakistan, and even North Korea and possibly Iran in an odd combination of rogue nuclear states only China could control.

For China to claim a primary interest in Russia as a strategic, economic, or political partner of choice when addressing the United States and Europe would not make much sense. This is not the Cold War: there is little prospect of diplomatic triangulation between the United States, Russia, and China because these powers can develop better relations with each other separately than together. In any case, should China seek triangulation away from, or at the expense of, the United States, Europe would be a better choice than Russia. If nothing else, more substantial economic advantages would ensue. The same is true for Russia: the European security architecture it favors is less designed to force America down than to bring Russia in while keeping China out. The Russian view is that these goals can be achieved best with the main European national capitals in Berlin and Paris than with the EU in Brussels. This is not all that different from the Chinese view: in 2011, Chinese companies were the top foreign investors in Germany—the first time China surpassed the United States by such a measure.[30]

Illusive Chindia

An effective counterweight to China because of its bulk, capabilities, and temperament, India, nuclear weapons and all, is a major bidder for Great

Power status in the emerging post-Western order. Hailed by Barack Obama as "a power that has already emerged" and thus worthy of U.S. support for its bid as a permanent member of the UN Security Council, India can also serve as a convincing substitute for a diminished Japan, which would be too small even if it had not become so much weaker over the past twenty years. Irrespective of its place in the West, with the EU and relative to the United States, Russia, too, would welcome India as a partner of choice in Asia: too much history stands in the way of other leading candidates like Japan and China. Russia, however, is not a card India is anxious to play. Larger and more reliable markets can be found elsewhere, including the United States and China (which is India's largest trading partner), and new and more reliable weapon systems can also be acquired readily from a well-disposed Euro-Atlantic West. In sum, already seduced by the United States, actively courted by the EU, and repeatedly engaged by Russia, India is much in demand. Not surprisingly, however, it shows little interest in responding precipitously and exclusively to any of its many suitors: forever it seems, nonalignment has been the Indian diplomatic tool of choice.

The Indian economist Jairam Ramesch has evoked a composite Asian giant comprising India and China, which he called "Chindia."[31] This grouping is also unlikely, however. Both countries are hungry consumers of global institutions, which they can manipulate on behalf of their respective interests better than any special partnership between them. During the Cold War, nonalignment, which India embraced more tightly than China to make maximum usage of the bipolar stalemate, never was much of a bloc nor even a cohesive movement, and it is not now either. There is a temptation to view the whole of Asia as an irresistible a-Western group of rising powers around which the post-Western world will be organized. Midway through the twenty-first century, Indonesia, Malaysia, and Thailand in addition to China and India—plus such Western derivatives as Japan and South Korea—will have a combined total population of 3.1 billion, and account for 45 percent of the world's GDP, according to the Asian Development Bank.[32] But this vision of a united Asia is equally far-fetched: rather, the Asian mass is a G-zero as its members, individually focused on their bilateral relations with the United States or Europe more than with one another, can be most influential with narrower coalitions of the willing that they compose on their own—as one coalition per issue and one issue per coalition.[33]

Both China and India have comparable size and population. (India is about to surpass China's population, but past the billion who is counting the additional tens or hundreds of millions?) Their economies grow at a pace that dwarfs that of all Western economies and enables them to absorb a rising share of the world's global output. There end the similarities, however. The two countries abhor any other state lecturing to them, which each nonetheless likes to do to the other and everyone else. More significantly, both are economic and strategic competitors and rivals rather than allies and partners. Even shared characteristics like a taste for global status and worldwide influence are adversarial and preemptive rather than cooperative or complementary. For example, India's bid for a permanent seat at the UN Security Council has been endorsed by the United States and other Western countries, but it is met in China with eloquent silence. Meanwhile China's relentless search for influence in the thirteen countries (plus India) with which it shares boundaries is followed by India with some concern and countervailing pressures. Finally, both welcome, and compete for, better and closer relations with the United States, though not to the point of providing it with more leverage on either of them. If anything, the Euro-Atlantic competition for influence in India and China is more intense than their competition for influence in either America or Europe, with India more skeptical of the EU than is China and China more distrustful of the United States than of Europe. As to Russia, it occasionally looks like a major neglected factor in this unfolding nuclear *pas de quatre*. Russia is a Eurasian country but Asia is not its primary strength: the region it most identifies with is Europe and the interlocutor it singles out most readily is the United States. Indeed, looking at India's proximity to two hostile, possibly desperate, and potentially aggressive nuclear powers (Pakistan and North Korea), and reflecting over China's neighbors (starting with India), Russia can feel relatively safe and even geopolitically content by comparison.

Trade does not say it all but it does say a great deal. Thus, according to the Indian Department of Commerce bilateral trade between China and India amounted to $63 billion in 2010 (from April to March): this was more than ten times larger than in 2002 but still well below potential for the two most populous countries in the world. By comparison, Chinese trade with the EU and the United States that year reached a combined total of nearly $1,000 billion, notwithstanding the smaller size of the Euro-Atlantic market relative to the size of the Indian market if measured by their populations. According to EU statistics, exports to China increased by 37 percent in 2010 relative to the previous year, which makes India all the more ambivalent about the EU; meantime, U.S. exports to China increased by an impressive 50 percent during the first three years of the Obama administration. India, the world's largest importer of arms, looks up to the United States and

Europe for most of its needs; this is a status to which China aspires but has been unable to achieve. Meantime, India accounted for barely 1 percent and China for less than 9 percent of Russia's foreign trade respectively in 2010, as compared to almost 47 percent for the EU share of Russia's trade. That is not likely to improve any time soon as Russia is unlikely to emerge as a primary energy supplier of either of these two Asian countries. Seemingly, both China and India would rather place a speculative bet on oil-rich Iran, whose historical narrative is closer to each of them than that of Russia, and even though they both show concern about Iran's nuclear aspirations, India more than China.

Perceptions, too, limit each nation's interest in making of the other its security interlocutor of choice. In 2006, 76 percent of all Indians believed that their country will be ahead of China (and also the United States) by 2020. This figure exceeded China's perception of its own status relative to the United States, which China, dismissive of India, viewed as its only possible competitor by that year.[34] In 2009, the Obama bounce that restored America's good name in much of the world did not reach China, where there had been some appreciation of George W. Bush, whose father is still well remembered for his moderate response to the 1991 Tiananmen crisis. In India, however, Obama's election produced a remarkable 76 percent pro-American sentiment. By comparison, only 46 percent of all Indians viewed China favorably in 2009, according to the Pew Global Attitudes Survey, down from 56 percent in 2005; the trend has worsened since, and a 2010 survey showed that India's image of China has turned negative (30 to 38 percent, with many more respondents than three years earlier). Completing the picture, India, maybe sensitive to Britain's influence, is more skeptical than China about Europe's stagnant economy and weak institutional foundation—a perception reinforced during the euro crisis to which India, less commercially active in Europe, is relatively less sensitive than China.

China's ascendancy does not raise the same demographic or economic risks for India as for Russia but it is cause for military and positional concerns. There are too many areas where India simply cannot compete with its neighbor. Consider, for example, that for the years 2009–2010 the Chinese lent more money to the developing countries than the World Bank: when that money goes next door—say, for a pipeline that will bring oil to China through the Bay of Bengals—there is a related surge of Chinese influence that leaves India predictably concerned. After all, the NATO countries, too, are concerned when China buys its way into Iceland for a tourism project that claims about 0.3 percent of the total area of this depopulated but strategically vital country; and, closer to home, there is concern in the United States, too, when allegedly private Chinese banks openly discuss the construction of a land-based rival to the Panama canal across Colombia, or move billions of dollars in the Caribbean in long-term economic ventures that offer the added benefit to acquire new allies on the cheap.[35] In spite of its enormous (and unmet) social agenda, the Indian government therefore privileges defense spending, scheduled to increase by 7 to 8 percent in future years for a projected expenditure of an estimated $100 billion modernization plan largely aimed at China's own military plans for the decade. The emergence of partially bipolar conditions in Asia is especially dangerous because ever since the disastrous border war of 1962, which India remembers pointedly well, both countries have generally sought to avoid tit-for-tat decisions. Hence, for example, India's decision to neglect Pakistan's strategic stockpile rather than risk a growth of the Chinese stockpile. China, meanwhile, does not privilege nuclear arms as weapons of choice: unlike Pakistan, China does not require a strategic equalizer, and unlike India, China does not need a psychological boost; all that matters for China is to maintain strategic capabilities sufficient for deterrence even if they remain inferior in numbers. But the ongoing development of Indian missiles able to reach China's main urban centers is a different matter.

While maintaining a loose strategic balance, India and China hold incompatible visions of a regional order in Asia; more specifically, they view differently the U.S. presence, which India mostly favors, unlike China, which views that presence as intrusive and even hostile. Nor do China and India have mutually acceptable views of their respective roles in a multipolar world order. Each country is aware of the other's hegemonic impulse, with India more affected because of China's tendency to dismiss India's capacity to live up to its potential.[36] Like Russia in Europe, Turkey in the Middle East, or Brazil in South America, the Indians want to be taken seriously—something which Clinton, the godfather of normalization with New Delhi, was the first U.S. president to understand in full. As to the Chinese they are less worried and would prefer to not be bothered so long as their trading routes remain opened and their identity respected.

The two countries are geopolitically exposed, and with both sensitive to each other's vulnerabilities neither could remain indifferent to a conflict involving the other. In other words, any military conflict involving either India or China with a third party could quickly escalate into a dangerous regional war. In spring 2010, the specter of Indian retaliation against Pakistan because of its alleged role in a terror attack on Mumbai raised Chinese concerns and, together with U.S. pressures, encouraged India's moderation.

When it comes to borders or the mere perception of its territorial integrity China is not a passive bystander: the United States learned this early and the hard way in Korea in late 1950, and, like many other states, has often been exposed to it since. The spillover of civil disorders or worse in Pakistan threatens India specifically and possibly most urgently, and conditions Delhi's manipulative presence in Afghanistan; this in turn affects directly China's own security calculations relative to India and Pakistan and, by implication, the United States, too.

India's fear of encirclement by China is exacerbated by Pakistan's reliance on Chinese weapons and dual-use nuclear technologies. Such reliance increased in 2011 when U.S. tensions with Pakistan grew to the point of halting its military assistance in July of that year. Also of concern to India is China's old-standing ambition to develop Pakistan as a hub for markets and production centers in the Middle East and Africa—with the port of Gwadar, the refurbishment of the Karakoram Highway, a railway linking both countries, and the trans-Karakoram pipeline. "We are like one nation in two countries," declared Pakistan's prime minister upon returning from a state visit in Beijing where his hosts' welcoming gifts included a promise of fifty fighter jets.[37] Memories of the 1962 war also keep India fearful of China's territorial claims on the northeastern Indian state of Arunachal Pradesh, a mountainous area that shares cultural ties with Tibet and lies next to the largest Indian state with a population twice that of Germany. These claims in turn feed internal tensions in India, whose postcolonial administrative map was designed by Britain's imperial authorities to manage the state's heterogeneity: its fourteen official languages and many more dialects feed emotive demands for statehood in areas that have been marginalized by uneven economic growth and social developments.

China's sense of encirclement also sharpened when the 2008 bilateral agreement on civil nuclear cooperation appeared to add India to a U.S.-drawn arc of democratic states, including Japan and Australia but also Vietnam and South Korea. The war in Afghanistan, with which China shares a short border, is viewed as a diversion of American power and a loss of American prestige. The benefits for China of strategic diversion also apply to India relative to Pakistan, which is a rapacious consumer of Indian capabilities and leadership, and to Japan and South Korea, through North Korea, now under suicide watch. In both countries, defense spending is increasing not only because of their added concerns about China—hardly a historic friend—but also because of the reduced credibility of U.S. guarantees, which would be questioned further should new instabilities and more violence in the Persian Gulf and the Middle East remain unanswered.

In sum, there is a lot of gunpowder between and around India and China. That much of that powder would be nuclear and, worse yet, that some of it would also be available to the failing state of Pakistan and the failed state of North Korea adds to the geopolitical fragility and geostrategic complexity of the entire region. After half a century of total wars in and for Europe, future global wars if any will likely be waged away from the Western world, and Asia is a good candidate to replace Europe as the central battlefield in a post-Western century of total wars. While the intensity of such wars in Asia will be total, even if kept below the nuclear threshold, their range need not turn global if Western powers, and especially the United States, abstain from direct military involvement. But even with Western abstention, the global consequences of an Asian war would be serious and cannot be measured any more effectively than, say, the consequences of World War I on Asia when the war erupted in Europe.

THE REST OF THE REST

Henry Kissinger's reported *bon mot* about the geopolitical significance of New Zealand—"a dagger pointed at the heart of Antarctica"—lacked taste, even as a poor imitation of Halford Mackinder's formula about the Heartland and the World Island, but it was accurate: some regions matter more than others, as do some states in each region, and their significance evolves over time. In the pre-American world that opened the twentieth century in Europe the Balkans were such a region, and in the American world that emerged during the Cold War Germany was one such state: the Balkans as an area where the falling Russian, Ottoman, and Austrian empires converged in the 1900s, and Germany as the only country that neither superpower could afford to lose in the 1950s.

Now, in the zero-polar structure left behind after a wasted unipolar moment, no region in the world is more central to the future of the post-Western world than the Greater Middle East, including the Persian Gulf, which extends into "the new Global Balkans" whose conflicts, fueled by ethnic and sectarian passion, have "a suction effect on major powers."[38] No region is more volatile—disruptive as a hub for global terrorism, dangerous as the stage for foreign and civil wars, unstable because of its unbearable socioeconomic conditions, as costly for peacekeeping as for peacemaking, and intrusive because of the internal dimensions of all policy decisions for the area. In the twenty-first century, this region offers an unsurpassed potential for exporting chaos and war on a global scale, including a highly volatile Central Asia—Afghanistan, Pakistan, and Iran. Because of this vital significance and explosive potential, and because current conditions will worsen before they can get better, it is there that a new world order will be tested most immediately, as well as most decisively: there, that is, that powers, old and new, great and small, influential and marginal, will be challenged most dangerously and most inescapably. When it comes to this region, there is no place for the world to hide and no time for the main world powers to run. With non-OECD (Organisation for Economic Co-operation and Development) countries expected to account for 90 percent of the growth in energy needs until 2035, and with much of the demand heavily dependent on suppliers from the Middle East and the Persian Gulf, it is there more than anywhere else that the post-Western world is coming, and indeed has arrived.[39]

The Fire Next Time

"For many centuries," wrote historian Bernard Lewis, "the world of Islam was at the forefront of civilization and achievement" but now "compared with its millennial rival Christendom, the world of Islam [has] become poor, weak, and ignorant." And Professor Lewis, a leading authority on Islam, asks provocatively: "What went wrong?" As can be expected, answers vary, but since the horrific events of 9/11 they have been increasingly sought in religious terms, and to some degree this seems due to alien ideas and practices that have seized authentic Islam and had a "retardative influence" on Arab intellectuals and the scientific community. In other words, notwithstanding legitimate reminders of what the West has done to Islam and its adherents, the question is not simply "What has Islam done to Muslims" but also "what have Muslims done to Islam?"[40]

Answers appear in the enormous development deficits left behind, by the West at the expense of Islam and by Islam at the expense of its people. Conditions used to be different: as noted by historian Richard Fletcher, Europe's "intellectual advances of the twelfth and thirteenth centuries," and its subsequent hegemony later in the sixteenth and seventeenth centuries, was achieved in large part "by acquiring what the Islamic world had to offer." Acquired initially but not shared subsequently, adds Professor Fletcher: "Muslim aloofness from Christendom had the effect of obscuring from view what was afoot" and it helps explain what followed afterward to the Ottoman Empire, still the most powerful European state in the sixteenth century, but soon to be "bullied, exploited and degraded by the arrogant westerners."[41] Entering the twenty-first century this degradation and its related deficits—in freedom, knowledge, women's empowerment, and more—were singled out as identifiable catalysts for extremism, terrorism, international crime, illegal migration, and more.[42] Heaps of data now describe a region overwhelmed by masses of people with too little hope from within and not enough respect from without, including many such people who moved to the West in order to regain both but found nothing and got nowhere, thus leaving more than a few with an unsuspected will to inflict indiscriminate deaths at the price of their own.

It is there, in the Middle East and in much of the Muslim world, that reside the new "wretched of the earth" who previously stood as the heroic figures of the Cold War debates in the 1960s. "Come close and listen [to] strangers gathered around fires," urged the French philosopher Jean-Paul Sartre in a preface written for Frantz Fanon's plea for the dispossessed of the Third World; for their "suppressed fury" and "irrepressible violence" will mean "the resurrection of savage instincts" not because of "resentment" but with the aim of "recreating" an identity.[43] These fires have been spreading everywhere, some out of the ashes of 9/11 but most lit with matches stored during several centuries of neglect and rising anger. For what was witnessed in the revolutionary fervor that erupted throughout the region in a few weeks in 2011 seemed so very unique as to defy the use of any precedent in modern Western history—from the revolutions of 1848, which unraveled the stable order engineered three decades earlier, to the revolutions of 1989, which ended the communist order imposed forty years before. After eight hundred years of decline and abusive victimization of the people by their rulers, and of the rulers by their foreign conquerors or sponsors, the long term ran out of time: a new era has started.

The emotional surge that seized the region during the Arab Spring of 2011 will endure for more than a season. "Arab pride" is back—though in what form and to what ends will take years and even decades to emerge: this is a generational problem, not only for the common good of 1.5 billion Muslims everywhere but also at the expense of 1 billion Westerners and another few billion people in Asia and everywhere else. "Are peoples in the Middle East," asked George W. Bush in November 2003, "somehow beyond the reach of liberty . . . condemned by history or culture to live in despotism? Are they alone never to have a choice in the matter?"[44] After the Cold War's failure of Arab nationalism, "peoples in the Middle East" are giving democracy one more chance as the best remaining alternative to the extremist version of the only political paradigm they have known—Islam.

How history could have been denied for so long and at the expense of so many is legitimate cause for debate. In the relatively short historical context of the past four decades, the world changed everywhere, mostly for the better, except in the Arab world. There it remained the same or turned worse, as unmovable and incompetent regimes brutally imposed inept policies and corrupt practices on their docile and subdued people. The condition lasted long enough to feed a belief that it might never end, thus setting the stage for the "surprising" events of 2011 when, in a matter of weeks or months, never-ending autocratic regimes fell in Tunisia, Egypt, Libya, and Yemen, and were threatened in Syria and elsewhere. Indeed, these events proved to be so astonishing as to leave them without a generic label that could apply to all. These have been the no-name revolutions of 2011.

The formative character of these revolutionary movements has been no less surprising—mostly young, always passionate, fairly spontaneous, remarkably courageous, and subtly nationalist. Combined, they expressed an Arab populism that was initially neither anti- nor pro-Western (in the sense of being genuine democratic movements), neither fundamentally religious nor secular (in the direction of, say, a Turkish or even Indonesian model), neither pro-Palestinian nor anti-war (meaning passively tolerant of Israel). Indeed, the benchmarks that were or could have been used for forecasting or explaining them have been at best irrelevant and often distortive. Even Iraq fails to figure: although the war was admittedly the catalyst for the reconfiguration of the global power structure, regime change in Baghdad was not a significant factor in enabling political changes in the Middle East, either as a democratic initiative, like the Bush administration hoped, or as a reminder of Western imperial brutality, like its critics feared. And by the time Osama bin Laden was killed in May 2011, he had long ceased to be a significant political actor in the Arab world and had become instead a bit of a footnote—no more than a source to be acknowledged for the horrific pain bin Laden and his few followers inflicted on the West rather than for the benefits they brought to Islam. As to al-Qaida, initially the central target of the post-9/11 War on Terror, it failed to emerge as an organization able to do for the people it professed to love and protect as much as it pledged to do to the people it was committed to hate and destroy—unlike Hezbollah and Hamas whose commitment to violence nevertheless came together with some aspiration to societal justice for their own people.

At first hearing, the political and social upheavals that transformed Europe in 1848 provide a tempting analogy for the Arab revolutions of 2011. Then as now, opposition to the regimes in place united many different groups that shared a deep resentment for their exclusion from political life and, for most of them, had produced much frustration over their inability to have sufficient income. Then as now, the depth and furor of that opposition were grossly underestimated by the rulers in place, as they had been on the eve of the French Revolution in 1789 or were to be again before the Russian Revolution in 1917—and again prior to the Eastern European revolutions in 1989. Then as now, food shortages were an important catalyst, including a potato famine in Ireland, but also famine in the Flanders, bread riots in France, and bruising potato wars in Berlin and Vienna. Finally, then as now, too, the goals initially pursued by the more rebellious groups were either modest or so unclear as to leave the most radical groups on the side while they waited for the postrevolutionary days when a more specifically political surge would cease the leadership of such modest popular outbreaks. In other words, regime change was not an immediate goal, which kept the rulers complacent. In 1848 public discontent took the form of banquets held in public squares: place de la Madeleine in Paris, for example, during three rainy days that can now be recalled like a very early dress rehearsal for the theatrics on Freedom Square in Cairo, which members of the Muslim Brotherhood attended rather silently but expectantly—until they returned later in an electoral season, which they were poised to exploit more openly and even dangerously this time.

Like the 2011 Arab Spring, though, the "revolutions" of 1848 had a specific character in each country. Then as now, the revolutionaries triumphed, occasionally in a matter of days, because they faced conservative forces whose long suppressed fears reached paranoid levels suddenly, and whose long repressive armies became as suddenly unwilling (though still able) to keep order by force. Had it been otherwise the revolutions would have been seriously compromised and probably failed, as was demonstrated by Czar Nicholas I in Russia. As noted by historian William Langer, "one of the striking features of the revolutions of 1848 was the failure of the authorities to use the means of suppression which were at their disposal."[45] Interestingly, though, in 2011 it is only after other rulers witnessed the humiliating fate of Presidents Ben Ali and Hosni Mubarak, who both resigned relatively peacefully and quickly, that the violence avoided in Tunisia and Egypt erupted elsewhere at levels near civil war in Libya and Yemen, which did not "save" their respective rulers, and escalated into crimes against humanity in Syria, increasingly plunged into a civil war with threatening consequences on the entire region.

There have been other tempting analogies, like the Spring revolutions in Eastern Europe that marked the end of the Cold War—a euphoric moment when the Western powers reigned supreme. But this analogy does not work either because the differences between these two moments, in 1989 and 2011, overwhelm a few superficial similarities, and also—most importantly—because the uniqueness of Islam and the diversity of the Middle East simply cannot fit any analogy: because Islam is an all-encompassing religion guided by a prophet who is also "statesman, judge, and general" and cannot be factored into patterns of modern Western history[46]; but also because the idea of Arab unity cannot cross the fault lines that fragment the Muslim world the way the idea of European unity did twenty years ago as an irresistible attraction for the post-Soviet European mosaic. Had there been one or more Arab de Tocqueville able to tell their people what transpired in their streets, like the celebrated Frenchman did in 1848, they would surely have been moved by the emotional nature of these revolutions: a sense of humiliation so intensely felt that it could not be reduced to any single issue or captured by any one group or, least of all, reported by any one Western observer.

Granted that the legacies of Western imperialism have caused problems for "the rest" of the world most generally, there is no need to worsen these legacies with misguided trials that would seek to impose harsh sanctions on those charged with the responsibility of the Arab predicament. In any case, with the West no longer guided by imperialist ambitions of control over distant Arab lands and cultures, it is those lands that now present a problem for Western countries left at the mercy of geopolitical conditions that can affect all aspects of their lives: monetary stability, economic growth, societal cohesion, security, and more—including a steady inflow of immigrants moving across the Mediterranean. As is often the case, the past serves as an echo chamber. One hundred years ago, a relatively small crisis in the Balkans derailed a confident Europe and recast the world for the decades that followed. Now, the second decade of the twenty-first century also opens with a crisis in a new pivotal region that will be the world's center stage for the years to come. At this decisive time in history, can the "We" of the West thus be summoned to action without the "They" of the rest, let alone against them—and can the foreign but human face of the West appear preferable to a God-inspired but man-made alternative of murderous martyrs? This is not Thomas Hobbes's "war of all against all" as was feared amid the burning ashes of September 11, 2001; but the fires lit in the freedom squares of Middle Eastern capitals in 2011 threaten to burn wild in Western capitals next time.

A Sarajevo Moment

In an increasingly conflicted Middle East, strenuous competition from and between the emerging powers like China (in Sudan, for example), new influentials like Turkey (in Syria) but also other states with lesser reach like Pakistan (in Saudi Arabia), can be expected. Irrespective of how the revolutions of 2011 work out—going from bad to better or worse but not the same—many of the states in the region will want new friends because they will demand more help and seek other security guarantees. Both as a matter of needs and capabilities, many more major players can now exert leverage in the region, especially as Western powers find words cheaper than action in a moment of worsening austerity. This is where the West and the rest best meet; but it is also there that conditions are best met for new rivalries and possible clashes.

Like elsewhere during the twentieth century, the primacy of the United States in the Middle East began with the collapse of the region's former imperial patrons in Europe. For those who might have missed it, final evidence of their collapse was provided with the failed Anglo-French intervention in Suez in the fall of 1956, which was meant as an imperial revival but proved to be a final imperial gasp. There had been other signs of spreading U.S. influence and interest before, including Truman's immediate recognition of the newly born state of Israel in 1948, and an early case of regime change in Iran engineered by the Eisenhower administration in 1953 to return to power a young deposed shah. But the Suez crisis was decisive: it signified the abdication of the former European imperial powers and the start of an era when the United States assumed at least partial ownership of the region, often in partnership with unsavory regimes that delivered several decades of relative stability but ultimately became the focus of latter day revolutions. During the Cold War, repeated Soviet attempts to assert a presence of their own confirmed the limits of Russian power and influence outside Europe. But paradoxically enough the Soviet role also limited the American vision of the region, which was reduced to a one-dimensional stage for a global bipolar conflict that had little to do with the specific conditions of more urgent local conflicts. Thus, Henry Kissinger identified the key to the U.S. strategy in the Middle East as the capacity "to wean the Arabs away from the Russians and to convince them . . . that they could not achieve their diplomatic aims with Soviet arms," which could only help wage wars but not win them before they "would turn to us" as the only actor who could end them.[47] That goal proved elusive, and the missing piece of a Middle East peace remained the U.S. inability to impose it on Arabs and Israelis alike. That still keeps conditions in the area more comparable to interwar Europe after 1919, when European leaders rejected an American involvement that would not be based on their own terms, than to postwar

Europe after 1945, when the United States could assert the terms of the institutional peace that now defines the European continent.

In the twentieth century Europe had two fault lines, Germany and Russia, which unification for the former and a revolution for the latter worsened but did not create. In the end, these were resolved a bit of each at a time, the Western half of Germany and the Soviet side of Russia during the Cold War, and the geographic and historical balance of each next—meaning, an orderly reunification of Germany and disintegration of the Soviet Union. The final plea—"guilty as charged"—did not come easily for either country. After World War I, the Germans denied defeat and claimed the civilians' betrayal of the military authorities as an explanation for their humiliation at Versailles, and thus as a justification of what followed—which, Hitler was still arguing in his Berlin bunker, had been democratically sanctioned by the German people in 1933. It is only in 1989, fifty years after a divided Germany had started to reinvent itself in order to overcome and forget its own collective shame, that a reunified Germany was reintroduced to its neighbors as a state that had not only mastered its past but had transcended it. In 1917, the newly established Soviet Union at first denied defeat against Germany but claimed instead a revolutionary victory for the Russian people, whom they rewarded with famines, gulags, and more war; the logic was repeated in 1989 when Soviet leaders denied the Western triumph and claimed instead liberation from communism for the peoples of the Soviet Union. After the Cold War, that claim alone left Moscow with the illusion that its confrontation with the United States had ended without winners or losers, a comfortable conclusion that caused much bitterness that still seems to linger in Vladimir Putin's Russia.

Moving into the twenty-first century, past the Cold War, beyond the consequences of 9/11, and notwithstanding the intense sectarian fault lines exposed throughout the Middle East since the 1979 Iranian Revolution and widened further since, Israel's conflict with its neighbors remains a precondition to the resolution of anything else. The stakes have become too high, and the risks too urgent, for its resolution to be postponed much longer. Moving into the decisive decade of the 2010s, this is another Sarajevo moment for Western powers, which means that looming ahead is the risk of premeditated action or fortuitous accidents that will serve as catalysts for conflict. To be sure, short of an act of terror initiated with weapons of massive destruction, the "accident" would be different from what took place in July 1914, when casualties were numbered in millions; and even if it were to precipitate a global conflict, that conflict would be fundamentally different from what occurred during the second half of the 1910s. Predicting the specific nature of that accident is not possible but forecasting its broader consequences is. For in the Middle East even more than anywhere else, every prediction sounds like an impertinence, and every predictor looks like an impostor. Suffice it to say, more modestly, that stopping first in the Middle East to settle the Israeli-Palestinian conflict will ease the unfolding journey to a post-Western order.

NOTES

1. Henry Steele Commager, *The Defeat of America: Presidential Power and the National Character* (New York: Simon & Schuster, 1968), p. 23; Francis Fukuyama, *The End of History and the Last Man* (New York: Free Press, 1992).

2. David P. Calleo, *Follies of Power: America's Unipolar Fantasies* (Cambridge: Cambridge University Press, 2009), p. 13; William Kristol and Robert Kagan, *Present Dangers: Crisis and Opportunity in American Foreign and Defense Policy* (San Francisco: Encounter, 2000), p. 22.

3. James Politi, "World Banks Sees End to Dollar's Hegemony," *Financial Times*, May 17, 2011.

4. Andrew Moravcsik, "Europe: Rising Superpower in a Bipolar World," in Alan Alexandroff and Andrew Cooper, eds., *Rising States, Rising Institutions; Challenges for Global Governance* (Washington, DC: Brookings, 2010), p. 152; and "Europe: The Quiet Superpower," *French Politics* 7, no. 3/4, 403–22. Mark Leonard, *Why Europe Will Run the 21st Century* (London and New York: Fourth Estate, 2005); Steven Hill, *Europe's Promise: Why the European Union Is the Best Hope in an Insecure Age* (Berkeley and Los Angeles: University of California Press, 2010).

5. Jolyion Howorth, "The European Union: A Power in the World—Not (Yet) a World Power," in Simon Serfaty, ed., *A Recast Partnership? Institutional Dimensions of Transatlantic Relations* (Washington, DC: CSIS Press, 2008), p. 96.

6. See Alan Milward, *The European Rescue of the Nation-State*, 2nd ed. (London: Routledge, 2000).

7. Vivien A. Schmidt, "Re-envisioning the European Union: Identity, Democracy, Economy," *Journal of Common Market Studies* 47 (annual review, 2009): 17–42; and "The EU as a Supranational Regional State: Rethinking What the EU Is and Where It Is Going," in *A Recast Partnership*, pp. 77–84.

8. Armando Garcia-Schmidt and Dominik Hierlemann, eds., "EU 2020—the View of the Europeans," results of a representative survey in selected member states of the European Union, Bertelsmann Stiftung, September 20, 2006.

9. Bruce Stokes, "What Europeans Think about the Eurocrisis: Doubts and Waning Faith in the European Project," EuroFuture Project, German Marshall Fund of the United States (January 2012). Support for the euro has remained firm

even as the crisis has seemed to worsen. See Paul Gettner, "Euro Seems Better than Alternative, Poll Finds," *New York Times*, May 29, 2012.

10. Richard Cooper, "The Post-Modern State and the World Order," *Demos* (January 2000).

11. François Duchêne, in Jan Orbie, ed., *Europe's Global Role: External Policies of the European Union* (Burlington: Ashgate, 2008), pp. 13–16; Hanns W. Maull, "Europe and the New Balance of the Global Order," *International Affairs* 81, no. 4 (July 2005): 775–94.

12. Transatlantic Trends, *Transatlantic Trends: Leaders, Key Findings 2011* (German Marshall Fund of the United States and Compania di Sao Paulo, 2011), p. 3.

13. "The Rise or Fall of the American Empire," with Daniel W. Drezner, Gideon Rachman, and Robert Kagan, *Foreign Policy*, February 14, 2012, http://www.foreignpolicy.com/articles/2012/02/14/the_rise_or_fall_of_the_american_empire?page=full. A few years earlier, Kagan was deploring the Europeans' unwillingness to "supplement American power with their own" with "the net result" of diminishing "the total amount of power that the liberal democratic world can bring to bear in its defense." Robert Kagan, *Of Paradise and Power: America and Europe in the New World Order* (New York: Vintage, 2004), p. 158.

14. Daniel Hamilton and Joseph Quinlan, *The Transatlantic Economy, 2010: Annual Survey of Jobs, Trade, and Investment between the United States and Europe* (Washington, DC: Center for Transatlantic Relations, 2010).

15. U.S. investments in China recovered in 2010, up an estimated 6.3 percent over 2009. Vikas Bajaj, "Foreign Investment Ebbs in India," *New York Times*, February 25, 2011.

16. John F. Kennedy, "The Goal of an Atlantic Partnership," July 4, 1962; Henry Kissinger, Address to the Associated Press Annual Luncheon, New York, April 23, 1973.

17. Tod Lindberg, "The Case against the Case against Europe," in Simon Serfaty, ed., *Visions of the Atlantic Alliance: The United States, the European Union, and NATO* (Washington, DC: CSIS Press, 2005), pp. 3–19.

18. Simon Serfaty, "The United States and Europe in a Multipolar World," in *A Recast Partnership*, pp. 3–30.

19. Zbigniew Brzezinski, "The Group of Two That Could Change the World," *Financial Times*, January 13, 2009. According to Giovanni Grevi, interpolarity means "multipolarity in the age of interdependence." *The Interpolar World*, EUISS Occasional Paper, no. 79 (June 2009), p. 5.

20. BBC World Service Poll, "Rising Concern about China's Increasing Power: Global Poll," March 27, 2011; also Bruce Stokes, "Friendship, Warily," *National Journal*, February 13, 2010, p. 31. See Satoru Mori, "Crisis Invigorates Japan-Europe Cooperation, But for How Long?," EuroFuture Project, German Marshall Fund of the United States (March 2012).

21. Richard M. Nixon, Address to media executives in Kansas City, July 6, 1971. Unknown at the time, the speech was delivered the day before Kissinger's first secret trip to Beijing, for what was to be the normalization of U.S. relations with China.

22. George Liska, *Nations in Alliance: The Limits of Interdependence* (Baltimore: Johns Hopkins University Press, 1962), pp. 16–17.

23. Richard N. Haass, "The Palmerstonian Moment," *National Interest* (January/February 2008); Charles Kupchan, *How Enemies Become Friends: The Sources of Stable Conflicts* (Princeton, NJ: Princeton University Press, 2010).

24. Consider Prime Minister Thatcher's concern over Germany's reunification in 1989: as she later remembered, French president François Mitterrand's shared concern was enough to make her like him—at least that one time. Margaret Thatcher, *The Downing Street Years* (New York: HarperCollins Publishers, 1993), pp. 796–97.

25. David P. Calleo, *Rethinking Europe's Future* (Princeton, NJ: Princeton University Press, 2005), p. 178; Anders Aslund and Andrew Kuchins, *The Russia Balance Sheet* (Washington, DC: Peter G. Peterson Institute for International Economics and the Center for Strategic & International Studies, 2009), p. 115.

26. Will Englund, "Candidate Putin Vows Defense Buildup," *Washington Post*, February 21, 2012.

27. Counting civilians, total fatalities in the post-Soviet period in North Caucasus could be as high as a hundred thousand. John W. Parker, *Russia's Revival: Ambitions, Limitations, and Opportunities for the United States*, Strategic Perspectives, no. 3 (Institute for National Strategic Studies, 2011), p. 4.

28. As suggested by assistant secretary of state for European Affairs, Philip Gordon, after the U.S.-Soviet Summit in Lisbon in November 2011. Interview, *Le Figaro*, November 24, 2010.

29. As stated by Foreign Minister Sergei Lavrov, quoted in Andrew C. Kuchins, "Russia, the 360-degree Regional Power," *Current History* (October 2011): 266.

30. Paul Gettner, "China, Amid Uncertainty at Home and in Europe, Looks to Germany," *New York Times*, April 23, 2012.

31. Jairam Ramesch, *Making Sense of Chindia: Reflections on China and India* (India Research Press, 2006).

32. Mohan Guruswamy, "India and the European Union: Dim Prospects," EuroFuture Project, German Marshall Fund of the United States (March 2012), p. 9.

33. Ian Bremmer, *Every Nation for Itself: Winners and Losers in a G-Zero World* (New York: Portfolio / Penguin, 2012).

34. *World Powers in the 21st Century: The Results of a Representative Survey in France, Germany, India, Japan, Russia, the United Kingdom and the United States*, Bertelsmann Stiftung, 2006, p. 17; also, Bruce Stokes, "Friendship, Warily," *National Journal* (February 13, 2010): 30–36; "Global Views of United States Improve While Other Countries Decline," BBC World Service Poll, April 18, 2010.

35. Geoff Dyer, "Signals of a Shift," *Financial Times*, January 31, 2011; Andrew Ward and Leslie Hook, "Chinese Tycoon's Planned $100 mi Tourism Project in Iceland Raises Security Concerns," *Financial Times*, August 30, 2011; John Paul Rathbone and Naomi Mapstone, "China in Talks over Panama Canal Rival," *Financial Times*, February 13, 2011; Randal C. Archibold, "China's Cash Buys Inroads in Caribbean," *New York Times*, April 7, 2012.

36. "The Chinese think of the Indians as incompetent, as unreliable payers of debts, and that they have no notion of time. India is perceived as a backward, untidy country with an outmoded transport system. In addition . . . relying too heavily on law . . . makes cooperation difficult and complicated." Thibaud Voita, adapted from Wen Zhougfa, "Ideas for Cooperation between the Indian and Chinese SME," *Nanya Yanjiu Jikan*, no. 1 (2009): 87–92, in *China and India: Rival Always, Partners Sometimes* (European Council on Foreign Relations and Asia Centre à Science Po): 8.

37. David Piling, "China's Masterclass in Schmoozing Pakistan," *Financial Times*, May 26, 2011.

38. Zbigniew Brzezinski, *Second Chance: Three Presidents and the Crisis of American Superpower* (New York: Basic Books, 2007), p. 153.

39. *World Energy Outlook*, 2011, p. 39. China's top ten oil exporters for 2009–2010 were (in millions tons): Saudi Arabia (45.3), Angola (40.8), Iran (21.1), Russia (15.2), Oman (15.2), Sudan (12.8), Iraq (10.6), Kazakhstan (10.0), Kuwait (9.7), and Brazil (7.9). Alexandros Petersen with Katinka Barysch, *Russia, China, and the Geopolitics of Europe in Central Asia* (London: Center for European Reform, December 2011).

40. Bernard Lewis, *What Went Wrong? The Clash between Islam and Modernity in the Middle East* (Princeton, NJ: Princeton University Press, 2002), pp. 1, 151, 156; John Cassidy, "Prophet Motive," *New Yorker*, February 28, 2011.

41. Richard Fletcher, *The Cross and the Crescent: Christianity and Islam from Muhammad to the Reformation* (New York: Viking, 2003), p. 160.

42. See "U.S. Working Paper for G-8 Sherpas," Dar Al-Hayat, February 13, 2004, at http://english.daralhayat.com/Spec/02-2004.

43. Preface by Jean-Paul Sartre for Frantz Fanon, *The Wretched of the Earth*, trans. Constance Farrington (New York: Grove Press, 1963), pp. 7–34.

44. George W. Bush, Remarks at the 20th Anniversary of the National Endowment for Democracy at the United States Chamber of Commerce, November 6, 2003.

45. William Langer, *The Rise of Modern Europe: Political and Social Upheaval, 1832–1852* (New York: Harper & Row, 1969), pp. 319–26.

46. Bernard Lewis, "What You Should Know about Islam," and Olivier Roy, "What You Should Know about Islam as a Strategic Factor," in Philip D. Zelikow and Robert B. Zoellick, eds., *America and the Muslim Middle East* (New York: Council on Foreign Relations, 1998), pp. 5, 33.

47. Aaron David Miller, *The Much Too Promised Land: America's Elusive Search for Arab-Israeli Peace* (New York: Bantam-Dell, 2008), p. 131; Dennis Ross, *The Missing Peace: The Inside Story of the Fight for Middle East Peace* (New York: Farrar, Straus and Giroux, 2004), p. 25; Henry Kissinger, *Years of Upheaval* (Boston: Little, Brown, 1982), pp. 201ff.

6

NO TIME FOR A TIME OUT

"**A** scholar's task," wrote Zbigniew Brzezinski, "is observing gradual change to determine, if possible, its direction and its likely future significance. In time even gradual evolution may produce a real discontinuity." Discontinuities, however, are unveiled abruptly. Added Brzezinski: "There is a qualitative difference between a boy and a man even though they are still the very same person."[1] The difference emerges retrospectively; it is a surprise—like locating "grains of gold in the river," said Lord Acton, in 1895.[2]

Much has been written and much more remains to be argued before history's new leaps in unexpected directions are lit up and completed.[3] At the very least it can already be agreed that a state no longer needs a Western label to seek and gain global influence, and possibly primacy. That alone would be a compelling change. For the first time in quite a while, the West cannot control the world, and there is no prospect of reversing that condition any time soon. The rest of the world is here to stay—meaning that it counts. But still, do not sell the West short. While there is no doubt that systemic changes are under way, there should also be little doubt that even a post-Western world will maintain a Western look after all. Somewhere in the post-Western world there stands a West restored.

It cannot be stressed too much that the rise of other powers must not be construed as the decline of, or a threat to, the United States and the rest of the West. Their trajectories are not parallel or complementary—one envisioned as irresistibly up, and the other said to be irreversibly down. Each trend is real but neither is caused or conditioned by the other. An inclusive recasting of the global system need not take the form of a hostile takeover of the West by a cluster of emerging powers, mostly in Asia. Rather, the Western powers can seize the moment as an opportunity to reposition themselves in a world they no longer dominate but can still influence more than any other group of states.

Whether that condition is really new relative to the most recent decades of Western preponderance is moot. While the United States extended Western leadership during the second half of the twentieth century, its preponderance was always a reality but its omnipotence always remained an illusion. One year after the 1956 Hungarian Revolution, Secretary of State John Foster Dulles forcefully warned against any such illusion: "We are not omnipotent," he wrote. "Our power and policy are but a significant factor . . . in combination with other factors."[4] The warning has been repeated since. It addressed what Henry Kissinger had called "a very critical failure" of the American hubris and its approach to international relations.[5] Claimed to have ended in Vietnam, the illusion of omnipotence was resurrected during the unipolar moment that followed the Cold War. With that moment passed, the facts of American superiority endure but, in the words of Secretary of State Hillary Rodham Clinton, they do not make an "argument to go it alone—far from it." The argument instead is to go it together: the United States together with the rest of the West, and the rest together with the West.

LEADERSHIP, STUPID

On the way to a post-Western order this is a pivotal moment, and there is too little time left to take a time out along the way. Nor is there any other way: a worse alternative to accepting the ongoing redistribution of power would consist in insisting that there is no power to cede and no influence to share. Clearly that is not the case. The example of China alone is enough: its share of world income (measured in purchasing power parity prices) has gone up from 2.2 to 14.4 percent during the three decades since 1980. Later on in the 2010s that share may well exceed that of the United States: what to make out of this statistic can be debated, but that it does reflect a transfer of power of some sort cannot.[6] What is needed, then, for the West to move confidently toward this emerging new world?

As a start, it should be clear that the point of maximum pressure is not external but internal. The trip to the post-Western world will be more difficult and less pleasant if the West does not regain its assurance and loses its cohesion. This means first the United States and the state of Europe, which together form the core of the Western core. Japan matters, of course, but over the past twenty years it has fallen behind—too small, too weak, too far, and now no longer rich enough to show the potential it once did. Yet on both sides of the Atlantic the risk of Western self-denial is discernible and even growing. There are too many doubts among Europeans about the United States, as well as about each other; and there are too many doubts, too, among Americans about themselves, but also about the states of Europe. These doubts are heard as an invitation to seek alternatives elsewhere—for the United States outside Europe, and for the states of Europe beyond their union. That would be repeating in the twenty-first century the fatal mistake that Europe made after 1919 when it attempted to keep going on its own and without its newly rediscovered partner across the Atlantic.

That Americans and Europeans are growing tired of each other after several decades of intimacy is probably true. But alternatives to their union would be worse and less rewarding—far too costly if with China, much more demanding if with India, and certainly less comfortable if with Russia. In a world recast the United States and Europe form an indispensable axis of stability, but however indispensable that axis may be it cannot be exclusive. In other words, America can be more of a trans-Pacific power without turning into less of a trans-Atlantic partner, and Europe can also renew its Asian vocation without turning its back on the Atlantic. History is knocking on the door: a civilian Europe is America's past, and America is Europe's future as a union.

Forget, then, about the "New World" getting old while the "Old World" gets older. Even as banalities these clichés have run their course. America has been called young for too long—and Europe has tamed its past convincingly enough to no longer resemble the old. In effect, they are both entering the same advancing age when sulking turns into a bad habit and bonding looks like a protective instinct, when giving up becomes increasingly tempting and memory lapses reflect a lack of interest and a shortage of attention—when resignation to relative decline is explained as overdue maturity and can even pass for serenity. But they have not reached the age of retirement. Rather, as Americans and Europeans look back, the reality is that their time together has been lived historically well and is a powerful motivation for moving forward: more specifically, too much has been achieved together during the twentieth century to dare travel separately or alone into the new century. In the 2010s, the disassociation of the Euro-Atlantic alliance or the disintegration of the European Union would hurt every state on both northern sides of the Atlantic, and would help no other state elsewhere.

For the West to put its house in order before it can best meet the challenges of a post-Western world will be neither easy nor quick. Western societies have been undisciplined for too long—permissive and profligate to the point of making everything seem permissible and affordable. Now, the first decade of this century has turned into an unexpected story of debt and punishment, first told in global battlefields where terror aimed to prevail, and most recently heard in the marketplace where austerity has been taking over. For Western societies to emerge out of an anxious era of unrestrained entitlements leadership is missing, money scarce, and values blurred. What is unveiled during this post-Western moment is less the evidence of decline than a sense of decadence: ambitions that overwhelm convictions, greed that prevails over compassion, and complacency that defies accountability.

Leadership matters—and under conditions of existential crisis, at home or abroad let alone both, it matters decisively. During the past century, the West produced all kinds of leaders. Some of them were so good as to look irreplaceable (which they never were) and others were so bad and even evil as to demand that the very good be urgently God-sent. In 1940, Winston Churchill stood as Britain's main asset until Franklin D. Roosevelt became Churchill's best asset; at that time, France's only strength came from a rebellious general, Charles de Gaulle, whose sole power attribute was Churchill and Britain's support; ten years later Konrad Adenauer emerged out of Germany's ruins to become Europe's most sturdy pillar, pending its reconciliation with France within a European community bent on renewal. Moving into a Cold War that the West did not start, the best and brightest of the postwar years helped history change its ways—by keeping America and Europe away from what they both had become historically used to: going home for the former, and going to war for the latter. Remember Harry Truman, initially miscast as "an ordinary provincial" who ultimately acquired greatness on the strength of his "exceptional qualities of character." What Truman and his counterparts across the Atlantic started, Ronald Reagan ended—himself a reportedly "relentlessly banal" man who felt the issues better than he actually understood them.[7] Now, a decade into this century and twenty years after the Cold War, good leadership is lacking: a few leaders inspire but do not lead, others lead but do not inspire, and most do neither.

"The true measure of nations," said Winston Churchill in 1919 "is what they can do when they're tired." That is especially true for democracies, where self-complacency serves as an irresistible excuse for doing nothing.[8]

The crossroads was missed after World War I: as the West got lost the cost proved to be high in the absence of any effective rescue party. Since then, there have been many more moments of exhaustion during which Western societies proved to be at their best—least willing to bend when things appeared to be taking a turn for the worse and the temptation to come home seemed irresistible. Remember the 1970s, when the Nixon administration engineered a policy overhaul in the dire circumstances of Vietnam, the outrages of Watergate, and the ruinous assault of OPEC. At that time, European leaders in a Hegelian mood also feared a hostile and dangerous world under demanding conditions of economic stagflation (meaning, little growth, rising inflation, and high unemployment) and political turbulence. But it is out of that turbulence that the Western leaders elected between 1979 and 1983, ranging from left to right, proved the declinists of the time wrong and made of the 1980s a winning decade for the West.[9] For the decisive decade of the 2010s, this is such a moment, and how well it is met in the West will also determine how good it is for the rest.

NEITHER MISANTHROPY NOR PHILANTHROPY

Good leadership in the West, as well as in Western institutions, will ease the post-Western moment, and make the journey into the post-Western world more comfortable. From within as well as relative to others, a new plural world should not be faced with self-serving claims of philanthropic benevolence and sporadically angry bursts of misanthropic resentment. Certainly, the West can no longer claim a right of birth to dominate and educate the rest—to lead a good and rewarding life while other states are left behind and in relative squalor until they learn how to elect good governments that obey Western rules of political governance and economic fair play. After three hundred years of Western primacy, that time is effectively gone. Remaining in place, though, there is a Western "package" that remains the best available set of economic, social, and political institutions and which "the Resterners" seek to emulate—as a goal that looks distant rather than the achievement some seem to make it already.[10] Here, then, are a few closing observations that touch upon some elements of the package.

First, even during an admittedly post-Western intermission this is still an American moment, as Secretary Clinton tells her domestic audiences: a moment when the world still "looks to us . . . to solve problems on a global scale, in defense of our own interests but also as a force for progress."[11] The facts of American power, as well as the broad legitimacy of its leadership, renewed with the Obama presidency, remain on the whole without rivals. For the world to be multipolar, noted Samuel Huntington more than a decade ago, there would have to be "several major powers of comparable strength that cooperate and compete with each other in shifting patterns." Professor Huntington was right then and he continues to be right now. There are many major states with the will to compete, but fewer, if any, with the global reach and capabilities to engage in the "shifting patterns" associated with the multipolar management of important international issues.[12] As argued, there is only one complete power—economic, military, diplomatic, ideological, technological, and cultural—which is the United States; and there is still only one reliable complete alliance—with common goals, overlapping values, compatible interests, and complementary interests—and that remains the U.S.-European alliance. That, however, points neither to the renewal of America's unipolar moment nor to the persistence of some exclusive Western primacy.

At Churchill's sixty-ninth birthday celebration in Tehran in 1943, Stalin toasted America as "a country of machines," which he described as "the most important thing in . . . war" and which only Americans could produce in sufficiently large numbers to not "lose this war."[13] In 1941, the policy that relied on that "thing" was called "Lend Lease," and an American warehouse full of "machines" helped Britain and Russia wage the war until the United States was literally forced, on December 7, 1941, to join it. The American warehouse is still open for business, and "leading from behind" gives privileged partners access to the tools they need to stand up to the regional bully tempted to invade its neighbors, or the local tyrants intent on killing their people. For this approach to work, however, other states are expected to move ahead of the peloton, which is what happened in Libya in the spring of 2011, but was not repeated with Syria in 2012 and will be missing in Afghanistan in 2013: military intervention in Libya made possible by the United States but initiated by a few European states (but not the EU), launched after the abstention of the BRIC powers at the UN, and fought in a NATO context; abstention in Syria after Russia and China vetoed an action that the Western powers were probably unwilling or unable to execute in any case; and evacuation in Afghanistan with a U.S. and Western withdrawal reportedly designed to delegate the lead combat role to local forces, and thus limit their mission to support and counterterrorism.

Whether in the lead or in a supporting role, the role of Europe will remain vital. Already, its transformation during the second half of the twentieth century has been historically extraordinary—from nation-states to client states and now member-states. Now the EU is a geopolitical megaphone that enables the national voices of its members to be heard by their senior partners.[14] A Europe that was reborn after it learned how to speak American as the junior partner of its alliance with the United States must now learn anew how to speak European as payment for its elevation as an equal partner and its completion as a world power. That demands more Europe, meaning, an institutional finality without which Europe will be too weak to colead with its senior partner, or even follow it: absent an ally with coequal potential, the United States would have to recast the West in some other ways, outside NATO and without the EU, or with other partners not equally capable (because divided) and not similarly compatible (because non-Western). That outcome, however, would deny the post-Western world the Euro-Atlantic axis of stability it needs for order.

For this pivotal moment to be lived better than the unipolar moment that preceded it, the United States must take the world seriously and overcome the reticence of its own public at home.[15] That will not be an easy task. Americans do not feel at home abroad in part because they are not especially well away from home. A public opinion poll taken in 2010 indicated that only two countries (China and Germany) were found "very important" by a small majority of the public (54 and 52 percent respectively). Outside of Canada, so cited by an even 50 percent, every other country, starting with Japan, was deemed to be very important by only 40 percent or less of the public, and only seventeen countries were so assessed by one out of ten Americans.[16] Fatigue with the world helps to widen further the gap between capabilities, commitments, and purpose: more commitments than available capabilities, and more of a purpose than readily made commitments. The gap can take the form of abusive claims or expectations about the nature or potential of friends and adversaries alike (as tends to be done with regard to Turkey, for example); exaggerated declaratory policies relative to the capabilities committed for their execution (as occurred with President Obama's celebrated reconciliation speech in Cairo in June 2009); pandering to large emerging powers (like rising China or India) for short-term profits coupled with too much indifference to smaller or poorer states (like Ukraine) that are not conducive to long-term gains.

Taking the world seriously begins in and with the Middle East, which stands out as the pivotal region of this pivotal moment. During the second half of the twentieth century, the U.S. leadership of the West in a region it hardly knew was surprisingly successful. The goals were limited, and mostly designed to preserve the status quo inherited from the European era: to keep the Soviet Union out, Israel up, and oil coming. To meet these goals, which were mostly designed to preserve the status quo in a new post-European era, the United States spent an estimated $200 billion—a modest expenditure relative to the interests that were at stake.[17] Occasional Soviet intrusions in the region were disruptive but rarely decisive because never sustainable; Western sponsorship helped Israel maintain an unchallenged superiority on its neighbors (at a deep discount after American diplomacy managed a peace treaty with Egypt in 1978); and for nearly half that period, up to 1973, oil prices were kept profitably low, while U.S. influence on Saudi Arabia kept them short of unreasonable highs for the rest of the time. Arab-Israeli wars occurred periodically—in 1956, 1967, 1973, and 1982—but Israeli superiority and American guarantees made their outcome predictable while keeping the wars short and their consequences manageable.

Now, however, the U.S. role in the region has become more difficult to assert, the goals more difficult to define, and the strategy—any strategy—more difficult to execute. After World War II, journalist Theodore White evoked the image of a beautiful white whale dying on a magnificent European beach and threatening to stink up all the continent and the entire world; by comparison, there are many such whales this time, not quite white and with many other species added, not all as big but all threatening to die on overcrowded beaches in the Mediterranean and the Persian Gulf, leaving the entire region desperate for help.[18] For the necessary cleanup American power matters but it can no longer be exclusive, and outside help must be differently calibrated. Turkey, for example, may have more influence than any of the leading EU members, and Russia in Syria or China over Iran may have more impact for what they do or fail to do than any Western state. In other words, neither the United States without the rest of the West, or the West without the rest nor the rest against the West will be enough to give the Middle East the stability it lacks; but there will be little post-Western order in the Arab world without it either.

The agenda is all the more daunting as its timetable is short. Consider: the ambiguous end of the contested U.S.-led war in Iraq, the critical confrontation with Iran over its quest for nuclear weapons, the unresolved Palestinian bid for statehood and its fragile stalemate with Israel, the stormy Arab Spring and its aftermath in Egypt especially, the one-sided civil war in Syria and the massacres engineered by a regime that is disavowed but spared, the threat of other civil wars in Yemen and Libya, the fracture of such states as Sudan and their drift to wars that will invite neighbors but also distant powers like China, the region's hold on the global energy market, and more—much more—are all issues that are running out of time. "When our interests and values are at stake, we have a responsibility to act," stated President Obama in the spring of 2011, with regard to Libya.

Predictably, the juxtaposition of interests and values at stake in the region produces serious inconsistencies as the latter are not always aligned with the former: "That is just reality," noted Hillary Rodham Clinton in an apparent attempt to explain nonintervention in Syria later that year and in 2012.[19] What is "just reality" on one side of the Atlantic can be just an illusion or worse on the other side of the Mediterranean, let alone elsewhere. Remember Yalta as the consequence of one of these realities at the start of another postwar geopolitical transition in 1945, when the West determined it was better to not look east too closely; or the Hungarian Revolution at the peak of the Cold War in 1956, when the Eisenhower administration determined that it was better to neglect past declaratory commitments to the "liberation" of Soviet-controlled territories. Words and the ideas they convey were betrayed on behalf of interests that were less glorious but more relevant. After or still in the midst of the Arab Spring, that is the risk faced by the United States and the West from Syria and Iraq to Afghanistan and Pakistan: betrayal that is understood in the West as a rational calculus of power but which, in the cultural context of the region, is equated with damaging charges of cowardice.

In a zero-polar moment of geopolitical transition, though, it is also time for the rest of the world, too, to get serious about America and the West. In the period of strategic uncertainties, economic austerity, and political foolishness that prevails in the West, that does not always seem to be the case, however. The geopolitics of power gave the West more imperial zeal than it needed to show, but now the geopolitics of emotions is giving it self-defeating deference while the rest engages in premature celebration.[20] This would not be the first time that a state's pretention of superiority paved the way for its subsequent humiliation.

Outside the Middle East it is when dealing with China that the timidity of the Western powers comes to the edge of mendacity and on occasion even threatens irrationality. Hear Vice President Joseph Biden telling his Chinese hosts in the spring of 2011, with nearly dismissive tones: "our advocacy of . . . what we [Americans] refer to as human rights" is "at best an intrusion, and at worst an assault on your [Chinese] sovereignty." This is too easy: there should be limits on obsequiousness, not only because of what America does, which is plenty good, but also because of whom Americans are, which is also plenty good. These limits are often exceeded by other Western powers: there is no need to build a case against the rise of the rest, but why make instead a case for the demise of the West? If nothing else, the first decade of the twenty-first century has confirmed—through 9/11, the wars in Afghanistan and Iraq, the great recession of 2008, the euro crisis of

2010, and the Arab Spring of 2011—that what is good for the West need not be necessarily good for the rest; but more decisively, the past decade has also shown that what is bad for the West is bad for others, too—at least equally bad and possibly worse.

Entering possibly an era of austerity, the U.S. temptation to stand aside and Europe's urge to remain aloof are real. Combined, these two trends add up to a form of Western neoisolationism that neither the West nor the rest can afford. To achieve an instant retrenchment from the world—its quarrels and its people, its goods and its evils—borders are closed for protection from unwanted consumers of scarce public goods; troops are withdrawn for separation from internal strife or out of exasperation over insufficient results. Meantime, aid is denied because of a growing lack of compassion no less than a deepening scarcity of resources. The paradox is for everyone to fear: globalization was mainly a Western creation, but de-globalization, should it occur, will likely be initiated in the West. Yet even this conclusion confirms that on the whole the rest is fighting to join a world made in the West, rather than to bring it down.

Do not bury the West, therefore: it has adapted before—from city states to nation-states, and now from nation-states to member states—and it can adapt some more. "Adaptive capability," wrote political scientist John P. Lowell four decades ago, "mean[s] those natural, material, human, and in-stitutional resources of the nation-state that comprise its potential over an extended period of time for coping with present and foreseeable demands from the geopolitical environment, and for exerting a measure of control over it."[21] That is another attribute that defines the completeness of U.S. power, and which no other state can match as well, except for its main Western partners that have been doing just that for over sixty years while transforming their nation-states into a European Union. What is found among the emerging powers looks more like an adoptive capability, mean-ing, the ability to adopt what is being done elsewhere. The label "made in China" says it all, and the then Chinese president Hu Jintao's boast to change the label to "created by China" remains to be proven.[22] And so does, for that matter, Chinese resiliency should the past thirty years of growing prosperity fail to be sustained or should current inequities fail to be re-duced as new Chinese leaders struggle to reform their country away from the model that took it selectively away from poverty and toward a model that would sustain its affluence more evenly. By comparison, or for inspira-tion, recall Japan again—not, however, its aborted rise late in the twentieth century but the mistaken predictions of its collapse after the 1929 Kyoto earthquake, which caused a 29 percent loss of the country's nominal GDP:

less than fifteen years later a presumably crippled Japan had recovered well enough to invade Manchuria and prepare for a devastating surprise attack on the United States and a war that caused a reported 86 percent level of damage, according to the Bank of Japan; yet a generation later the "new" remade-in-the-USA Japan was challenging America's economic supremacy.

The capacity to adapt is also what characterizes Europe and its union. Selling it short would be a mistake as well: for this union is what emerged after all hopes had died, and we ought to remember that, too. End the EU, and there will be nothing left to take its place—which is why its end, repeatedly announced as imminent, could never materialize. More than four decades ago, German-born, American political scientist Carl Friedrich, who was calling Europe an "emerging nation" even before a small Common Market had been completed, wrote with some early exasperation, "It is part of being clever nowadays to talk about the 'end' of European integration, about 'dead alleys,' 'crises,' and 'impending collapse.'"[23] The skeptic's tale has been proven repeatedly wrong over the past four decades, and yet it continues to be told, whether in the context of the single currency or in that of an elusive common defense policy. "The party is clearly over, the bill has come due," claim the permanent prophets of Europe's demise while the euro crisis is played out.[24] The *déjà dit* of this refrain may be for the better after all: there is room for constructive pessimism during such "moments of anticipation"—which was Hannah Arendt's phrase.[25] This is not to suggest that Euro-skeptics have been the true believers in European integration. But it is to recall that the most skeptical European leaders have often presided over the most significant advances in the European process—including de Gaulle in the 1960s for the takeoff phase, Thatcher in the 1980s for the pre-union phase that launched the single market and its currency, and now Angela Merkel, who inherited the mantle of skeptic-in-chief when her colleagues were torn between the different meanings of an impending institutional *finalité* for Europe.

For all the talk about the irresistible rise of the non-Western rest of the world, and for all the aggregate data and expert analysis put forward to make it look irreversible, the global transfer of power that is forecast is only beginning to emerge—a history to be lived before it can become a tale to be told. If anything, the competition between the West and the rest remains a mismatch, while rivalries within the rest threaten to be less peaceful than in or with the West. Most of the richest, industrially advanced, democratically stable states are in, or affiliated with, the Western world, where there is also the largest accumulation of hard power the world has ever seen. Much is written about economic growth in Asia, but its new wealth has been acquired in, and depends on, the West—its consumers, its technologies, and its capital. Further evidence is provided by the immediate effects of Western institutions on its newest members: in 2010, Europe's five best economic performers were all new EU members including the three Baltic states that used to pass as Soviet republics, as well as Poland, at the center of Moscow's Cold War empire, and Finland, which had helped define Soviet intimidating influence since 1941. Meantime, the countries of South and Central America, led by Brazil and including Mexico, which easily qualifies also as a new influential, have joined their northern partners to form an unprecedented continent-wide zone of political stability, sovereign security, and economic affluence.

Standing ahead are many years and even decades of uncertainty for the main bidders for preponderant, or at least significant, global status. The most universal lesson to be remembered from past events is that inevitability has a poor record in history: when picking winners and losers, best to hedge your bets. The risk is not for the rest to succeed when rising relative to the West; the greater risk is for the West to fail before the rest is ready. Keep on watching, there and elsewhere. No verdict can be expected for a while—and many hung juries are likely to be heard before any final judgment can be rendered on the final form of a post-Western world.

NOTES

1. Zbigniew Brzezinski, *The Soviet Bloc: Unity and Conflict,* 2nd ed. (Cambridge, MA: Harvard University Press, 1966), p. ix.

2. Quoted by Dean Acheson, "History as Literature," in *Fragments of My Fleece* (New York: W.W. Norton & Company, 1971), p. 82.

3. Isaiah Berlin, *Four Essays on Liberty* (New York: Oxford University Press, 1969), pp. 43–48.

4. John Foster Dulles, "Challenge and Response in United States Policy," *Foreign Affairs* (October 1957): 25–26.

5. Richard M. Pfeffer, ed., *No More Vietnams? The War and the Future of American Foreign Policy* (New York: Harper & Row, 1968), p. 13.

6. Gideon Rachman, *Zero-Sum Future: American Policy in an Age of Austerity* (New York: Simon & Schuster, 2011), p. 10.

7. David McCullough, *Truman* (New York: Simon & Schuster, 1992), p. 525; Harvey Sicherman, "The Rest of Reagan," *Orbis* (Summer 2000): 477–99.

8. Quoted in Edward Hallett Carr, *Conditions of Peace* (New York: Macmillan Company, 1942), p. xiv.

9. The list would include, but not be limited to, Britain's Margaret Thatcher (1979), Ronald Reagan (1980), France's François Mitterrand (1981), Spain's Felipe Gonzales (1982), and Germany's Helmut Kohl (1983)—not to mention Pope John XXIII.

10. Niall Ferguson, *Civilization: The West and the Rest* (New York: Penguin Press, 2012), p. 323.

11. "A Conversation with U.S. Secretary of State Hillary Rodham Clinton," Council on Foreign Relations, Washington, DC, September 8, 2010.

12. Samuel P. Huntington, "The Lonely Superpower," *Foreign Affairs* 78, no. 2 (March/April 1999): 35–36.

13. Quoted in Jon Meacham, *Franklin and Winston: An Intimate Portrait of an Epic Friendship* (New York: Random House, 2004), p. 264.

14. Jeremy Shapiro and Nick Whitney, *Towards a Post-American Europe: A Power Audit of EU-US Relations* (London: European Council on Foreign Relations, 2009), p. 16.

15. Richard N. Haass, *The Reluctant Sheriff: The United States after the Cold War* (New York: Council of Foreign Relations, 1997), p. 140; and *The Opportunity: America's Moment to Alter History's Course* (New York: PublicAffairs, 2005), p. 199.

16. *Constrained Internationalism: Adapting to New Realities*, results of a 2010 National Survey of American Public Opinion (Global Views, 2010), p. 18.

17. William B. Quandt in David W. Lasch and Mark L. Haas, eds., *The Middle East and the United States: History, Politics and Ideologies* (Boulder, CO: Westview Press, 2012), p. 511.

18. Theodore White, *In Search of History: A Personal Adventure* (New York: Warner Books, 1978), p. 275.

19. Barack Obama, March 28, 2011. Hillary Rodham Clinton, quoted by Karen DeYoung, "Clinton Defends U.S. Stance on Syria, Bahrain," *Washington Post*, November 7, 2011.

20. See Dominique Moisi, *The Geopolitics of Emotion* (Baltimore: Johns Hopkins University Press, 2009).

21. John P. Lowell, *Foreign Policy in Perspective: Strategy, Adaptation, Decision-Making* (New York: Holt, Rinehart & Winston, 1970), p. 146.

22. Quoted by Jackie Calmes, "Obama Sees Opening in China Trade," *New York Times*, November 13, 2011.

23. Carl J. Friedrich, *Europe: An Emerging Nation?* (New York: Harper & Row, 1969), p. 196.

24. Kathleen R. McNamara, "The Eurocrisis and the Uncertain Future of European Integration," Council on Foreign Relations, September 2010.

25. Hannah Arendt, *The Origins of Totalitarianism* (San Diego: Harcourt: 1995), p. vii.

BIBLIOGRAPHY

Acheson, Dean. *Fragments of My Fleece* (New York: W.W. Norton & Company, 1971).

Adler, Selig. *The Isolationist Impulse: Its Twentieth Century Reaction* (New York: Free Press, 1957).

Alexandroff, Alan, and Andrew Cooper, eds. *Rising States, Rising Institutions; Challenges for Global Governance* (Washington, DC: Brookings Institution Press, 2010).

Arendt, Hannah. *The Origins of Totalitarianism* (San Diego: Harcourt, 1995).

Armitage, Richard L., and Joseph S. Nye, Jr. *CSIS Commission on Smart Power* (Washington, DC: Center for Strategic & International Studies, 1997).

Aron, Raymond. *The Century of Total War* (Garden City, NY: Doubleday, 1954).

———. *Peace and War among Nations: A Theory of International Relations* (Garden City, NY: Doubleday & Company, 1967).

Aronson, James. *The Press and the Cold War* (New York: Bobbs-Merrill, 1970).

Ash, Timothy Garton. *Free World: America, Europe, and the Surprising Future of the West* (New York: Random House, 2004).

Aslund, Anders, and Andrew Kuchins. *The Russia Balance Sheet* (Washington, DC: Peter G. Peterson Institute for International Economics and the Center for Strategic & International Studies, 2009).

Aslund, Anders, and Gary Clyde Hufbauer. *The United States Should Establish Permanent Normal Trade Relations with Russia* (Washington, DC: Peter G. Peterson Institute for International Economics, 2012).

Baker, James. *The Politics of Diplomacy: Revolution, War & Peace, 1989–1992* (New York: G.P. Putnam & Sons, 1995).

Baldwin, Hanson W. *World War I* (New York: Grove Press, 1962).

Bailey, Thomas A. "America's Emergence as a World Power," *Pacific Historical Review* 30, no. 1 (February 1961): 1–16.

Bailyn, Bernard. *To Begin the World Anew: The Genius and Ambiguities of the American Founders* (New York: Alfred A. Knopf, 2003).

Basu, Kaushik, et al. *The Evolving Dynamics of Economic Power in the Post Crisis World. Revelations from a New Index of Economic Power*, India's Ministry of Finance (2010).

Berlin, Isaiah. *Four Essays on Liberty* (New York: Oxford University Press, 1969).

———. "The Silence in Russian Culture," *Foreign Affairs* 36, no. 1 (October 1957).

Bertelsmann Stiftung. *Who Rules the World? Conclusion from and Results of a Representative Survey in Brazil, China, France, Germany, India, Japan, Russia, the United Kingdom, and the United States* (Brussels, 2005).

Boot, Max. *The Savage Wars of Peace: Small Wars and the Rise of American Power* (New York: Basic Books, 2002).

Bremmer, Ian. *Every Nation for Itself: Winners and Losers in a G-Zero World* (New York: Portfolio / Penguin, 2012).

Brown, Seyom. *New Forces, Old Forces, and the Future of World Politics* (Glencoe, IL: Scott Foresman, 1988).

Brzezinski, Zbigniew. "Delusions of Balance," *Foreign Policy* (Summer 1972): 54–59.

———. *The Geostrategic Triad: Living with China, Europe, and Russia* (Washington, DC: CSIS Press, 2001).

———. *Out of Control: Global Turmoil on the Eve of the 21st Century* (New York: Charles Scribner's Sons, 1991).

———. *Second Chance: Three Presidents and the Crisis of American Power* (New York: Basic Books, 2007).

———. *The Soviet Bloc: Unity and Conflict*, 2nd ed. (Cambridge, MA: Harvard University Press, 1966).

Bugajski, Janusz, with Marek Michalewski, eds. *Toward an Understanding of Russia: New European Perspectives* (Washington, DC: Council on Foreign Relations, 2002).

Bush, George, and Brent Scowcroft. *A World Transformed* (New York: Vintage Books, 1999).

Bush, Keith. *Russian Economic Survey* (Washington, DC: U.S.-Russia Business Council, May 2007).

Calleo, David P. *Follies of Power: America's Unipolar Fantasies* (Cambridge: Cambridge University Press, 2009).

———. *Rethinking Europe's Future* (Princeton, NJ: Princeton University Press, 2005).

Carr, Edward H. *Conditions of Peace* (New York: Macmillan, 1942).

Caryl, Christian. "Unveiling Hidden China," *New York Review of Books*, December 9, 2010.

Cassidy, John. "Prophet Motive," *New Yorker*, February 28, 2011.

Chicago Council on Global Affairs. *Constrained Internationalism: Adapting to New Realities*, results of a 2010 National Survey of American Public Opinion (Global Views, 2010).

Cline, Ray S. *World Power Assessment, 1977: A Calculus of Strategic Drift* (Boulder, CO: Westview Press, 1977).

Cohen, Craig S., ed. *Capacity and Resolve: Foreign Assessments of U.S. Power* (Washington, DC: Center for Strategic & International Studies, 2011).

Cohen, Saul Bernard. *Geopolitics: The Geography of International Relations* (Lanham, MD: Rowman & Littlefield, 2009).

Commager, Henry Steele. *The Defeat of America: Presidential Power and the National Character* (New York: Simon & Schuster, 1968).

Comparative Atlas of Defense in Latin America and the Caribbean (Buenos Aires: Red de Seguridad y Defensa de América Latina, 2010).

Cooper, Richard. "The Post-Modern State and the World Order," *Demos* (January 2000).

Cordesman, Anthony H., et al. *The Real Outcome of the Iraq War: US and Iranian Strategic Competition in Iraq* (Washington, DC: Center for Strategic & International Studies, December 21, 2011).

Craig, Gordon A., and Alexander L. George. *Force and Statecraft: Diplomatic Problems of Our Time*, 3rd ed. (New York: Oxford University Press, 1995).

Custine, Marquis Astolphe-Louis-Léonor. *Empire of the Czar: A Journey through Eternal Russia* (New York: Anchor Books, 1989).

DaVanzo, Julie, and Clifford Grammick. *Dire Demographics: Population Trends in the Russia Federation* (Santa Monica, CA: Rand Press, 2001).

Deutsch, Karl. *The Nerves of Government* (San Francisco: W.H. Freeman and Company, 1963).

Ding, Sheng. "Analyzing Rising Power from the Perspective of Soft Power: A New Look to China's Rise to the Status Quo Power," *Journal of Contemporary China* 19, no. 64 (2010): 255–72.

Dorff, Robert. "Responding to the Failed State: The Need for Strategy," *Small Wars and Insurgencies* 10, no. 3 (1999): 62–81.

Doyle, Michael W. *Empires* (New York: Cornell University Press, 1986).

Duchacek, Ivo, with Kenneth W. Thompson. *Conflict and Cooperation among Nations* (New York: Rinehart and Winston, 1967).

Dulles, John Foster. "Challenge and Response in United States Policy," *Foreign Affairs* (October 1957).

Fakiolas, Tassos E., and Efstathios T. Fakiolas. "Domestic Sources of Russia's Resurgence as a Global Great Power," *Journal of International and Area Studies* 16, no. 2 (2009).

Fanon, Frantz. *The Wretched of the Earth*. Translated by Constance Farrington; preface by Jean-Paul Sartre (New York: Grove Press, 1963).

Fearon, James D. "Rationalist Explanations for War," *International Organization* 49, no. 3 (Summer 1995): 379–414.

Feis, Herbert. "Is the United States Imperialist?" *Yale Review* (September 1951).

Ferguson, Niall. *Civilization: The West and the Rest* (New York: Penguin, 2012).

———. *Colossus: The Price of American Empire* (New York: Penguin, 2004).

———. "A World without Power," *Foreign Policy*, no. 143 (July/August 2004).

Fletcher, Richard. *The Cross and the Crescent: Christianity and Islam from Muhammad to the Reformation* (New York: Viking, 2003).

Friedman, Thomas L., and Michael Mandelbaum. *That Used to Be Us: How America Fell Behind in the World It Invented and How We Can Come Back* (New York: Farrar, Straus and Giroux, 2011).

Friedrich, Carl J. *Europe: An Emerging Nation?* (New York: Harper & Row, 1969).

Fu, Zhengyuan. *Autocratic Tradition and Chinese Politics* (New York: Cambridge University Press, 1993).

Fukuyama, Francis. *America at the Crossroads: Democracy, Power, and the Neo-Conservative Legacy* (New Haven and London: Yale University Press, 2006).

———. *The End of History and the Last Man* (New York: Free Press, 1992).

———. *State-building: Governance and World Order in the 21st Century* (Ithaca, NY: Cornell University Press, 2004).

Gaddis, John Lewis. *George F. Kennan: An American Life* (New York: Penguin Press, 2011).

———. *We Now Know: Rethinking the Cold War* (New York: Oxford University Press, 1997).

Garcia-Schmidt, Armando, and Dominik Hierlemann, eds. "EU 2020—the View of the Europeans." Results of a representative survey in selected member states of the European Union, Bertelsmann Stiftung, September 20, 2006.

Garrison, Jim. *America as Empire, Global Leader or Rogue Power* (San Francisco: Berrett-Koeler, 2002).

Garthoff, Raymond L. "Estimating Soviet Military Force Levels," *International Security* 14, no. 4 (Spring 1990).

Gelb, Leslie H., with Richard K. Betts. *The Irony of Vietnam: The System Worked* (Washington, DC: Brookings Institution Press, 1979).

Gelernter, David. "The Roots of European Appeasement," *Weekly Standard* 8, no. 2 (September 23, 2002).

Global Firepower. *World Military Strength Ranking, 2011*, at http://globalpower.com.

Gopnik, Adam. "Decline, Fall, Rinse, Repeat: Is America Going Down," *New Yorker*, September 12, 2011.

Gould-Adams, Robert. *John Foster Dulles: A Reappraisal* (New York: Appleton-Century-Crofts, 1962).

Grevi, Giovanni. *The Interpolar World: A New Scenario*, Occasional Paper, no. 79 (Paris: European Union Institute for Security Studies, June 2009).

Guruswamy, Mohan. "India and the European Union: Dim Prospects," EuroFuture Project, German Marshall Fund of the United States (March 2012).

Haas, Mark. "A Geriatric Peace: The Future of U.S. Power in a World of Aging Populations," *International Security* 32, no. 1 (Summer 2007).

Haass, Richard N. "The Age of Nonpolarity," *Foreign Affairs* 87, no. 3 (May/June 2008): 44–56.

———. *The Opportunity: America's Moment to Alter History's Course* (New York: PublicAffairs, 2005).

———. "The Palmerstonian Moment," *National Interest*, January 2, 2008.

———. *The Reluctant Sheriff: The United States after the Cold War* (New York: Council on Foreign Relations, 1997).

Hamilton, Daniel, and Joseph Quinlan. *The Transatlantic Economy, 2010: Annual Survey of Jobs, Trade, and Investment between the United States and Europe* (Washington, DC: Center for Transatlantic Relations, 2010).

Harper, John Lamberton. *The Cold War* (Oxford and New York: Oxford University Press, 2011).

He, Lichal. "Ready to Become a Great Power? The Recent Nationalist Movement and China's Evolving National Identity," *Journal of International Affairs and Area Studies* 16, no. 2 (2009).

Herstgaard, Mark. *The Eagle's Shadow: Why America Fascinates and Infuriates the World* (New York: Farrar, Straus and Giroux, 2002).

Hill, Steven. *Europe's Promise: Why the European Union Is the Best Hope in an Insecure Age* (Berkeley and Los Angeles: University of California Press, 2010).

Hinsley, F. H. *Power and the Pursuit of Peace* (London: Cambridge University Press, 1963).

Hobsbawm, Eric. *The New Century: In Conversation with Antonio Polito*, translated by Allan Cameron (London: Abacus, 2001).

Hoffmann, Stanley. *Gulliver's Troubles, or The Setting of American Foreign Policy* (New York: McGraw-Hill, 1968).

Holborn, Hajo. *The Political Collapse of Europe* (New York: Alfred A. Knopf, 1951).

Huntington, Samuel P. "The Lonely Superpower," *Foreign Affairs* 78, no. 2 (March/April 1999).

Ignatieff, Michael. *Empire Lite: Nation-Building in Bosnia, Kosovo, and Afghanistan* (New York: Penguin, 2003).

Ikenberry, G. John. *After Victory: Institutions, Strategies, Restraint and the Rebuilding of World Order after Major Wars* (Princeton, NJ: Princeton University Press, 2001).

Ikenberry, G. John., Thomas J. Knock, Ann-Marie Slaughter, and Tony Smith. *The Crisis of American Foreign Policy: Wilsonianism in the Twenty-First Century* (Princeton, NJ: Princeton University Press, 2010).

Isaac, Jeffrey C. *Arendt, Camus and Modern Rebellion* (New Haven, CT: Yale University Press, 1994).

Isler, Matt. "Graying Panda, Shrinking Dragon: The Impact of Chinese Demographic Changes on Northeast Asian Security," *JFQ*, no. 55 (2009): 101–3.

Jackson, Richard, Keisuke Nakashima, and Neil Howe. *China's Long March to Retirement Reform* (Washington, DC: Center for Strategic & International Studies, 2009).

Jackson, Robert H. *Quasi States Sovereignty, International Relations, and the Third World* (New York: Cambridge University Press, 1990).

Jacques, Martin. *When China Rules the World: The End of the Western World and the Birth of a New World Order* (New York: Penguin Press, 2010).

Joffe, Josef. *Uberpower: The Imperial Temptation of America* (New York: W.W. Norton & Company, 2006).

Joffe, Julia. "Net Impact," *New Yorker*, April 4, 2011.

Judt, Tony. "What Have We Learned, If Anything?" *New York Review of Books*, May 1, 2008.

Kagan, Robert. "The Benevolent Empire," *Foreign Policy*, no. 112 (Summer 1998): 24–35.

———. *Dangerous Nation: America's Place in the World from Its Earliest Days to the Dawn of the Twentieth Century* (New York: Alfred A. Knopf, 2006).

———. *Of Paradise and Power: America and Europe in the New World Order* (New York: Vintage, 2004).

Kaplan, Robert D. *The Coming Anarchy: Shattering the Dreams of the Post Cold War* (New York: Vintage, 2000).

Kennan, George F. *Memoirs, 1925–1950* (Princeton, NJ: Princeton University Press, 1967).

Kissinger, Henry. *Diplomacy* (New York: Simon & Schuster, 1994).

———. *White House Years* (Boston: Little, Brown, 1979).

———. *Years of Upheaval* (Boston: Little, Brown, 1982).

Kjetsaa, Geir. *Fyodor Dostoyevsky, A Writer's Life*. Translated from the Norwegian by Siri Hustvedt and David McDuff (New York: Viking Penguin, 1987).

Krasner, Stephen D., and Carlos Pascual. "Addressing State Failure," *Foreign Affairs* (July/August 2005): 153–63.

Krauthammer, Charles. *Democratic Realism: An American Foreign Policy for a Unipolar World* (Washington, DC: American Enterprise Institute, 2004).

———. "The Unipolar Moment," in "America and the World," supp., *Foreign Affairs* 70, no. 1 (1990/1991): 23–33.

———. "The Unipolar Moment Revisited," *National Interest* 70 (Winter 2002/2003).

Kreijen, Gérard. *State Failure, Sovereignty and Effectiveness* (Leiden: Koninklijke, 2004).

Kristol, William, and Robert Kagan. *Present Dangers: Crisis and Opportunity in American Foreign and Defense Policy* (San Francisco: Encounter, 2000).

Krugman, Paul. *Pop Internationalism* (Cambridge, MA: MIT Press, 1997).

Kuchins, Andrew C. "Russia, the 360-degree Regional Power," *Current History* (October 2011).

Kupchan, Charles A. *How Enemies Become Friends: The Sources of Stable Conflict* (Princeton, NJ: Princeton University Press, 2010).

———. *No One's World: The West, the Rising Rest, and the Coming Global Turn* (New York: Oxford University Press, 2012).

Lake, Anthony. "Confronting Backlash States," *Foreign Affairs* 73, no. 2 (March/April 1994): 45–56.

Langer, William. *The Rise of Modern Europe: Political and Social Upheaval, 1832–1852* (New York: Harper & Row, 1969).

Layne, Christopher. "The Unipolar Illusion: Why New Great Powers Will Rise," *International Security* 17, no. 4 (Spring 1993): 7–10.

Leonard, Mark. *Why Europe Will Run the 21st Century* (London and New York: Fourth Estate, 2005).

Lesch, David W., and Mark L. Haas, eds. *The Middle East and the United States: History, Politics and Ideologies* (Boulder, CO: Westview Press, 2012).

Lewis, Bernard. *What Went Wrong? The Clash between Islam and Modernity in the Middle East* (Princeton, NJ: Princeton University Press, 2002).

Lieber, Keir A., and Gerard Alexander. "Waiting for Balancing," *International Security* (Summer 2005): 109–39.

Lieberthal, Kenneth, and Wang Jisi. *Addressing U.S.-China Strategic Distrust*, John C. Thornton China Center, Brookings Institution, Monograph Series, no. 4, March 2012.

Liska, George. *Imperial America: The International Politics of Primacy* (Baltimore: Johns Hopkins University Press, 1967).

———. *Nations in Alliance: The Limits of Interdependence* (Baltimore: Johns Hopkins University Press, 1962).

Lo, Bobo. *China and the Global Financial Crisis*, CER Essays (London: Center for European Reform, April 2010).

Lowell, John P. *Foreign Policy in Perspective: Strategy, Adaptation, Decision-Making* (New York: Holt, Rinehart & Winston, 1970).

Lum, Thomas, et al. *China's Foreign Aid Activities in Africa, Latin America, and Southeast Asia*, Congressional Research Service, 7–5700, R40361 (February 25, 2009).

Luttwak, Edward. *The Grand Strategy of the Byzantine Empire* (Cambridge, MA: Harvard University Press, 2009).

———. *The Grand Strategy of the Roman Empire: From the First Century A.D. to the Third* (Baltimore: Johns Hopkins University Press, 1976).

Macmillan, Margaret. *Paris, 1919* (New York: Random House, 2003).

Maddison, Angus. *The World Economy: A Millennial Perspective* (OECD: Development Center Studies, 2006).

Mahbubani, Kishore. *The New Asian Hemisphere: The Irresistible Shift of Global Power to the East* (New York: PublicAffairs, 2008).

Mandelbaum, Michael. *The Frugal Superpower: America's Global Leadership in a Cash-Strapped Era* (New York: PublicAffairs, 2010).

Mann, Robert. *A Grand Delusion: America's Descent into Vietnam* (New York: Basic Books, 2001).

Maull, Hans W. "Europe and the New Balance of the Global Order," *International Affairs* 81, no. 4 (2005).

May, Ernest R. *Imperial Democracy: The Emergence of America as a Great Power* (Chicago: Imprint Publications, 1991).

May, Ernest R., and Philip D. Zelikow. *The Kennedy Tapes: Inside the White House during the Cuban Missile Crisis* (Cambridge, MA: Belknap Press of Harvard University Press, 1997).

Mayers, David. *The Ambassadors and American Soviet Policy* (New York: Oxford University Press, 1995).

McDaniel, Tim. *The Agony of the Russian Idea* (Princeton, NJ: Princeton University Press, 1996).

McClory, Jonathan. *The New Persuaders II: A Global Ranking of Soft Power* (Harvard University and the Institute for Government, 2011).

McCullough, David. *Truman* (New York: Simon & Schuster, 1992).

McFaul, Michael, and Kathryn Stoner-Weiss. "The Myth of the Authoritarian Model: How Putin's Crackdown Holds Russia Back," *Foreign Affairs* 87, no. 1 (February/March 2008).

McNamara, Robert S. *The Essence of Security: Reflections in Office* (New York: Harper & Row, 1968).

McNamara, Robert S., with Brian VanDeMark. *In Retrospect: The Tragedy and Lessons of Vietnam* (New York: Random House, 1995).

McPherson, James M. "What Drove the Terrible War," *New York Review of Books*, July 11, 2011.

Meacham, Jon. *Franklin and Winston: An Intimate Portrait of an Epic Friendship* (New York: Random House, 2004).

Mead, Walter Russell. *Special Providence: American Foreign Policy and How It Changed the World* (New York: Alfred A. Knopf, 2001).

Mearsheimer, John. *The Tragedy of Great Power Politics* (New York: W.W. Norton & Company, 2001).

Miller, Aaron David. *The Much Too Promised Land: America's Elusive Search for Arab-Israeli Peace* (New York: Bantam-Dell, 2008).

Milward, Alan. *The European Rescue of the Nation-State*, 2nd ed. (London: Routledge, 2000).

Mistral, Jacques. "La réorientation de la croissance chinoise: Sa logique, ses enjeux et ses conséquences," Centre des études économiques, Institut français des relations internationales (March 2011).

Moisi, Dominique. *The Geopolitics of Emotion* (Baltimore: Johns Hopkins University Press, 2009).

Montbrial, Thierry de. *L'action et le système du monde* (Paris: Presses Universitaires de France, 1992).

Moravcsik, Andrew. "Europe: The Quiet Superpower," *French Politics* 7, no. 3/4 (2009): 403–22.

Morgenthau, Hans J. *Politics among Nations: The Struggle for Power and Peace*, 4th ed. (New York: Alfred A. Knopf, 1966).

———. *Scientific Man versus Power Politics* (Chicago: University of Chicago, 1948).

Mori, Satoru. "Crisis Invigorates Japan-Europe Cooperation, But for How Long?" EuroFuture Project, German Marshall Fund of the United States (March 2012).

Motyl, Alexander J. "Why Empires Re-emerge: Imperial Collapse and Imperial Revival in Comparative Perspective," *Comparative Politics* 31, no. 2 (January 1999).

Mueller, John. "The Iraq Syndrome," *Foreign Affairs* 84, no. 6 (November/December 2005): 44–55.

Nye, Joseph S., Jr. *Bound to Lead: The Changing Nature of American Power* (New York: Basic Books, 1990).

———. *The Future of Power* (New York: PublicAffairs, 2011).

———. *Soft Power: The Means to Success in World Politics* (New York: PublicAffairs, 2004).

Odom, William E., and Robert Dujaric. *America's Inadvertent Empire* (New Haven, CT: Yale University Press, 2004).

O'Neil, Shannon K. *U.S.-Latin America Relations: A New Direction for a New Reality*, Independent Task Force, no. 60 (New York: Council on Foreign Relations, 2008).

Orbie, Jan, ed. *Europe's Global Role: External Policies of the European Union* (Burlington: Ashgate, 2008).

Osgood, Robert E., and Robert W. Tucker. *Force, Order, and Justice* (Baltimore: Johns Hopkins University Press, 1967).

Pape, Robert A. "Soft Balancing against the United States," *International Security* 30, no. 1 (2005).

Parker, John W. *Russia's Revival: Ambitions, Limitations, and Opportunities for the United States*, Strategic Perspectives, no. 3 (Washington, DC: Institute for National Strategic Studies, 2011).

Parmar, Iderjeet, and Michael Cox, eds. *Soft Power and U.S. Foreign Policy: Theoretical, Historical and Contemporary Perspectives* (New York: Routledge, 2010).

Pastor, Robert A., ed. *A Century's Journey: How the Great Powers Shape the World* (New York: Basic Books, 1999).

Pentagon Papers, based on investigative reporting by Neil Sheehan (New York: Bantam Books, 1972).

Petersen, Alexandros, with Katinka Barysch. *Russia, China, and the Geopolitics of Europe in Central Asia* (London: Center for European Reform, December 2011).

Pfaff, William. "Wise Men against the Grain," *New York Review of Books*, June 9, 2011.

Pfeffer, Richard M., ed. *No More Vietnams? The War and the Future of American Foreign Policy* (New York: Harper & Row, 1968).

Phillips, David L. *Losing Iraq: Inside the Postwar Reconstruction Fiasco* (Boulder, CO: Westview Press, 2005).

Piazza, James A. "Incubators of Terror: Do Failed and Failing States Promote Transnational Terrorism?" *International Studies Quarterly* 52, no. 3 (2008).

Poggio Teixeira, Carlos Gustavo. "Brazil and United States: Fading Interdependence," *Orbis* (Winter 2010): 156–57.

———. *Brazil, the United States, and the South American Subsystem: Regional Politics and the Absent Empire* (Lanham, MD: Lexington Books, 2012).

Porte, Anton de. *Europe between the Superpowers* (New Haven, CT: Yale University Press, 1979).

Quinlan, Joseph. *The Rise of China: A Brief Review of the Implications on the Transatlantic Partnership* (Washington, DC: German Marshall Fund, 2006).

Rachman, Gideon. *Zero-Sum Future: American Policy in an Age of Austerity* (New York: Simon & Schuster, 2011).

———. *Zero-Sum World: American Power in an Age of Anxiety* (New York: Simon & Schuster, 2011).

Ramesch, Jairam. *Making Sense of Chindia: Reflections on China and India* (India Research Press, 2006).

Rice, Condoleezza. *No Higher Honor: A Memoir of My Years in Washington* (New York: Crown Publishers, 2011).

"The Rise and Fall of the American Empire," with Daniel W. Drezner, Gideon Rachman, and Robert Kagan, *Foreign Policy*, February 14, 2012, http://www.foreignpolicy.com/articles/2012/02/14/the_rise_or_fall_of_the_american_empire.

Ridgway, Matthew B. *The Korean War* (Garden City, NY: Doubleday, 1967).

Ross, Dennis. *The Missing Peace: The Inside Story of the Fight for Middle East Peace* (New York: Farrar, Straus and Giroux, 2004).

Rossiter, Clinton, and James Lare, eds. *The Essential Walter Lippmann* (New York: Random House, 1963).

Rostow, Eugene V. *A Breakfast for Bonaparte* (Washington, DC: National Defense University Press, 1995).

Rotberg, Robert I., ed., *State Failure and State Weaknesses in a Time of Terror* (Washington, DC: Brookings, 2003).

———. *When States Fail: Causes and Consequences* (Princeton, NJ: Princeton University Press, 2004).

Royal Society. *Knowledge, Networks, and Nations: Global Scientific Cooperation in the 21st Century* (London: March 2011).

Russett, Bruce, and Harvey Starr. *World Politics: The Menu for Choice* (New York: Basic Books, 1981).

Santayana, George. *Skepticism and Abnormal Faith* (New York: Scribner, 1923).

Schama, Simon. *Landscape and Memory* (New York: Vintage Books, 1985).

Schlesinger, Arthur. "The Making of a Mess," *New York Review of Books* 51, no. 14 (September 23, 2004).

Schmidt, Vivien A. "Re-envisioning the European Union: Identity, Democracy, Economy," *Journal of Common Market Studies* 47 (annual review, 2009): 17–42.

Scott, George. *The Rise and Fall of the League of Nations* (New York: Macmillan, 1974).

Scowcroft, Brent. "Foreign Policy in an Age of Austerity," *American Interest* (Winter [January/February] 2010).

Sen, Amartya. "Quality of Life: India vs. China," *New York Review of Books*, May 12, 2011.

Serfaty, Simon. *Architects of Delusion: Europe, America, and the Iraq War* (Philadelphia: University of Pennsylvania Press, 2008).

———. "The Folly of Forgetting the West," *Policy Review*, no. 174 (August & September 2012): 35–48.

———. *The Elusive Enemy* (Boston: Little, Brown, 1972).

———. "The Limits of Audacity," *Washington Quarterly* 33, no. 1 (January 2010): 99–110.

———. "Memories of Leadership," *Brown Journal of International Affairs* 5, no. 2 (Summer/Fall 1998): 3–16.

———. "Moving into the Post-Western World," *Washington Quarterly* 34, no. 2 (Spring 2011): 7–23.

———. *The Vital Partnership: Power and Order; America and Europe beyond Iraq* (Lanham, MD: Rowman & Littlefield Publishers, 2005).

Serfaty, Simon, ed. *A Recast Partnership? Institutional Dimensions of Transatlantic Relations* (Washington, DC: CSIS Press, 2008).

———. *Visions of the Atlantic Alliance: The United States, the European Union, and NATO* (Washington, DC: CSIS Press, 2005).

Shambaugh, David. "Coping with a Conflicted China," *Washington Quarterly* (Winter 2011): 7–27.

Shapiro, Jeremy, and Nick Whitney. *Towards a Post-American Europe: A Power Audit of EU-US Relations* (London: European Council on Foreign Relations, 2009).

Sicherman, Harvey. "The Rest of Reagan," *Orbis* (Summer 2000): 477–99.

Snyder, Timothy. "Hitler vs. Stalin: Who Killed More," *New York Review of Books*, March 10, 2011.

Stokes, Bruce. "What Europeans Think about the Eurocrisis: Doubts and Waning Faith in the European Project," EuroFuture Project, The German Marshall Fund of the United States (January 2012).

Talbott, Strobe. *The Russia Hand: A Memoir of Presidential Diplomacy* (New York: Random House, 2002).

Taylor, A. J. P. *Bismarck: The Man and the Statesman* (New York: Vintage Books, 1967).

Thatcher, Margaret. *The Downing Street Years* (New York: HarperCollins Publishers, 1993).

Tilford, Simon. "Turning Japanese?" Center for European Reform, *Insight*, April 30, 2010.

Tombs, Robert, and Isabelle Tombs. *That Sweet Enemy: The French and the British from the Sun King to the Present* (New York: Alfred A. Knopf, 2007).

Trenin, Dmitri. "Russia Leaves the West," *Foreign Affairs* 85, no. 4 (July/August 2006).

Truman, Harry S. *Memoirs*, vol. 1: *Year of Decision* (Garden City, NY: Doubleday, 1955).

Tsygankov, Andrey P. "If Not by Tanks, Then by Banks? The Role of Soft Power in Putin's Foreign Policy," *Europe-Asia Studies* 7, no. 58 (2006).

Walt, Stephen M. *Taming American Power: The Global Response to U.S. Primacy* (New York: W.W. Norton & Company, 2005).

Waltz, Kenneth W. *Man, the State, and War* (New York: Columbia University Press, 1969).

———. "The Stability of the Bipolar World," *Daedalus* 93, no. 3 (Summer 1964).

———. *Theory of International Politics* (Reading, MA: Addison-Wesley Publishing, 1979).

White, Theodore. *In Search of History: A Personal Adventure* (New York: Warner Books, 1978).

Wilmot, Chester. *The Struggle for Europe* (New York: Harper & Brothers, 1952).

Wolfowitz, Paul. "Realism," *Foreign Policy* (September/October 2009): 66–72; and comments in "Is Paul Wolfowitz for Real?"; Stephen M. Walt, "Just Because He Walks Like a Realist . . ."; David J. Rothkopf, "A Neocon in Realist's Clothing"; Daniel W. Drezner, "Capitalization Matters"; and Steve Clemons, "Failing to Note the Difference When the U.S. Power Tank Is Full or Near Empty," http://www.foreignpolicy.com/articles/2009/08/27/why_paul_wolfowitz_should_get_real?page=0,0.

Wolpert, Stanley. *India and Pakistan: Conflict or Cooperation?* (Berkeley: California University Press, 2010).

Yuan, Jing-Dong. "The Dragon and the Elephant: Chinese-Indian Relations in the 21st Century," *Washington Quarterly* (Summer 2007): 131–44.

Zakaria, Fareed. *The Post-American World, Release 2.0* (New York: W.W. Norton & Company, 2011).

Zelikow, Philip D., and Robert B. Zoellick, eds. *America and the Muslim Middle East* (New York: Council on Foreign Relations, 1998).

Zweig, Stefan. *Memories of Yesteryear* (Lincoln: University of Nebraska Press, 1964).

INDEX

Page numbers of figures (tables, charts, etc.) are italicized.